KU-413-031

MACMILLAN MODERN DRAMATISTS

CONTEMPORARY IRISH DRAMATISTS

Michael Etherton

First published 1989

Published by
Higher and Further Education Division
MACMILLAN PUBLISHERS LTD
Houndmills, Basingstoke, Hampshire RG21 2XS
and London
Companies and representatives
throughout the world

Printed in Hong Kong

British Library Cataloguing in Publication Data
Etherton, Michael
Contemporary Irish dramatists.—(Macmillan
modern dramatists).
1. English drama—Irish authors—
History and criticism   2. English drama
—20th century—History and criticism
I. Title
822'.914'099415   PR8789
ISBN 0–333–40928–0
ISBN 0–333–40929–0 Pbk

Contents

Contents

List of Plates

1. *The Freedom of the City*, Royal Court Theatre, London, 1973. Photo: Donald Cooper
2. *Translations.* Field Day Theatre Company, 1980, Ann Hasson as Sarah, Mick Lally as Manus. Photo: Rod Tuad.
3. *The Communication Cord*, 1982. Field Day Theatre Company. Photo: Thaddeus Sullivan.
4. *The Communication Cord*, 1982. Field Day Theatre Company. Photo: Thaddeus Sullivan.
5. *Double Cross*, 1986. Field Day Theatre Company. Stephen Rea as William Joyce. Photo: Fergus Burke.
6. *Double Cross*, 1986. Royal Court Theatre, London. Kate O'Toole and Stephen Rea. Photo: Donald Cooper.
7. *The Great Hunger*, 1986. Almeida Theatre, London. Dermod Moore, Vincent O'Neill, Conal Kearney, Tom Hickey. Photo: Donald Cooper.
8. *Observe the Sons of Ulster*, Hampstead Theatre, London, 1986. John Bowe. Photo: Donald Cooper.

9. The Field Day Theatre Company in 1986. Richard Howard, Lisa Stifler, Douglas Laing, Ursula McAllister, Julie Barber, Joe McGrath, Kate O'Toole, Consolata Boyle, Fiona Macmillan, Jim Sheridan, Stephen Rea, Jane Perrott, Brian Friel. Photo: Larry Doherty.

Acknowledgements

It is a privilege for me to have been able to write this book. A number of people in Ireland welcomed me and generously gave me their time to discuss a range of ideas related to their own writing and activism in Irish theatre: I would especially like to thank Brian Friel, Seamus Deane and Thomas Kilroy who each generously offered me new insights not only into their work but also into my own Third World theatre commitment. I am also grateful to Frank McGuinness for discussing his work with me and allowing me to read some of his unpublished manuscripts; and to Margaretta D'Arcy and John Arden for their willingness to discuss at length with me the new directions in their work. I have a special debt of gratitude to Mark Cohen: initially he helped me to focus my ideas, and then subsequently offered encouragement and criticism through all the stages of revising the manuscript. Without his friendship and advice the book would not have been written. I am also very grateful for the critical comments given me by John Reed, Chris Dunton and Ronald Ayling on early drafts of the manuscript. Their rigorous assessment of my text is something I appreciate more than I can adequately express. I am further indebted to Ronald Ayling whom I recently spent some time with in Canada

Acknowledgements

and who first awakened me to the richness of Irish theatre when I was his student. It is an interest and commitment which has latterly been enriched by the welcome and affection of neighbours and friends in Caherdaniel, County Kerry; in particular by Jer Galvin and Maurice Carey. I am deeply grateful to my wife Mary not only for her support throughout the preparation of the manuscript but particularly for her professional scrutiny of the final drafts and her invaluable advice. Finally, I want to thank Peggy Vowles, and my Drama colleagues and students for their sustaining enthusiasm and material support.

M. E.

For
Jer 'Derby' Galvin
and
John Reed

Editor's Preface

The *Macmillan Modern Dramatists* is an international series of introductions to major and significant nineteenth- and twentieth-century dramatists, movements and new forms of drama in Europe, Great Britain, America and new nations such as Nigeria and Trinidad. Besides new studies of great and influential dramatists of the past, the series includes volumes on contemporary authors, recent trends in the theatre and on many dramatists, such as writers of farce, who have created theatre 'classics' while being neglected by literary criticism. The volumes in the series devoted to individual dramatists include a biography, a survey of the plays, and detailed analysis of the most significant plays, along with discussion, where relevant, of the political, social, historical and theatrical context. The authors of the volumes, who are involved with theatre as playwrights, directors, actors, teachers and critics, are concerned with the plays as theatre and discuss such matters as performance, character interpretation and staging, along with themes and contexts.

BRUCE KING
ADELE KING

Introduction

This book aims to present an analysis of some of the most significant developments in drama and theatre in Ireland now. The idea of a 'significant drama' contains a particular view of drama, as well as a view of what constitutes 'significance'. A significant drama enables us to come upon a deeper understanding *collectively*. It is this collectivity which makes drama (and its manifestation in the conventional forms of theatre) different from other literatures, for drama comes out of what the Africans call 'orature': a live, spoken literature, presented vocally to an audience. Good drama needs to have deep significance for its assembled audience.

Reaching a deeper understanding is a process. There is the 'shock of knowing': we in the audience had previously felt, but not been able to express, what we are now hearing and seeing on the stage. At a certain point in the social emergence of dramatic art, this 'shock of knowing' is full of delight: the status of the new knowledge does not depend on its sacredness or on our belief in it. Its very profanity is powerful. But beyond receiving this deeper understanding, really good drama gives us the language to go out of the theatre and express it for ourselves. We are actually given the linguistic tools to make that wider grasp of our social reality our own.

This is the ideal, or the idea, or *ideology*, of a significant drama. In First World societies today, within the metropolitan cultures of the Superpowers, it is difficult to reach the ideal. Our dramatic art, like any aspect of our culture, is socially produced. It is commoditised: both the products ('plays', 'performances') and the talents of its makers. Furthermore, and as part of the political and social totality of dramatic art today, in what has been called a 'one-world economy', our culture is dominated by literacy. Within the First World especially, our art is more deeply literate, more bound up in writing, than in any other period of the history of man. The analysis of this phenomenon does not lie within the scope of this book; but the relationship of the written and published text to the live performance underscores much of what is written.

The relationship of the *reader* to the significance of drama cannot be brushed aside; and this book, which is itself a 'text', would be dishonest if it ignored the written texts of plays which it attempts to analyse as performance. The aim, therefore, is to avoid prioritising one over the other – reading a play/seeing it in performance; writing a play/developing it by collective creation – but instead to show how deeply problematic is the relationship between artistic 'text' and social change.

In fact, despite my own preference for collectively created drama, the focus of this brief study of contemporary Irish drama has been on individual playwrights, rather than on groups involved in collective creation either purely with the company itself or with the target community audiences for whom the drama is intended. Such a focus accepts the continuing dominance of authorial insights in the creation of a significant drama in Ireland, both north and south of the Border. I have tried to develop this focus in order to try to contextualise what in my view is the extraordinary achievement of the work of Brian Friel, and also of the work of Thomas Murphy.

In doing so I am aware that I have simply ignored a number of interesting and significant achievements by companies like the Irish touring company, Theatre Unlimited (based in Kilkenny) and its Polish artistic director, Maciek Reszczynski; and TEAM Theatre Company, with whom Frank McGuinness worked in developing his plays, and who presented Neil Donnelly's play *Blindfold*, co-authored with the company, at the Dublin Theatre Festival in 1986. Also omitted are the inventive and often philosophically substantial one-person shows, such as the satirical work of Sydney Bernard Smith, based in Sligo and touring widely in both rural areas and to Dublin, whose satire has a significant political edge to it; and the very different work by the Belfast actress, Briege Arthurs, in *Only the Rivers Run Free*, directed by Siobhan Dunne, who together founded in London the Simply Now Theatre Company. These people, and the many others in determined small drama groups in the 1980s, have an important double commitment: to what they want to communicate to audiences, and to the dramatic art they must develop in order to do it.

I did not intend to offer a survey of contemporary theatre practice in Ireland. I am aware that for a number of readers the most useful thing a critic can do is offer information on the state and ethos of the big theatres and their artistic management. In fact, most established theatres tend to do this themselves: the Abbey's history is regularly up-dated; the Druid in Galway offered a survey of their first ten years in 1985; the Pike, in Dublin, in a book by Carolyn Swift, *Stage by Stage*, which was also published in 1985, by Poolbeg Press in Dublin. The 'Theatre of the Image', developed by Patrick Mason, Tom MacIntyre and Tom Hickey in the Abbey's experimental theatre space needs much more detailed analysis than I have been able to give in this book. My chief regret, however, is not to have written at greater length on the Project Arts Centre, Dublin, which in many ways has offered real alternatives to the social production of the arts in the 1970s and 1980s, at least in Dublin.

My emphasis has not been on the Dublin theatre, or on the theatre in Belfast, but on the perspectives from the rural West of Ireland. I make no apology for this. I hope that for at least some readers the arguments which I have attempted to pursue will be proven, or, even better, found interesting enough to develop further. I find that all over Ireland, North and South, there is burgeoning of drama which will soon be seen to be much more significant, as the expression of a new Irish nationalism, or identity, than the work of Yeats, Lady Gregory, Synge, the Fays, Lennox Robinson and O'Casey. A more difficult and intractible reality is now being depicted: Ireland as part of a world threatened by neo-colonialism and by the gross and increasing imbalance between rich and poor nations. Irish audiences are finding through this new drama a new expression of their greater understanding.

1
Dublin and Belfast

Irish theatre today might still be seen to be centred upon Dublin. Any state capital in Europe in the latter half of the twentieth century quite literally capitalises on artistic developments in that country, and Ireland is no exception. It is in the metropolis that theatre professionals find the funding and the audiences, as well as the infrastructure of their profession: theatres, agents, contacts, academies. Because of this, any new drama in the metropolis is *noticed*, in both the formal and informal sense of that word: written up in reviews and published.

Dublin, too, and not Belfast, should obviously be the locus of dramatic representations of new Irish realities, in the context of the continuing political and social divisions in the island. However, a closer analysis of the relationship of Irish drama to Irish realities today, in terms of a developing drama aesthetic which seeks to express these realities, and in terms of an audience's understanding of the plays performed, reveals a drama which unites rather than divides Dublin and Belfast. Furthermore, the avant-

1

garde theatre in both Dublin and Belfast, whilst stressing
its Irish dilemmas, has a tendency to embrace the various
materialist discourses of British drama since 1957.

The real locus of contemporary Irish drama is not
Dublin or Belfast but the rural West of Ireland. In this it
is not at all like the founding days of the Abbey Theatre.
Although the Irish drama there in the early years of the
twentieth century appeared to have its aesthetic rooted in
the rural *Gaeltacht*, it was very much an urban Dublin
theatre. Anglo-Irish playwrights such as W. B. Yeats and
J. M. Synge used the West as an Irish emblem of their
own urban intellectual, *European*, sensibilities. Yeats'
repeated battles with his Abbey Theatre's audiences was
as a result of the quite different sensibilities of the urban
Irish who 'read' this emblematic Irish theatre much more
directly. In a way, the people of the rural West of Ireland,
in themselves, were not represented in this early Dublin
theatre. Nor were they in the audience. Their appearance
as characters in the plays was very much a cosmopolitan
or urban view of rural Irish communities. The real
communities have subsequently found their own
playwrights, most notably George Fitzmaurice, John B.
Keane and M. J. Molloy. The awkward substance of
people's lives – not their romantic shadows – are
transformed by these playwrights into drama; but their
plays remain unrecognised – not *noticed* – even in Dublin;
and certainly not in Britain.

In its discourses and in its aesthetic, their rural theatre
offers a modest but persistent challenge specifically in the
way it works upon the imagination of the people whom it
plays to and depicts. Here are plays which are, at one and
the same time, ordinary and yet saying something new. A
performance goes beyond the written text: a new text is
made, collectively, in the imaginations of the watching

audience. Such performances reassert the art of a much more ancient and effective theatre: one in which audience and actors, together, can suddenly perceive a deeper truth, way beyond the established text, and through an active imagination gain confidence to act – socially and politically – upon this understanding. This is a theatre which is closer to the dynamics of the new activist theatre among politicised Third World peasants.

The challenge of such a theatre is threefold. First it challenges the death of the imagination in European intellectual thought. Secondly, it challenges the State and commercial funding by which an increasingly uncertain European drama is realised in performance – of plays which, paradoxically, seek to depict the materialist realities of society. Thirdly, it challenges this very post-industrial materialism by reinstating culture and metaphysics *within* the materialist discourse.

What makes this challenge so significant in contemporary Irish drama today is that some of the best playwrights presently writing in the English language have taken it up, to produce a profound Irish understanding of European sensibilities. Brian Friel, Tom Murphy, Thomas Kilroy, and in a different way the collaborative authorship of John Arden and Margaretta D'Arcy, have perceived in this drama a sensibility which cuts right across contemporary European dramatic sensibilities. It has pointed the way to a truly radical drama in terms of that deeper understanding actors and audiences realise, together, in live performances.

To some extent, these playwrights have influenced the professional theatre in Dublin, and in Belfast. But in so far as the Dublin and Belfast playwrights have drawn closer to the intellectual mainstream of British drama (e.g. David Edgar, Edward Bond, David Hare) they have been forced into a dialectical relationship with the West of Ireland playwrights, especially since the resurgence of violence in Northern Ireland after 1969. The plays of, for example, Hugh Leonard, or Graham Reid, Stewart Parker or Martin Lynch, are popular with both Irish and non-Irish audiences, and often successful commercially. Their plays are important, and they develop the aesthetics of theatre quite significantly. But in being 'about Ireland', and responding however obliquely or directly to events in the North since 1969, they all seem contained and closed-off from anything other than an objectively realised 'Ireland' on the stage. Ironically, in their objective view of Ireland they are oddly close to a British sensibility which likewise tends to categorise, or name, experience.

Friel's plays, as well as the plays of Murphy, Kilroy, and Arden and D'Arcy, are not 'about Ireland' in this categorical sense. Nor are they 'an Irish view'. They are about other things: an opening-up of ideas about which they and their Irish audiences need to reach a greater understanding, a deeper truth. The other playwrights often complain that it is difficult to know what their plays 'mean', while Friel might contend that a play with an obvious 'meaning' has no meaning at all. A written play text has no meaning until it is made in the imaginations of the audience. The problem, of course, is to know what makes 'meaning' in drama.

This chapter attempts to tackle this issue by analysing the authorial intentions for some of the most popular plays which have emerged from the Dublin and Belfast theatres since 1969. There are some common denominators here. In every instance the plays are concerned to find a theatrical correlative for the intellectual and political crises which grip the Irish, the British–Irish and the Anglo-Irish people both north and south of the Border. This is the

4

case whether the playwright's view is oblique or direct. If he or she tries to avoid it, a palpable unease in the theatrical aesthetic of the piece seems to creep in. Secondly, most of the serious playwrights are demanding of their audiences that they discover a less partial and less compromised understanding of history. In one way or another, the plays seek to expose the problems in a familial view of history, specifically where fathers pass on a view of tradition to sons or grandsons.

Finally – though less crucial in terms of the scope of this book – is the fact that all the plays are performed to Irish audiences who, like all European audiences, are now accustomed to seeing much less drama in the theatre than they do on television: in series, serials and soap operas, as well as in televised plays.

Incidently, in the context of the development of contemporary drama in the 1980s in Dublin and Belfast, a depiction on television of a new Irish reality has obviously been seen by a number of leading Irish dramatists as deeply problematic, politically and aesthetically. There is a striking imbalance between the resources for television drama production in Belfast and in Dublin. Belfast can draw on the combined and competing resources of British broadcasting through the commercial channels of ITV and the public service channels of the BBC. However, although the provision for production is lavish, it is still subject to the overt and covert controls of the British state. RTE (*Radio Telefis Eireann*), the combined government and commercial television broadcast system of the Irish Republic, has very limited resources by comparison. However, even these resources are still subject to state controls – this time the controls of the Irish state.

Two of the most popular Irish plays in the mid-1970s were *Da* by High Leonard and *Spokesong* by Stewart

Parker. Their popularity with audiences on both sides of the Atlantic has continued and they are now established in the professional and amateur repertoire. In their appeal to audiences, and in their content and theatrical form, they can be seen retrospectively to have signalled a transformation of Irish drama north and south of the Border over the next decade. A comparison of these two plays makes an appropriate starting point: *Da* represents the view from Dublin; *Spokesong* represents the complementary view from Belfast. What they were saying in the mid-1970s, and the theatrical ways in which they were saying it, indicate what was to become the dominant authorial discourse in the mid-1980s: how changing Irish realities can be turned into theatre art. The theatre's task is to *name* that reality. The plays are as much about 'theatre' as they are about any 'reality'.

It is interesting to note that while both playwrights have successful careers as scriptwriters for television – Hugh Leonard especially – both plays are quintessentially theatrical. They have been successful in live performance. It is possible that their popularity reflects the matching of the particular sort of dramatic craftsmanship of the two playwrights with the audience's experience of a changing drama aesthetic on television.

Dublin: Hugh Leonard, 'Da'

Hugh Leonard was born in 1926, in Dalkey, Dublin. 'Hugh Leonard' is the pseudonym for John Keyes Byrne (Brady and Cleeve, *Biographical Dictionary of Irish Writers*) or John Joseph Byrne (Fintan O'Toole, *In Dublin*, 30 Sept. 1982). He had already established himself as a professional playwright with plays for the live theatre in the late 1950s and early 1960s, when British playwrights such as Bolt and Pinter were also developing an entertaining and serious psychological theatre. These early plays were *The Big Birthday*, *A Leap in the Dark*, *Madigan's Lock* and *A Walk on the Water*. Then, for Granada Television in Britain, where he worked on contract, he wrote for a number of series and serials, both conventional comedy (*Me Mammy*) and adaptations of established English novels (e.g. Dickens's *Nicholas Nickleby*).

Da was premiered at the Olney Theatre, Maryland, USA on 7 August 1973. It was first performed in Ireland at the Olympia Theatre, Dublin, on 8 October of the same year. Both productions were directed by James Waring. A revival in 1978 in New York won the Drama Critics Award, and 4 Tony Awards including one for Best Play of 1978.

The success of *Da* confirmed his pre-eminence as a craftsman of drama. He has the ability to structure narrative and character, irony and paradox, wit and dialogue into plays which demonstrate a completeness. This completeness does not come from an over-riding scheme or patterning of actions, emblems and characters. It comes instead from the seemingly effortless and economical way in which Leonard reveals complex psychological motivation of characters in the minutiae of their day-to-day behaviour. He deftly flicks back the layers of pretence; and suddenly we have an insight into a character's aching self-awareness. We match this with our own sudden self-recognition. The revelation of a subtle psychology – in us as much as in his characters – is the cornerstone of his dramatic art. It is the basis of the dramatic impact of *Da*. This revelatory psychology confirms the ideas we have of ourselves and our relationships in society today.

The psychological base of *Da* is its dominant structural element. The narrative is slight: a middle-aged fellow, Charlie, has returned from England to Dublin to bury his 82-year-old foster father, Da, of the title. The action in the play's present time is the few hours Charlie spends in his deceased father's council house, clearing out the paltry remains of a long life of poverty. Charlie is visited briefly by his former school-mate Oliver, and by his first employer, Mr Drumm. Both have small materialist motives for calling: Oliver would like Charlie to try and get the house allocated to him; Drumm returns to the son the only two material possessions Da ever had: the melted remains of 30 pairs of spectacles from the San Francisco earthquake of 1906, and all the money which Charlie has ever sent him, saved up and now returned.

This present time of the play – which is given in the stage direction precisely as May 1968 – is penetrated by memories of Charlie and his family in a past time. They occupy his mind. They are realised physically on the stage, concretely and directly. There are no stagey theatrical devices. Leonard does not want us to explain them (as flashbacks or as a sort of metaphysical present-in-the-past, an historical determinism) but simply to accept their representation on the stage as a given and to enjoy the ironical exchanges which follow. What depth of meaning there is comes from an exploration, with hindsight, of a relationship between father and son which spans the 35 years of Charlie's life. Both the dead Da and the living Charlie are reviewing the relationship. Thus, although Da is referred to in the text as being in Charlie's mind, the evidence of the drama is to the contrary. Da is a separate entity, on a par with Charlie, and in his own way reflecting as much upon the relationship as Charlie himself is. As members of the audience, we hold in view the fact that

Da is now dead, and we enjoy the redefinition of his influence over Charlie '*as if*' he were still present.

This whimsical 'as if' is important. If Da was still alive the relationship could not be redefined by Charlie: the living presence is far more inhibiting than the 'dead' presence. A dead Da is freed from his dotage. Charlie is also free to find an ideal expression of Da's personality. This process leads, in an ironic twist at the end of the play, to Charlie realising that far from burying his foster father and burning all his papers and the memory of him, the old man has now decided, against Charlie's express instructions, to accompany him back to England – something he would never do whilst he was still alive. It is as though the relationship has been prised out of Ireland, and cut loose from a cloying Irish, or Dublin, specificity.

Although the ideal state of the relationship between Da and Charlie rejects its Irishness, it specifically does not reject the historical class basis. Da is a jobbing gardener, working for 54 years with a Quaker family, forelock-tugging, grateful to be pensioned off with a pittance. There is a hint that Charlie, being bright and bookish as a young man, has escaped to England to become a successful writer in his 40s. In doing so, he has also escaped his class destiny as a white-collar clerk.

His distance from Catholic *petit bourgeois* Ireland in the late 1960s is depicted in the ambiguous and distanced relationship he has now with the two people, other than his fostering Mother and Da, who mattered in his life as a young person and who now call in at the house in the present or real time of the play: his discontented and frustrated first employer, the chief clerk, Mr Drumm; and his school-friend Oliver. Both are quintessentially *petit bourgeois*. Charlie's relationship with these two deepens our understanding of the terms of the central relationship

9

between Charlie and his Da. This is a 1960s reworking of the late-nineteenth-century alliance between the alienated intellectual and the former serf against the steely-eyed clerks and small businessmen, and other *petit bourgeois* Irish. Charlie reminds Da that at the age of 68 he, Da, went to work for the upwardly-mobile Catholic schoolteacher and his wife who owned a fashion-shop, and who bought the house from the Quakers:

> CHARLIE: . . . And then you put in another four years, toiling for the Catholic but somewhat less than Christian Diors of Grafton Street.
>
> DA: 'Tynan,' says that bitch's ghost to me, and him only a schoolmaster, 'I want more honest endeavour from you and less excuses.' 'Do you see this fist?' says I to him.   (*Da*, Newark, Proscenium Press, 1975, p. 61)

Early in the play Charlie sums up Da's influence over him:

> You banjaxed me, you know that? Long after I had quit the job and seen the last of Drumm, I was dining out in London: black dickie-bow, oak panelling, picture of Sarah Bernhardt at nine o'clock: the sort of place where you have to remember not to say thanks to the waiters. I had just propelled an erudite remark across the table and was about to shoot my cuffs, lose my head and chance another one, when I felt a sudden tug as if I was on a dog-lead. I looked, and there were you at the other end of it. Paring your corns, informing me that bejasus the weather would hold up if it didn't rain, and sprinkling sugar on my bread when Ma's back was turned. . . .
>
> . . .
>
> And it was more than a memory. She was dead then,

and at that moment I knew you were sitting here on your own while the daylight went. Did you think bad of me? (p. 27)

The ultimate impression from this little speech is that Charlie was not banjaxed at all. On the contrary, Da's influence is perceived by Charlie to be the necessary and saving influence of his working-class origins against intellectual pretentions – 'codology' – and the *petit bourgeoisie*, especially as he rises up in the world. The implication is that through Da, Charlie maintains the common touch.

The seriousness of Charlie's criticism of Da is belied by the consistent, affectionate tone throughout the play. Indeed, Mother appears much less and is summarily dismissed. This occurs in the scene in the past in which Mr Drumm calls, with a view to offering the young Charlie, fresh out of school, a job. Mother and Da, in different ways, show an extraordinary lack of sensitivity, education and nous on this occasion. Leonard deliberately depicts this embarrassment for young Charlie as a failing of their class. By way of conversation with Mr Drumm, Da makes *ad hoc* and ignorant speeches in support of Hitler (the scene is taking place at the end of the Second World War); and, seemingly to cover up for the embarrassment caused, Mother launches into her well-rehearsed account of how, against advice, she took Charlie in as a foundling and raised him. The middle-aged Charlie, surveying the scene, finds Mother's behaviour more indictable, simply because it is loveless. Although Da's ignorance is not disputed, it is shot through with his unconscious and unreflecting love for the young lad he is helping to rear. In the re-run of the scene now, the hurt of the past is salved in the present time of the play. The tone is softer:

DA: (*Softly*) You're a comical boy.

CHARLIE: (*Almost an appeal*) You could have stopped
  her.   (p. 21)

Mother is also given a very limited vocabulary. Her
speech is unusually restricted; much more so than Da's.
There are a range of language registers in the play. Oliver
comments on having taken elocution lessons, and his
phrasing patterns reflect this. Charlie corrects the utterance
of young Charlie. Mr Drumm is absorbed in ironic
aphorisms reminiscent of Oscar Wilde. Their register is
an indication of their class. The particular ambivalence of
Charlie's class affiliations is consciously pointed to in the
letter-writing episode in which young Charlie is made to
write and re-write a letter to some middle-class people
who have inquired after him. He has compared himself to
Micawber, and this has stuck in Mother's throat. Language
and class are effectively elided in this little scene:

MOTHER: Write it out again and do it proper.
  . . .
YOUNG CHARLIE: There's nothing wrong with it. Maybe
  you don't understand it, but the Jacobs will. It's
  meant to be funny, they'll laugh when they read it.
MOTHER: Aye, to be sure they will. At you, for setting
  yourself up to be something you are not.
CHARLIE: It's my letter. You're not writing it: I am.
MOTHER: Then write it proper.
YOUNG CHARLIE: Proper-*ly!*
MOTHER: Don't you pull *me* up. Don't act the high-up
  lord with *me*, not in this house.   (p. 42)

In pent-up fury, young Charlie writes a parody of a letter,
made up entirely of cliché-ed working-class phrases. He

is appalled when both Mother and Da indicate that this is exactly what they wanted him to write.

There are some elements of autobiography in the play: Charlie, like Leonard himself, was born in 1926, a foundling, and adopted by a working-class couple in Dalkey. There may be a more directly personal element in the relationship depicted. In which case, the writing of the play is a writing-out of an emotional debt. There are one or two instances in which the writing of the play is reflexive, that is to say, when the subject-matter of the play is no longer class, or the psychology of a relationship between two characters, but simply writing-a-play:

> CHARLIE: . . . it was easier and funnier and more theologically orientated to say that the angels were having a pee.
> DA: You ought to put that down in one of your plays.
> CHARLIE: I'd die first. (p.10)

At the end of the play Da rather archly repeats the line that Leonard/Charlie will never put into a play. There is a sense in which the play seems to get out of control. Certainly it gets out of Charlie's control. One can pinpoint the moment when Da takes over: it is when Charlie tells him that he has burned all his documents:

> CHARLIE: I got rid of them. You're gone, now they're gone. So?
> DA: (*Nodding*) Ah, sure what the hell good were they anyway.
> CHARLIE: Eh? (p. 62)

This is the first hint that Da has a strategy all worked out. Young Charlie flies off to his wedding in Brussels, and the end of this is strangely conflated with Da asking Charlie, whom he seemingly mistakes for Mother's father, for his daughter's hand in marriage. There is an even stranger stage direction given at this moment:

(*Charlie stares at him. [Note: this is not a flashback to Da as a young man; it is Da in his 80s, his mind wandering.]*) (p. 67)

There is no other stage direction like this in the whole play. It is as though the writing of the play has taken over Leonard himself, that the character of Charlie's/Leonard's Da has achieved a certain autonomy, recalled a moment of fulfilment in the midst of disintegration. Leonard then writes some dialogue in which he seems to give back the initiative to Charlie's Da:

DA: I never carried on the like of that.
CHARLIE: How?
DA: Astray in the head. Thinking it was old God's time and you were herself's da.
CHARLIE: Oh, didn't you!
DA: And you're not a bit like him. (p. 68)

The sentient, all-knowing Da has been reclaimed from his dotage. I am not sure how convincing this reclamation is. Certainly, in the passage before it, when Da seems to lose his wits – and become, paradoxically, an objective reality – it does seem as though an unplanned and unintended bit of text was permitted to intrude and, in the revisions of the play, allowed to remain.

The narrative presses on. Drumm comes to the house at this point, with Da's will, his money and the spectacles from the San Francisco earthquake. Da, the dead Da, not

14

the personality of the idealised relationship, has actually put one over on Charlie. This is the ironic climax of the play, which Leonard planned, constructed dramatically, and wrote. In writing this play, did he, could he have anticipated the success and popularity of it? Or planned the autobiographical implications, which, in its very success, have been read into it?

We can now link the notion *within the play* of Charlie's Da going back with him to England, to the notion that the actual subject-matter of this play is *Leonard writing it*. The play's very success, together with the audiences' insistence on its semi-autobiographical content, mirrors Charlie's Da returning with Charlie, against his will, to England, permanently. Through the writing of this play, and through audiences and readers subsequently 'reading' an autobiographical meaning into it, Leonard's Da is now permanently lodged in his oeuvre. But what if the play is not autobiographical? What if Leonard deliberately made it all up, an act of the imagination, deliberately making it seem – through the corroborative evidence of other pieces of his writing – as if it was partly or even wholly autobiographical? It makes no difference, because ultimately there is no objective reality to which this dramatic work of the imagination can refer. It refers only to what is written within it, or to what is written elsewhere.

Belfast: Stewart Parker, 'Spokesong'

Stewart Parker was born in Belfast in 1941. In the late 1960s he published his poetry in Belfast in two collections: *The Casualty's Meditation* (1966) and *Maw* (1968). In 1970 he edited and introduced the late Sam Thompson's seminal play of a decade before, *Over the Bridge*. In the 1970s and 80s he wrote plays for television, radio and for the theatre.

Spokesong, or *The Common Wheel*, was presented at the John Player Theatre at the Dublin Theatre Festival in 1975. It is a musical, with music by Jimmy Kennedy and lyrics by Stewart Parker. The American premiere of the play was at Long Wharf Theatre, New Haven, Connecticut, on 2 February 1978; and at The Circle in the Square Theatre, New York, on 15 March 1979.

Spokesong is thematically and structurally similar to *Da*. The central character, Frank Stock, runs a bicycle shop in Belfast and is obsessed, as he approaches middle age, with the memory of his grandfather, Francis, who with his wife Kitty set up the bike shop in the 1890s. They raised Frank, and his adopted brother Julian, after Frank's parents had been killed in an air-raid in the Second World War. The context for Frank's obsession with their memory is the sectarian bombings in Belfast in the early 1970s. Frank cannot seem to come to terms with the disintegration of his social and moral values. He is also mired in two relationships in the present time of the play. He is courting a young Belfast schoolteacher, Daisy Bell; and he is trying to cope with his cynical foster-brother from England who is selling the bike shop over his head.

The play's structural links with *Da* are seen in the way in which the characters from the past are directly presented on the stage alongside those in the present. They are not flashbacks, in that they do not correlate with an objective historical reality. They are clearly a subjective impression or memory of what happened in the mind of the character Frank. The incidents in the grandparents' lives, which obviously took place before Frank was born, are still his imagination recreating what he remembers having been told. It is the exiled-in-England Julian who eventually

makes the audience question the validity of what has been
so straightforwardly depicted on the stage:

JULIAN: You still miss them.

FRANK: Deeply.

JULIAN: You're a liar to yourself, Frank. They weren't
in the smallest degree like that. Your memory's an
entire school of romantic fiction.

FRANK: It's not a question of remembering. They are
me. A big part of me. You too.

JULIAN: He was a vain and obsequious little Ulster
tradesman, a crank and a bore, going over and over
the same dog-eared tales of his youth and his war-
experiences.

FRANK: Let's drop it.

JULIAN: She was a spoiled daughter of the regiment,
slumming it in the quaint backstreets and in her
ridiculous lace-curtained nationalism.   (p. 60)

However, there is a crucial structural difference, for
unlike *Da* there is no communication between those in
the present and those in the past. The relationship which
Frank creates in his imagination with his grandparents
may be idealised – and fictional – but they make no
contribution to it. Unlike the past in *Da*, the past for
Frank seems to have no inner dynamism. It seems unable
to interact with the present. This indicates, perhaps, that
at a deeper level Frank is already recognising the problem
of the past being carried in him.

In the one scene, towards the end of the play, in which
Frank appears to have a conversation with his granda
Francis, this lack of communication becomes very clear.
Francis is repeating his story of how he was the first person
to win a race riding on Mr Dunlop's pneumatic tyres.

Indeed, Dunlop's invention in Belfast in the 1890s of the pneumatic tyre is the one reference to an objective historical reality upon which the whole fiction of the play is hung. Frank tries to break into Francis's reminiscence:

> FRANK: It's not just the same as it was for you. There's no simple enemy. There's no Back Home. No Boche. And no Blighty.

and a few moments later:

> I don't know what to do, Granda. I'm lost for something to do. I'm lost for words. I'm lost. (p. 65)

Francis is not lost for words, however; and Frank falls silent. His statement, linking the loss of a *raison d'être* with a loss of words – a loss of language – is significant. He goes out, gets drunk, and when he returns he launches into a long monologue which is part of a complex theatrical image of his *Angst*. He concludes with an attempt to relate his present suffering to a loss of a sense of the past. There can no longer be a positive engagement with history. At the same time he demonstrates that he does not have the language or the words to express the understanding he perceives:

> What I want to know is . . . your past . . . the past, I'm talking about . . . the air's full of it . . . you have to breathe it . . . but you can't grab hold of it . . . you see what I'm saying . . . it's everywhere but you can't locate it . . . you see where I'm driving . . . how can something that's fundamental . . . be irrecoverable . . . and uncontrollable . . . answer me that . . . you take the point . . . how are you supposed to live? (p. 71)

18

Dublin and Belfast

To appreciate the full meaning of this climactic but seemingly undramatic moment, we need to take account of the tone and the theatrical style of the play. Tone and style are perhaps summed up in the presence and function of the Trick Cyclist. He echoes the vaudeville, with his trick cycling as well as with his singing of the songs, which also echo the music-hall. In this way he provides a theatrical link between the Victorian past and the Absurdist present. He plays a number of small characters: Ulstermen, mainly, who set the scene or who are part of the narrative.

In these roles he speaks, obviously. But his overall role is visual. He is a performer, creating the images which make the meaning of a scene apparent. During Frank's monologue the Trick Cyclist performs 'a running commentary in mime', as the stage directions indicate. For the reader of the play it is a little difficult to create in the mind's eye exactly what this miming figure does. (For example: *The Trick Cyclist bounces and cracks* . . . reading it, one has to pause and think about the total stage image.) The point of this is made apparent in the words quoted above: Frank is telling the Trick Cyclist *and the audience* that they can actually see on the stage what he cannot say just in words, in a verbal language. A physicalised language of theatre has taken over. Prior to Frank's monologues, he (and the Trick Cyclist) have vaporised Francis and Kitty, who had become frozen theatrical emblems on stage in the manner of Renaissance theatre. The link with the past is broken in the imagination. But this break is communicated to audiences in the physical images of the theatre.

This rupture of Frank's sense of the past, and with it his lack of purpose and the words to express the fracturing of the imagination, is mirrored by the way in which the reality of Belfast after 1969 penetrates the text of the play. The text of the play is what is created in the imagination of audiences and readers: its world of the fiction, and its theatricality. The reality of violence in Belfast undermines it. Stewart Parker intends the text of the play to be undermined. Daisy, the schoolteacher with whom Frank falls in love, offers the first indication that the fiction (including herself) and the theatricality of the piece cannot remain hermetically sealed against the world in which Parker is writing his play. After Frank and Daisy meet the second time, and as they are making rather stilted conversation with each other, she lightly mentions that the children she teaches have just taught her how to booby-trap a car. He continues to talk enthusiastically about the history of the bike, and only much later returns to her casual comment:

FRANK: . . . Who told you how to make a booby-trap?
DAISY: I had forgotten that . . . I've got a hooligan class of 14-year-olds. I was trying like a conscientious fool to get them talking about their own interests. Before I know where I am, this pathetic pixillated child is halfway through a description of how to booby-trap a car. Some others were correcting him on points of detail . . .
. . . They're the same on guns and explosives as you are on boneshakers and ball-bearings. (p. 20)

Frank is still trying to enthuse about bicycles as she is trying to tell him of her own crisis of understanding:

DAISY: . . . It's beginning to get rather foolish, me standing up there saying, 'Now, class, open your books at the Wars of the Roses . . .' and them fresh

in from stoning soldiers, and setting fire to shops.
They've already got more history than they can cope
with out in the streets.

FRANK: That's not history, that's depraved folklore . . .
bogeyman stories.

DAISY: It's got more appeal than the truth, Frank,
whatever that is.   (p. 35)

Frank presses on with his own version of history: the
story of his Granda and John Boyd Dunlop. His own crisis
comes later, after Julian has undermined his belief in the
'. . . blocked-up latrine of your own memories'. Julian
cynically continues: 'That's what memories are, big
brother, that's what the past is, history, the accumulated
turds of human endeavour' (p. 61). Towards the end of
the play an objective Belfast reality seems to have taken
over the text entirely. Frank is invited to join the Protestant
direct action and is threatened when he says he will not.
The pet shop just down the road from his bike shop is
bombed. Daisy threatens to go to England with Julian.
This is the point at which he dismisses the emblems of his
grandparents, and faces up to the loss of his own sustaining
fiction. However, it is the objective reality which is not
sustained in the ending of the play. The fictional world
reasserts itself through the play's narrative: Daisy buys
the bike shop from Julian, conveniently sees off the
Protestant intimidation, and moves in with Frank. They
ride off the stage on a tandem – singing 'Daisy, Daisy,
give me your answer do . . . On a bicycle made for two'!
The text of this musical and love story is satisfactorily
concluded.

In terms purely of narrative, the text offers us a complete
piece of theatre. However, the tone of the ending is not
really 'happy'. In contriving a parody of the music-hall

song we are forced away from any possible reality into something which is purely theatrical. In a way, this is an admission of failure by the playwright: no 'real' solution to the problems of a real Frank and Daisy can be represented on the stage. The only thing that can work by way of a conclusion is a theatrical reference to an earlier piece of theatrical escapism.

The objective reality, to which a piece of theatre might refer in seeking to make representations of it on the stage, is never complete. Interim solutions may emerge, things come together, tragedies occur: they all immediately raise new situations and new problems. The logical outcome of fracturing the narrative of a play text with an intrusive and undermining political reality would be to abandon the text and allow the play simply to end. Audiences tend to find this unsatisfactory. A grim reality of poverty or violence in their lives often predisposes them towards a theatre where the text (narrative, character, theatricality and style) remains optimistically sealed against an external reality. When the external world is allowed to threaten the validity of the interior fictions of the play, audiences still expect an aesthetic completeness.

Hugh Leonard achieves this in *Da* through the psychological awareness of his characters: they appear to reveal all the complexities in a particular relationship, and our self-recognition, in the process, completes the piece. He does this through his skill as an ironist. He pursues a psychological reality through irony and paradox, which he realises in the dialogue he writes for the characters. His debt to Oscar Wilde is apparent, and not just in the characterisation of Mr Drumm.

Indeed, there is another kind of Wildean development in a subsequent play which Leonard wrote in which Drumm is the central character. *A Life* was first produced for the Abbey Theatre in October 1979. With a few weeks to live, Drumm reviews his life – or rather, he recalls that time in early adulthood when the promise of sexual fulfilment invades all the possibilities for one's future. In retrospect, how was this optimism destroyed? Being able to answer this question in the theatre requires a verbal adroitness: an ironic wit. That the clerkiarchy can find their failed lives funny redeems them somewhat. Their ironical awareness is their saving grace.

Stewart Parker is also an ironist in *Spokesong*, though somewhat more self-consciously so. Oscar Wilde is actually referred to twice; and the characters of Kitty, Daisy and Julian all have an obvious Wildean wit, although Julian's is shaded into a more bitter cynicism. What is interesting is that the awareness of a more insistent Irish political reality after 1969 makes both popular playwrights echo a writer who tended to reveal the ambiguities, dubious motivations and contradictions in reality rather than clear-cut commitment.

The beginnings of a direct reaction to the events in the North can be seen in *Spokesong*, and the beginnings of an indirect reaction in *Da*. As the political reality seeps into the fabric of plays in Ireland in the mid-1970s, it subverts the inherited structures of drama. Even if the violent rupturing of normal social interaction does not become the subject-matter of a play, the dramatic form and aesthetic are both inevitably penetrated, in the different ways that *Da* and *Spokesong* demonstrate.

The moment of contemporaneity in Irish drama is 1969, with the resurgence of violence in the Province of Northern Ireland. The traumas of the next three years were a watershed for playwrights who were already being published and performed. This was particularly so for playwrights from the North who still live there, and especially for Brian Friel whose work forms the subject-matter for two later chapters; but the impact on playwrights in the Republic was equally important. It seemed to highlight a malaise and an emotional inertia at the heart of what constituted Irish literature and drama – even in the concept of 'Irishness'.

Ironically, the years of civil unrest in Northern Ireland since 1969, emergency legislation and the presence of the British Army there to enforce its provisions, have been matched by increasing material prosperity, at least for those in employment, in both Britain and the Republic of Ireland. This seeming paradox heightened the sense of alienation felt by intellectual playwrights who perceived a growing cultural and social indifference to suffering and hardship. In the 1980s, too, the monetarist policies of the radical Right, in government in Britain since 1979, redistributed wealth from the provision of social welfare to individual high earners. This found an echo in the policies of successive Irish governments, who saw the Irish cost of living rise in sharp disproportion to Britain and to the United States. Residents in the South crossed the border into the North in order to do their shopping; and, in the 1980s, emigration of young Irish people to Britain and the USA increased considerably. The materialism which made a united Ireland a less attractive goal also revealed that in other respects the Republic was not much different from the British state. Indeed, it had its own repressive legislation which was directed at the same targets as the emergency legislation in the North. This paradox, as well, was not lost on some Irish playwrights. The individual now, rather than the Irish Free State, Eire, the Republic, could determine what 'being Irish' meant (Field Day Pamphlets 10–12: *Emergency Legislation*).

In this period, being a Dublin Irish playwright (like

Hugh Leonard), or a Belfast Irish playwright (like Stewart Parker) meant writing for British television, with little contractural or cultural difference. Despite providing the playwright with a wage – perhaps even because of it – the materialist British state is deeply alienating. But so is the Irish state, during the 1970s, torn as it is between materialism and conservative rural Catholicism. And, in the 1980s, another kind of Irish alienation becomes more widely recognised. The Ulster Protestant playwright finds himself or herself severed from the community, from the Northern Irish (sub)state which is revealed as flawed by opposite aspirations: to sustain an ancient dissenting history within *petit bourgeois* commercialism.

Sam Thompson's play of the 1950s, *Over the Bridge*, which was eventually staged in 1960 at the Empire Theatre in Belfast, despite Protestant opposition to it, presaged this Irish Protestant *Angst*. Stewart Parker's *Spokesong* approached the Irish Protestant dislocation, but then retreated, with an embarrassed laugh, into the purely theatrical. The 1980s articulation, in drama, of a crisis of identity in the work of a number of younger playwrights is covered in the extensive summary of Ulster drama by Philomena Muinzer. In her analysis of the whole range of Ulster drama over the past decade she combines the idea of a new *Aisling* poetic drama with the self-characterisation by Ulster Protestants of themselves as members of tribe, moving into their Pagan pre-history. (Philomena Muinzer, 'Evacuating the Museum: the Crisis of Playwriting in Ulster', *New Theatre Quarterly*, III, 9, Feb. 1987, London, Cambridge U.P., pp. 44–63. The Irish *Aisling* poetry is a neo-Romantic dream-vision of Ireland as mother or the beautiful young woman. In this characterisation she embodies state, home, family, history, identity.)

Belfast: David Rudkin, 'Cries from Casement as his Bones are Brought to Dublin'; 'Ashes'

Two plays by David Rudkin, in 1973 and 1974, throw this recent work into sharp perspective: the BBC Radio 3 drama: *Cries from Casement as his Bones are Brought to Dublin* (transmitted on 4 February 1973); and *Ashes*, premiered at the Open Space Theatre, London, on 9 January 1974. Rudkin is regarded in Britain as an English playwright, though he is, in fact, half English and half Northern Irish Protestant. In a quoted comment in the published text of *Cries from Casement . . .* he states his 'need to write a large piece that gave utterance to my Northern Irish Protestant identity as opposed to my English one'. He states, in another comment, in the text of *Ashes*,

I believe the dramatist's function in a society to be to transmute the idiosyncracies of personal life-experience into metaphors of public political value to mankind.

These two comments suggest the playwright has resolved his diverging cultural allegiances in an all-embracing higher allegiance to the role and commitment of being a dramatist. However, the discourse which he has sustained through the writing and production-into-performance of both these plays suggests that the matter is not so easily resolved; and some of his more recent writing and production – his BBC television drama, *Across the Water*, transmitted on 10 January 1983, for instance – would seem to bear this out.

Briefly, *Cries from Casement . . .*, a vast play for radio, and published as a text of the BBC transmission, is about Roger Casement who had a glittering career in the British

Foreign Office, revealing to a shocked readership in
Europe atrocities in the Belgian Congo and Peru, where
he was investigating forced labour; until he committed
himself, an Ulster Protestant, to the Republican struggle
and, during the First World War, smuggled arms from
Germany into Ireland to aid the 1916 Uprising. A
collection of Diaries, purportedly his, revealed him to be
a homosexual with descriptions of sexual activity. He
was tried, hanged, and buried in quicklime. The later
independent Irish government put pressure on the British
to allow his remains to be interred in Dublin. *Ashes*, the
stage-play of the following year, is about a couple who
are childless, though sexually active. The man, Colin, is
bisexual; and he is a Northern Irish Protestant. The play
specifically does not present either his background or his
sexuality as a problem to either him or his wife, Anne.
They submit themselves to all manner of humiliating
modern medical means to achieve conception, which
eventually does happen – but then Anne loses the foetus.

The discourse which these two plays represent is the
intersection of sexual identity (anthropological and
mythical, rather than Freudian) with a political identity
(derived from English political philosophers, rather than
from Marx and Lenin). The merging of the two reveals
the potential of drama to present private and unresolved
crises in the public domain. This results in a facing up to
the problem of identity, and eventually understanding
what was previously not understood at all. In the process,
the crises are related to the common weal, to the wider
community of humankind, which can collectively resolve
them through their common culture. The drama renders
the private torturing of ourselves redundant, even though
the problems may not yet be resolved.

Obviously, such a drama discourse requires the *writing*

of the play – a private act – to be carried through into its realisation as *public performance*. Rudkin was able to persuade the BBC that the conjunction of the homosexual and republican themes in the life of the Protestant Roger Casement, in *Cries from Casement* . . ., 'a large piece that gave utterance to my Northern Irish Protestant identity', was worth two and three-quarter hours of national air-time on radio with a large cast of professional actors. It was subsequently given an experimental stage production by the Royal Shakespeare Company. *Ashes*, which juxtaposes sex in a marriage in an extraordinarily frank and theatrically uncompromising way with opaque violence in Ulster separate from it, has had success in London and New York.

In each of these two plays there is a set piece at the end: a sort of epilogue set in Ulster today in which the central character – Casement in the one, Colin in *Ashes* – confronts what the playwright perceives to be the Protestant reality in Northern Ireland. The change in tone in the final scene of *Ashes* from that of *Cries from Casement* . . . is marked.

In the scene at the end of *Cries from Casement* . . . the tone is positive. Casement's bones are finally laid to rest in Dublin; he should have been buried in Belfast. Last to remain by his grave is an Irish Protestant youth, 'bleeding, maimed from an explosion. . . . A patriot not yet born'. Alienated in the Irish Republic, he tells Casement:

> But I'm a hated man here. I'd rather be outright English when I am here than what I am; a man of any colour I'd liefer be, a leper or a dwarf even, to feel less foreign than the thing I am. Boys, but when I'm south here, I'd give anything, anything to be anything other than

the hated thing I am. I feel so hated here, so unwhole;
to belong here I would give my heart.   (pp. 77–8)

Casement urges him to give his heart to Ireland, to say 'I
am of this land': a sense of belonging to this land, i.e. this
patch of earth, is set against the *Aisling* tradition. 'Tear
this old bitch Erin off your backs,' he tells the youth.
'She'll squeal and claw off skin and flesh from your bones,
but rip her off, be free of her: trample her down where
she belongs, beneath your feet, to be the land you live
from, not your incubus and curse' (p. 78). But even in
this passage, which condemns a Romantic nationalism,
the image of the wounded youth in the hero's graveyard
is still just that: nationalism romanticised.

In *Ashes*, the bleakness of the Ulster funeral set-piece
is matched with a more negative tone. Colin is describing,
in a long monologue, the funeral of his Uncle Tommy
which he went over to Ulster to attend. His uncle had
been blown up in a crowd of shoppers by a bomb. Colin
describes his cousin Sammy:

He stood beneath the picture of the Duke of Edinburgh
and the Queen: in his anorak, cap, dark glasses; with
his stick. 'It's well for you,' he said, 'across the water.
We here have to fight. To save the land we love.'

(p. 47)

Colin recounts how the men stopped him carrying the
coffin. Sammy tells him:

'You'll carry no Ulsterman's coffin to no grave. Stay
her wi' the weemen.' The drum beat. Up the street, to
the Orange Hall then to the grave, went with that coffin

all my – belonging. . . . The women did not speak to me. I felt so severed. (*No self-pity, but an absolute new clear-seeing:*) I know it is the strongest feeling in the world, to be alone. And I did feel strong. Yet, the land, from whose earth I belong, the clan, from whose loins I come, had turned me out; to my own loins no child of tomorrow shall come; and I felt so – (*at last*) severed. . . . So. There's another – 'self' for the rubbish heap with all the rest. My self as 'tribal son'.   (pp. 48–9)

This account of a funeral signals a disengagement with Ireland; Casement's threnody was for the opposite: a more compelling engagement. The emblem of the 'bleeding youth' by Casement's Dublin grave has also given way to a naturalistic description of the awful aftermath of the bombing of shoppers in a crowded street. Colin returns to England, his wife Anne and their personal problem of a childless marriage. This is not the optimistic narrative conclusion – the happy ending – of *Spokesong*; but it is a similar avoidance of the ultimate dislocation of the text by violence in Northern Ireland. Again this is dictated by the structure and impetus of the drama. There is no easy or immediate resolution to the violence; but the ruptured narrative structure of the play demands an ending, a conclusion. Just as Frank, with Daisy, goes back to running his bike shop, so Colin, with Anne, goes back to pursuing the ultimate purpose of their marriage and their lives together. The final tone direction of Rudkin's play stresses the positive nature of this: . . . *and now he must learn to look at her, frank in his inadequacies, his reality, just as he is, all male personae shed. A Beginning* (p. 51). Curiously, this resolution and optimism does not seem to be reflected in either the spoken words or any other visual performance images in the play itself. The tone direction places a great burden on the actors who must accept it as the authorial voice within the text as a whole.

Although these two plays of the early 1970s present a dramatic vision of Irish attitudes which are more appropriate to the mid-1980s, they are nevertheless keyed into an English drama discourse, rather than an Irish one. This is not necessarily because of their delineation of an Irish dissenting *Angst* – indeed, this is now part of the Irish dramatic discourse – or because of the insistent male homosexuality, defended and upheld in both plays as a socially positive sexuality; but rather because the intersection of the sexual and the political themes, in the drama, is grounded in a philosophical view which is uniquely English: libertarian, pragmatic, non-ideological. It is the composure of a dominant, colonising culture. The disparaging use of the word 'tribal' by Rudkin, through his central character, Colin, at the moment of climax of the play, justifies a retreat to another kind of self-awareness, and is perhaps a reflection of Rudkin's more dominant English sensibilities.

'Tribe' is the word used by people of the dominant culture to describe the behaviour of dominated peoples who, against all economic logic, refuse to give up their own cultural behaviour which is considered as quaint, odd, illogical, and ultimately irrelevant. Philomena Muinzer appropriately draws our attention to the 'regression' to the pagan tribe in the work of many contemporary Ulster dramatists. The coloniser's notion of the unsentient tribe justifies his 'civilising' cultural imperialism; his triumph is to get the colonised to believe that they are indeed unsentient, with atrophied sensibilities. During the period of English colonisation of Ireland, the Catholic Irish found themselves characterised as 'tribal'; and now the Northern Irish Protestants, who see themselves betrayed by *petit bourgeois* British pragmatism which they had supported, accept the tribal disparagement of their reawakened dissenting identity by English and Irish alike.

These ideas are extended in the plays of the late 1970s and 1980s of the Ulster playwright, Brian Friel, whose work as a whole is considered later in the book. He is not only an outstanding Ulster playwright and a major influence on the direction of Irish theatre today, but also one of the most significant playwrights presently writing in the English language. Like that other Irish playwright, Samuel Beckett, Friel has extended the art of theatre to express the crisis of modern European sensibility, the death of the imagination; and like the plays of the German playwright, Peter Handke, and of the Nigerian playwright and Nobel prize-winner, Wole Soyinka, Friel's work discovers, through the specifics of colonised violence on Irish land, the political limitations of drama. It is these political limitations which concern us here.

Rudkin claimed that the dramatist translated personal life-experiences into 'metaphors of public political value to mankind'. Yet, like the plays we considered of Hugh Leonard and Stewart Parker, which show only a political awareness rather than a political commitment or intent, Rudkin's own dramatic structures work against a politicised drama. Rather than a political commitment to Northern Ireland, his two Ulster plays of the early 1970s return us to the Romantic paradigm of the search for the true self – Ibsen's *Peer Gynt* peeling away of the onion layers of 'Selfhood'. Rudkin's Irish plays are an extension of his English plays: a categorisation of his Irish experience. The plays may describe Irish politics, but they are not plays which commit their audiences to any political meaning for them.

Belfast: Graham Reid, 'Remembrance'; Martin Lynch, 'The Interrogation of Ambrose Fogarty'

Two working-class Belfast playwrights of the 1980s, Graham Reid and Martin Lynch, each, in different ways, in their plays and their professional careers as dramatists, offer us insights into the problems of politicising drama. Graham Reid, born in 1945, who ran away to join the British Army at 15, and took his university degree in his late 20s, is now an established dramatist, writing extensively for the BBC and commercial television in Britain, with his play-scripts published in London, and his stage plays performed in both Belfast and Dublin.

Martin Lynch, born in 1950, also in Belfast, worked in the Belfast Docklands and developed his playwriting through community theatre groups. He is less noticed than Reid, mainly because he has not had the extensive broadcast transmission or London publication of his work which Reid has. Both playwrights, however, are keyed into the British state patronage network of the Northern Ireland Province: they have both received financial assistance from the Northern Ireland Arts Council, and have held Writerships-in-Residence at the Lyric Players Theatre (Lynch), at Queens University, Belfast (Reid), and the University of Ulster, Coleraine (Lynch).

Reid's recent stage-play, *Remembrance*, premiered at the Lyric Theatre on 10 October 1984, and Lynch's only published play to date, *The Interrogation of Ambrose Fogarty*, also premiered at the Lyric, on 27 January 1982, both deal with a similar theme: the role and behaviour of the security forces, and in particular the Royal Ulster Constabulary (RUC), in administering Section 11 of the Northern Ireland (Emergency Provisions) Act of 1978. Lynch's play is set inside the Police Station: reception, cells and interviewing room. The violence is physical and on-stage. In Reid's *Remembrance*, the action ranges between the kitchens of two homes: Protestant and Catholic; and the graveyard. One character only is a policeman, and his violence is off-stage, though his account of it is ironically exaggerated.

Both plays are concerned to make apparent the very ordinariness of the people who, as custodians of the peace, systematically beat up other people. They are deliberately portrayed as not being pathological in their physical and mental abuse of others. They are shown as having exactly the same sensibilities as those people who observe them askance, with horror, including the playwrights themselves, whether they be Protestant or Catholic. This is the obverse of depicting their violent behaviour as indicative of the tribe, casting itself outside 'civilised' society. It is an attempt to show intimidation and torture, lies and abuse, as part of ordinary British and Irish society. Indeed, it goes further and shows that the enforcement of the laws and restrictions of the dominant society specifically requires this behaviour. Both playwrights show the policemen caught up with defending an imposed 'civilising' order on elements who quite logically seek to destabilise that order.

Lynch's characters precisely demonstrate this: the various members of the security forces who come in and out of the police station during the day show a range of ordinary attitudes, even including the instinctively physical and anti-intellectual plain-clothes policeman Jackie who seems to be longing to beat up the two IRA suspects, Ambrose Fogarty and Willie Lagan. It is Lynch's characterisation of these two suspects which is most downbeat. In the early stages of his 3-day interrogation, Fogarty seems to be a non-person, worrying about what physical aspects of the impending torture he will not be able to bear, trying to do press-ups, insisting on his rights and then almost giving up on them. It is deliberately made unclear in the early part of the play whether he is an active member of the IRA, whether he participated in a bank robbery, indeed, whether he is a terrorist suspect at all.

Towards the end of the play it becomes obvious that he is just an ordinary unemployed fellow who actually shows extraordinary endurance of a physical beating up by the brutal Jackie. This is not the climax of the play, however. Fogarty is taken back to his cell and makes a formal complaint to the Station Sergeant (a quite sympathetically-drawn policeman). Fogarty questions the nature of a society which can make such ordinary men do daily violence on their fellows as a job. The Sergeant is phlegmatic. This scene is intercut with the three special branch officers talking together in the aftermath of their brutal assault on Fogarty. While their reasoning is flawed and their justifications lame, they are re-established, after unacceptable violence, as part of the same materialist British (and Irish) society to which we, the audience or readers, belong.

The play's achievement is to make all the characters seem not much different from ourselves, even including the other suspect, Willie Lagan, who is recognised by all as 'not the full shilling'. The way Willie is drawn makes the most telling indictment of contemporary affluent Western society. He is a victim; and even to the audience he is not particularly likeable. He is not blessed with intelligence or even native wit – despite his endless jokes – and he is even more gratuitously beaten and abused than Fogarty.

The play ends with Willie Lagan being charged with three offences: this is vindictive and mean behaviour by the law-enforcement officers, simply because he is a man who is innocent, but irritatingly inadequate and unable to fight back.

Graham Reid's *Remembrance* depicts a rather awkward and unexpected love-affair of sorts between a Protestant man and a Catholic woman, both in their 60s, who meet in the graveyard where each has a son buried, murdered by the 'other side'. Their age has softened their prejudices; but not, the play shows, the prejudices of their surviving offspring. The man, Bert, has served in the British Army; his son, Victor, is presently serving with the RUC Special Branch, interrogating 'terrorist' suspects under Section 11 of the Emergency Powers Act. Victor is marginal to the narrative of the play – the adult daughters of the woman, Teresa, turn out to be more integral – but his brooding presence permeates the play. In the first scene he informs his father he is emigrating to South Africa – 'Good cops are appreciated over there. Kick the black bollocks off the nigs and nobody says "boo" to you' (p. 13) – and this is told, with embellishments, to others. When he meets the Catholic Theresa – whose son was shot by the RUC – she asks him if he is a policeman:

> VICTOR: A torturer, actually. That's why I'm exhausted tonight. Do you know, I've spent the whole day trying to coax a prisoner to jump out through the window? But the ungrateful bastard wouldn't jump. We haven't had a suicide for months. It implies our methods don't work. We're way behind some of the top British police forces. . . .
>
> THERESA: It must be a terrible job.
>
> VICTOR: Must it? No . . . I like it. I enjoy it.
>
> BERT: Victor, give it a rest.　　　　　　　　　　(p. 33)

Victor's estranged wife, Jenny, has earlier confirmed the tone of his utterances:

> JENNY: . . . don't try to fool me with your 'thick peeler's' routine. That's the one thing I dislike most about you. This attempt to portray yourself as a working-class thickie.
>
> VICTOR: I am working class.
>
> JENNY: You've had an education. You're an intelligent or at least a well-educated man. That job has destroyed you. I don't think you are doing Sam – or the memory of Sam – any good by pretending to be an unthinking fascist thug. (p. 30)

The ironical effect of Victor's edgy, satirical tone is to make the brutal and violent man seem ordinary, no different from his counterparts in the English constabulary. The viciousness is not denied; but its exaggeration shifts it from the man on to the society he 'protects'. Within the specific narrative of the play, that is, the story of Victor's father falling in love with an elderly Catholic woman, Victor does not appear as threatening. Indeed, towards the end of the play, he actually is about to date Deidre, Theresa's daughter, whose husband has been tried and imprisoned as an IRA killer. The audience even begin to feel comfortable with him, despite his uncomforting presence. In an interview, Graham Reid has described his own response to the men of violence:

> One of the most vicious men I ever met, he was paralysed in a shooting incident, he was a Provo, but I mean he was the life and soul of the hospital, you know, you couldn't dislike him. And for a while, until I

recognised this I felt very, very guilty. I'd go home at night thinking, I laughed at that bugger today, or I spoke to him today. I'd feel very uptight about that. And it was a recognition in different times, in a different environment – and I had worked with people like him in England – they were very ordinary people. Frighteningly ordinary.

(quoted in the *Guardian*, London, Manchester, 12 Nov. 1985)

These two plays are not necessarily representative of the best work of either dramatist. Reid's television trilogy, *Billy: Three Plays for Television*, was widely reviewed and praised; Martin Lynch, on the other hand, has generated interesting and important drama work with groups and within communities which has tended not to be noticed. But *The Interrogation of Ambrose Fogarty* and *Remembrance*, separately and together, indicate a developing drama discourse on the political future of Northern Ireland, which has more to do with politics and less to do with theatrical representations of an Irish polity. This new political intention is located in the confrontation between those charged with upholding law and order and those dissenting from those particular laws and that particular order. Repressive legislation is not orderly but vengeful.

Belfast: Ron Hutchinson, 'Rat in the Skull'; Anne Devlin, 'Naming the Names'

This new Ulster drama shows that even as the security forces seek to stand above the political implications of sectarian violence in their seeming ordinariness, so,

38

ironically, they are forced to reveal the political nature of the struggle. The need for very violent maintenance law and order raises the questions: Whose law? And what order? Continuing to insist on the impartiality of violent and brutal orderliness reveals the hidden and greater protagonist. The Northern Irish Protestant reaction to the Anglo-Irish Agreement (signed by the Irish and British governments in 1985) is a reaction not only to the idea of a united Ireland but also to Britain from which they are alienated. This is partly reflected in two Northern Irish plays screened on British television in 1987: *Rat in the Skull* by Ron Hutchinson, and *Naming the Names* by Anne Devlin.

Rat in the Skull was first performed at the Royal Court Theatre in London in 1984, and subsequently produced for British television. It was first screened in January 1987. An RUC interrogator is brought over to England to interrogate Roche, an IRA suspect of a London bombing. This is seemingly a confrontation between two antagonists. However, the shadowy and half-hidden third force of British law and British order is represented by the English police station, where the interview takes place, with its impartial English police superintendent and marginally venal and prejudiced constable. Their bafflement with and dislike of both interrogator and interrogated reflects the English point of view.

The constable, who is supposed to see that the interrogation is conducted by 'normal', 'civilised' procedures, finally allows himself to be persuaded to step outside the cell: by Roche, on the RUC man's insistence. Roche knows he will be beaten up by the latter. But his injuries at the hand of his interrogator will then force his release. For what? A later armed confrontation on Northern Irish soil. The English police cannot understand this palimpsest of a personally vengeful order on their own legal system. What these Englishmen cannot see is that it is originally their order and their laws.

Anne Devlin's play, *Naming the Names*, which was also broadcast on British television in 1987, was originally a short story (published in *The Way Paver*, London, Faber, 1987) and follows her earlier stage play, *Ourselves Alone*, which was staged during the filming of *Naming the Names* at the Royal Court Theatre. The play is about Finn McQuillen, a Belfast woman who pursues a liaison with the son of a Protestant judge in order eventually to lure him into his murder in an IRA trap. The play is set within the frame of her interrogation by members of the security forces. They are portrayed as ordinary and appalled by her action. Again, they reflect the British television viewers' dominant point of view. She does not seek to justify what she did; but, in a series of flashbacks, we see her absorbed into a personally vengeful order, overlaid upon the particular laws and particular order of the British state, materialist and predominantly male. The television play tries to make the specific obsessions of the 'normal', 'ordinary' polity apparent.

It is worth noting that in the BBC hype for the screening of the play the acting art of the non-Irish actress who played Finn was highlighted, rather than the achievement of the playwright herself. For example:

> Despite this, her [the actress's] normal accent is unaffected Home Counties – but it is not the accent to be heard in this week's *Screen Two* film, *Naming the Names*. In this she adopts a Belfast brogue and the Troubles in Northern Ireland are central to the drama in which she stars with . . .
>
> (BBC *Radio Times*, 7–13 Feb. 1987)

This sort of journalism is a continuation of what the play is attempting to criticise. It is an ironical and unconscious reflection of an actual element in the narrative of the play: one of the earlier boyfriends of the central character in the play, Finn, is an English journalist sent over to cover 'the Troubles' who later intervenes during the interrogation on behalf of the 'appalled' British. In a seeming parody of this, the BBC hype describes the actress playing Finn as going to Belfast for 'a short trip' and finding it a welcoming city: 'But filming near the end of a rifle – the way normal life continues in what is effectively an occupied city – rather disturbed me,' she is reported as saying.

None of these writers whose work confronts the paradox of aggressive and coercive policing in an affluent and 'free' materialist society presumably harbours any illusion that they can intervene as playwrights in the situation which personally affects them so greatly. On the other hand, they obviously hope to raise the political consciousness of their British audiences through the enhanced understanding of a situation of which those audiences are not so pressingly aware.

Dublin: Brendan Behan's 'The Hostage' in retrospect

On the surface it may seem as though there has been little development from Brendan Behan's *The Hostage*, as it was realised in Joan Littlewood's notable production of 1958, in which an English 'Tommy' – a regular soldier – is taken hostage by the IRA for one of their men who is to be hanged in a Belfast gaol. The hostage is holed up by his captors in a Dublin brothel, amongst whose residents he finds some support. Behan's play is a translation of his

Irish play *An Giall*. He was inspired by Frank O'Connor's short story 'Guests of the Nation', as well as being influenced by the theatre perspectives of the director, Joan Littlewood.

Behan himself served borstal and prison sentences for his boyhood membership of the IRA, and later in Dublin for shooting at a policeman. He writes directly out of his life experience; whether it be in prose fiction or reminiscence, or in drama. To some extent, professional theatre directors such as Joan Littlewood have put other writers to work on his text while it has been in production. In doing this they may have unfortunately and unintentionally excised from his drama its originality and the particular strengths of its dramatic structural *naïveté*.

The play's achievement is to make the British soldier and the IRA gunmen seem as ordinary as the Dublin whores and tenement residents who provide them with their credible urban context. 'Ordinary' in this context means as colourful and flamboyant as the writer himself. However, any similarities between that 1950s play and the Ulster drama today – of Reid, Lynch, Devlin, Friel and others – is only on first glance. Behan, and Littlewood as his equally ebullient director, together set a Dublin *élan*, or style, against the dourness of life in the British-occupied North. Dublin, they seem to be saying, can turn the IRA – and death – into wit and theatre. By contrast, Britain is orderly, and boring.

It is this positive anarchic Dublin alternative which the writers today find has evaporated. A dour and partial affluence is now seen to spread in a line from London to Dublin. It must be violently sustained – in a struggle at present conveniently located in Belfast and Northern Ireland.

A sense of the harsh realities of urban Ireland generally

has made an equal impact on both the style and content of Irish drama being developed by the professional theatre in Dublin. In some ways, this disillusionment is stylishly expressed by Leonard in his mocking of the upwardly-mobile young Dublin professionals and *petit bourgeoisie*. But his very style, his acute observation, ensures paradoxically that Dublin continues to exist as a cultural entity, as a more self-aware and witty alternative to London. In this he is like his literary mentor, Flann O'Brien (a pseudonym for Brian O Nuallain: *b*. 1912 in Strabane; *d*. 1966, Dublin; another pseudonym is Myles na Gopaleen.) This literary Dublin continues to appeal to intellectuals abroad.

Dublin: Jim Sheridan, 'Mobile Homes'

Two Dublin theatre directors provide an alternative materialist discourse to the shrewd and introverted psychology of Hugh Leonard's particular materialist discourse: Jim Sheridan and Patrick Mason. Both have encouraged younger Irish writers keen to bring a modern Ireland onto the stage for a non-literary Irish audience and to find new theatrical ways for doing so. Jim Sheridan, together with his brother Peter Sheridan, has been closely associated with the Project Arts Centre which was founded in Dublin in 1967 as a radical force for change in the Arts in Ireland:

> Originally a gathering of visual artists based in a single room, Project is now [1978] an organization of artists, musicians, writers, actors, directors, designers, film-makers and others who work in their own building, with its own gallery, cinema and performing space. They

present new Irish work which reflects and challenges the aspirations of the young, urbane and progressive population of Ireland today.

(Jim Sheridan, *Mobile Homes*, Co-op Plays, 1978)

Jim and Peter Sheridan founded the Project Theatre Company in 1977 at the Project Arts Centre. In the mid and late 1970s Project encouraged the talents of writers such as the Sheridans and Bernard Farrell. Jim Sheridan has worked also with the Lyric Players Theatre in Belfast, with the Abbey Theatre; with the Royal Court and the Institute of Contemporary Arts in London; and, since 1981, with various Off-Broadway theatres and the Irish Arts Theatre in New York, and with the Field Day Theatre Company in Derry. In Easter 1975 he co-directed, with the authors and Robert Walker, the single 26-hour performance in Dublin of Margaretta D'Arcy's and John Arden's *The Non-Stop Connolly Show*. In 1976 his own play, *Mobile Homes*, was directed by his brother Peter at Project. It is interesting to compare the tone and political intent of this play with the plays from Ulster.

Like *The Non-Stop Connolly Show* by D'Arcy and Arden, *Mobile Homes* advertises its political intentions in an explanatory preface in the published text which gives the factual reference for the fiction of the play, and points to the political significance in the reality which the play now hopes to make more explicit. It uses, as the microcosm of an exploitative social system, an illegal mobile homes site where, generally speaking, young couples purchase their first home and are variously exploited by salesmen, landlords and the Dublin Corporation. The play tries to show how by organising themselves on the site the young people could counteract their real oppression.

The tone of the play, like the tone of Lynch's *The*

Interrogation of Ambrose Fogarty, is very down-beat, deliberately avoiding a precocious intellectual wit in the characters, a 'cleverness' by which they might bamboozle their oppressors. The latter, too, are underdrawn: landlord and bureaucrats are neither well-organised nor effectively pragmatic. Furthermore, Sheridan does not seek to create an inventive dramatic structure which will draw attention to a compelling narrative and away from the almost insoluble problems of getting people together so that they can start to win their battles with the authorities by their collectivity. The result is a play which draws a spare and depressing picture of Dublin, without undervaluing the potential of the young Dubliners in it. The written text of the play is dedicated to the real Dubliners on whose actions the play is based.

Dublin: Patrick Mason at the Abbey: Theatre of the Image

Patrick Mason has been responsible for the development in performance of the creative playwriting talents of Thomas Kilroy, Tom Murphy, Graham Reid, Tom MacIntyre and Frank McGuinness, who greatly respect his theatrical vision. A great deal of the work has been developed at the Abbey's studio theatre, the Peacock, and then taken on tour, north and south of the Border, and to England. One example of his interactive work with playwrights and actors has been the 'Theatre of the Image', developed with Tom MacIntyre and the actor Tom Hickey, through the production of three of MacIntyre's plays: *The Great Hunger* (1983); *The Bearded Lady* (1984); and *Rise Up Lovely Sweeney* (1985).

The Great Hunger, which is based on Patrick Kavanagh's poem of the same title, was widely toured in 1986 and then had a run at the Almeida Theatre in London. The play is set in the early 1940s, during the Second World War, when Eire was neutral. In production the play works, not through verbal language but through powerful visual images of the spiritual and material desolation of the lives of peasant farmers in rural Ireland, set apart from world history at that point in time, fearful of women and sexually frustrated.

In the production at the Almeida Theatre the whole of the back of the stage was a towering wall of corrugated zinc, blackened and rusting, against which male characters hurled objects which crashed against it and resounded hollowly. The centre of the stage was a field of potato ridges running back to a fence; and, around the edges of this, interiors were created by a single object – such as a hearth, or an altar-rail. The acting company, from the Abbey, created, as an ensemble, sound and visual images – of gulls, for example, swooping across the front of the carthorse as the field was ploughed – and these images created resonances for the audience, rather than a meaning which comes from the syntax of sentences.

The Mason–Hickey–MacIntyre 'Theatre of the Image' obviously owes something to similar developments in theatre in Europe, in the work of Leopold Grotowski, Eugenio Barba, Peter Brook, and in Research Theatre generally, as well as to the theorising of this in theatre semiotics (as outlined, for example, in Keir Elam's *Semiotics of the Theatre*, London, Methuen, 1980). One problem of this is that, like opera, such drama cannot really exist independent of its performance in a written text. It tends, therefore, to get overlooked in a critical text like this. Unlike opera, or ballet, however, it lacks the sort of notation on the one hand, and the extensive and acceptable patronage on the other, which will ensure continual and repeated performances. It is 'High Art': it pushes out the limits of theatre and drama and so addresses itself to those who are interested in the art of theatre, as much as in the meaning and significance of the reality it depicts.

Dublin and Belfast: Frank McGuinness, 'Observe the Sons of Ulster, Marching Towards the Somme'

Mason directed Frank McGuinness's first major play, *The Factory Girls* at the Peacock in 1982, and in Australia the following year. In 1985 he directed both McGuinness's *Baglady/Ladybag* and his major work to date, *Observe the Sons of Ulster, Marching Towards the Somme*. In between these formal productions of his written play-texts, McGuinness worked with TEAM, a Theatre-in-Education and community theatre company, producing two texts, *Borderlands* (1983) and *The Gatherers* (1984). In 1986 his latest play *Innocence* was produced at the Dublin Theatre Festival, at the Gate Theatre, a play based on the life of the Renaissance painter Caravaggio. He acknowledges the influence of the play, *Demetos*, by the South African playwright Athol Fugard on the writing of this play; also of the Catholic Church and his Donegal peasant background.

Frank McGuinness has emerged now as one of the most important younger playwrights in Ireland today. *Observe the Sons of Ulster, Marching Towards the Somme* has won a number of prizes and, after the closing of Mason's Abbey production which extensively toured Northern Ireland with great success, it has already had an English production in London, at the Hampstead Theatre, directed by Michael Attenborough.

The play is about a group of young Ulstermen – Loyalists who go off to fight for British King and British Country in the First World War, and who die on the Somme. Except one: Kenneth Pyper, who, now an old man in the North, calls up the ghosts of his slaughtered companions, and attempts to restate in some forgotten way what constituted their loyalty to Ulster, to Protestantism and to Britain; but above all, to each other.

This central figure of Pyper is the catalyst who generates the ironies and contradictions within the play. As the only member of the Northern Protestant Ascendancy, Pyper is a young man in 1914: overbred, effete and nihilistic. He is in an emotional and mental *cul-de-sac* by virtue of his background and his history. He self-consciously parodies himself and mocks the others.

These others are working-class Ulstermen: Protestant, innocent and naïve. Two pairs are already friends when they enlist in the British army, one pair from Belfast, the other pair from Coleraine. Another man, older and self-absorbed, is or was a Presbyterian preacher; he soon seeks to protect the youngest and most innocent man amongst them. Pyper himself finds friendship with the son of a blacksmith who is increasingly perceptive and secure. Although they bring conventional Loyalist values into their platoon, they have widely different personalities, and, in coming from different parts of the Province, they consciously show off their rivalry of each other. What the war does is suddenly to deepen their camaraderie into intense and specific male friendships. The friendship is homosexual in the case of Pyper and Craig, but not so in the other relationships. These pairs of relationships serve as a structural framework and positive context for the analysis of their cultural backgrounds. The humanity and heroism of the men, and of their sensibilities, force a reassessment of history, allegiances and affinities.

This reassessment is ironically overturned at the end of the play by Pyper as an old man. As a young man he was at first the only one among them who understood and forced the reassessment on the others. Pyper's survival at the Somme when all the others perished leaves him with the memory of those intense friendships and acts of heroism, and this subsequently makes him defend fanatically what he felt defined them together: Protestant and Loyalist sympathies.

This moment of contradictory understanding is precisely judged in the theatre. McGuinness's act of writing such a play as this challenges Loyalist and Republican sentiment, north and south of the Border. The ending of the play draws together the theme of Irish identity, the function of theatre and the function of language. It is the inclusion in the drama discourse of the function of language which makes the play so significant. Other plays have hinted at the inadequacy of the verbal languages we have and use to get our minds around the realities of our world today – *Mobile Homes* even has a crucial passage on this at the moment of the climax, while *The Great Hunger* avoids sentences and verbal syntax altogether – but McGuinness builds this problem into the very structure of the play.

The characters initially and consciously define themselves in front of each other within the fiction of the play. They also define themselves to us, the audience. These spoken definitions are made easy by their common Loyalist background – a shorthand of abuse of Catholics and Nationalists. The characters are then required by their new circumstances to redefine themselves. The shorthand is no longer available. They are forced to define themselves *by actions*, which, in a composite expressionist scene, we as audience see taking place on stage. However, in order to be accomplished, this action needs to be spoken.

In this crucial scene they are on home-leave from the Front, just before the Battle of the Somme, each with his special friend, in different parts of the Province. All have already been traumatised by their experiences at the Front, and all know inwardly that the worst lies ahead of them. In each pairing one man needs to cope with an expression of a deeper crisis in his friend, and in each pair there is an act of friendship which is both a physical act and an act of speaking about it: one man *talks* the other man in crisis through to safety – though in the case of Anderson and McIlwaine, 'talking' is stretched to mean the beating of the Lambeg drum, and the unchanged speech of the Orange Parade to celebrate the Battle of the Boyne.

These several crises, as well as the collective trauma of the war, can only be handled in dialogue that occurs within the framework of a person's cultural references: here, as male; Loyalist; Protestant; Ulstermen. Cultural categories have positive and negative capabilities. Male relationships can be macho and competitive; they can also become loving and caring.

In the same way, nationalism, tribalism and religious bigotry can be transformed at certain adverse historical moments into the mainsprings of self-sacrifice and a deeper understanding. These alternatives need, in reality, to be both acted out and talked through. In the fictions in the theatre both need to be represented in precise dramatic structuring.

The audience arrive at the theatre to see the play with their particular structure of understanding. There *was* a real Battle of the Somme: subsequent generations have been made aware of the carnage and culpability of that

event. Ulster Loyalists *were* slaughtered there: memories
and monuments commemorate their sacrifice. To this
knowledge of historical events we add our divergent
understanding of Ulster (Northern Ireland) today. This is
in counterpoint to the play's own fictive account of the
'Somme', the 'Sons of Ulster', the 'Marching Towards . . .'
something (friendship, understanding, death, memory).

The play does not intend historical accuracy because
the playwright actually intends the opposite: to indict
history, dramatised as Pyper's regression into Unionist
activism in order to preserve the historical significance of
the sacrifice of his Loyalist friends. McGuinness's play
seeks instead to remember the friendship as an expression
of sensibilities which transcend limiting historical
archetypes.

To many who saw the play, either north or south of the
Border, it was about the Loyalists and about the First
World War in a destabilising way, especially in the way
it depicts changes in ordinary people's sensibilities. It
undermines the present cliché-ed debate about Catholics
and Protestants, about Republicanism and Loyalism from
inside those very clichés. It does this through actions on
the stage which force out of the characters on the stage a
new expression to match newly-discovered sensibilities.
The linking of speech to action to achieve a more profound
articulation of the sensibilities *of the audiences* is the
particular accomplishment of this play.

Dublin: Thomas Kilroy, 'Talbot's Box'; 'Double Cross'

Mason directed Kilroy's *Talbot's Box* in 1977 – a very
different play from Kilroy's highly successful play of nearly
a decade earlier, *The Death and Resurrection of Mr Roche*

(1968), which, like a number of important new Irish plays, was originally premiered and noticed at the Dublin Theatre Festival.

Kilroy was born in County Kilkenny in 1934. He has been Professor of Modern English at the University College, Galway, for the past 10 years. His participation in the Dublin literary scene, dominated by urban Dublin and Belfast perspectives, has been, perhaps, from a distance: he has a rural West of Ireland perspective and an uncompromising intellectual commitment to the processes of history: to historiography. His plays after the successful *Death and Resurrection of Mr Roche* – which was very much a modern urban Dublin play, observing a new materialism – have turned more to ideas and history. They have not been quite as successful in Dublin. His highly praised, award-winning novel, *The Big Chapel*, is specifically concerned with the relationship between history and fiction. Kilroy's intellectual critique of the personal introverted discourses of urban drama has lately influenced Dublin theatre. To some extent, Frank McGuinness has inherited this orientation from him. It is discernible in *Observe the Sons of Ulster . . .* and *Innocence*, his play out of the life of the Italian Renaissance painter Carravagio. The Field Day Theatre Company, of which he is not a member, have been influenced by the scope of his thought.

Talbot's Box is based upon the life of Matt Talbot who lived in Dublin from 1856 to 1925. For nearly 40 years of his adult life he had been a worker living in grinding poverty in a room in a Dublin tenement. He had bound his body up with chains, which had eaten into his flesh, while he followed a rigid daily regime of prayer and self-inflicted physical punishment. There is a movement in

Ireland to have him canonised. He would become the first urban working-class saint of Roman Catholic Ireland. In a *Note on Matt Talbot*, Kilroy sets out his authorial intentions for the play he has written and which Mason produced for Dublin audiences. Kilroy perceives as a single phenomenon the known facts of Talbot's life and the subsequent intentions of others to make him into a saint. Talbot lived through a crucial period in Irish history which was focused upon Dublin: the Great Lock-out in 1913, the Easter 1916 Uprising, the creation of the Irish Free State and the subsequent troubles in the 1920s. His adult life coincides with an historical period when Ireland changed its governing and commercial elites. Kilroy's first intention therefore is to show how the new elites, the Catholic *petit bourgeoisie*, who emerged from that historical upheaval needed – and still need – to validate themselves as the true heirs of the idealism which ultimately brought them to power. This is a political discourse, grounded in materialism. In the Author's Note Kilroy describes it thus:

> In the beginning I was possessed by the crude manipulation of an eccentric, inaccessible man by forces which sought a model for the purposes of retaining power.
>
> (Thomas Kilroy, *Talbot's Box*, Gallery Press, Dublin, 1979)

There are elements of this vision of the hegemony of the new Irish state in all but the concluding sections of the play. The most obvious is the section leading up to the dramatisation of 'Bloody Sunday' in Dublin, 1913, which closes the first half of the play:

PRIEST FIGURE: The people were misled. Agitators, proselytisers, terrorists. There is always a cost to fighting the godless.

FIRST MAN: (*Matter of fact*) There's always a Bloody Sunday, a Bloody Friday, somewhere or other. St. Petersburg, Dublin, Derry, Santiago. It happens. It passes. Can you name the names of the dead? No. Only the names of places. (p. 36)

The First Man has been playing a William Martin Murphy sort of figure: a Catholic capitalist who even before 1913 is beginning to see his power and political clout increase on the backs of the urban poor of Dublin. This is an obvious stereotype. The Priest Figure is much more complex. He takes on a number of different kinds of priestly roles, as well as the often conflicting characters of the different kinds of men who become priests. So the figure throughout the play is represented – or rather presented – both emblematically and psychologically. In the scene quoted above he is marked by an ordinary psychology: half with the people, half with the new Catholic bosses, constantly finding words and sentences to cover the contradictions in his role in the changing historical conditions. Later, as the play moves towards its climax, his role becomes emblematic:

PRIEST FIGURE: (*Slowly in a whisper*) What do you want of me Matt Talbot?

TALBOT: An' who are you?

(*Behind him* Priest Figure *disrobes to an* Old Woman, *long dress, long grey hair. She places her hands on* Talbot's *shoulders, gently rocking him from side to side.* Talbot *closes his eyes and rocks silently for a*

*little while. The sound of a thumping heart-beat begins
again.*)
Oh, Mother! Mother! Mother! Oh, Mother of God!
(p. 58)

Finally, at the very end of the play, this emblematic
figure of the Virgin Mary, representing Mother Church
and creating an image of Catholic piety, gives way to a
far more problematic figure:

TALBOT: (*Gesturing back to the other figures.*) Leave me!
Leave me to go it alone! Leave me! (*The two men
and the woman slink through the openings of the box,
leaving it altogether.* Talbot *staggers forward and
kneels. The* Priest Figure *has come down behind him,
a grotesque old crone, attending but rigid.*) (p. 62)

This figure has now become deeply ambivalent. Its
significance is perceived by intuition rather than by
explanation. This reflects the deep and unavoidable
ambiguity in Kilroy's purpose in writing the play and
reveals a metaphysical core at the heart of materialism.
Kilroy states in the Author's Note:

I wanted to write a play about the mystic and the
essentially irreducible division between such extreme
individualism and the claim of relationship, of
community, society . . .
. . . What I think I wrote was a play about aloneness,
its cost to the person and the kind of courage required
to sustain it.

There is an admission in this comment that the play to

some extent has written itself. This is born out by the ending. A purely materialist play would have driven the priest out of Talbot's Box as well as the others. But our last image is of a rigid old crone – that we know to be the transformed Priest Figure – locked in his box with him.

There is a further disjunction in the text towards the end. Throughout the play Matt Talbot has challenged the Priest Figure from within the dogma of the Church. He offers an oblique view of Christian belief – one which emerges, paradoxically, out of his working-class directness. This is the same working-class directness, in theatrical terms, to that given to the characterisation of the atheistic John Connolly in Arden's and D'Arcy's *The Non-Stop Connolly Show*. As Matt approaches death he tells the priest that all he ever wanted was to work with timber:

PRIEST FIGURE: Timber?
TALBOT: Ay. Timber. I used to walk round an' round
   the sheds when the fresh lumber used to come off the
   boats. Piles and piles to the roof. 'N I'd run me hand
   along the grain. 'N I'd fill me smell with the sap. Long
   ways away they came from where there's big woods.
   'N I'd see the trees 'cause timber never dies when 'tis
   cut, only changin' with age.   (p. 58)

There are strong echoes in this of Bertolt Brecht's early poetic play, *Baal*. Brecht's young anarchic hero is so precisely the opposite of Kilroy's Matt Talbot that they begin paradoxically to glide into each other. Baal's rampant atheism translates into a fanatical commitment to himself, to his sexual appetites without responsibility for the relationships, and to the skies and the forests. This could be the paradigm for Kilroy's Christian zealot. The central existentialist figure around which they have

structured their respective dramas takes them away from
their authorial intentions. Brecht's nascent materialism
and violent anti-Romanticism only reveal a new Romantic
archetype: the man who had been carried in his mother's
womb away from the forests into the cities dies back in
those forests, gazing at the stars in the doorway of a
wooden shack. He is among non-caring woodcutters who
remark on his stench of death but who will, nevertheless,
bury him.

Kilroy's initial commitment to the cruder operations of
capitalist hegemony is likewise changed in dramatising
Matt Talbot. The passion his drama discovers within the
man is not just a response to a denial of material well-
being. It is a passion which has its own path, and enables
the man to persist in seeing timber as the wood of forests,
which calls forth mankind's creativity and appreciation, as
well as his destructiveness. It is not just lumber, with a
price on it – a price, moreover, which has been depressed
by market forces. The contradiction which Kilroy's poetic
vision ultimately makes Talbot express is one which comes
out of human passions and a deep moral commitment to
our community and to whatever makes us human. The
dramatic structure convincingly makes this contradiction
lie beyond the other, materialist, contradiction inherent
in the capitalist mode of production. Kilroy's Talbot, like
Brecht's Baal, dies aware, finally, of his earth-bound
engendering. He is content. For his more materialist
neighbours, however, he has become just a stinking
corpse.

In 1969 Vincent Dowling directed Kilroy's play *The
O'Neill* at the Peacock in Dublin. Whereas the later play,
Talbot's Box, is about Irish history at the beginning of this
century, *The O'Neill* treats with an equally significant but
much earlier moment of history: the 'pacification' of

Ireland by the English Elizabethans. The English succeeded in their immediate objectives; but they had deadened the land they had 'pacified'. The difficulty for an Irish playwright is the dramatic structuring of the effect of the undisputed Elizabethan brutality and its equally indisputable success upon a brutalised and cowed population. Nothing which the drama could portray could match either the excesses by men who have subsequently been revered by (English) history: Sir Humphrey Gilbert, Sir Walter Raleigh, Arthur Grey, Edmund Spenser the poet, and many others.

Historically we are presented today with the evidence of immorality's undoubted success. It is very difficult to represent this success in performance to Irish audiences who have had to live with their brutalised failure for the past four centuries. This is precisely because of the *moral* protoculs of drama. To avoid becoming mawkish, Irish playwrights could all too easily come to blame people like the O'Neill for not being as immoral as the English – whose ascendant materialist morality linked 'good' to political purpose and economic success, and expressed it in a concept of 'civilisation', in much the same way as the Afrikaners in South Africa use 'civilisation' to justify apartheid today. Kilroy's play avoids such blame, and embraces a difficult and ambiguous characterisation of Hugh O'Neill. The publication of the play now, nearly 20 years after its first performance, and its revival in a new production would substantially add to the re-viewing of history which the Field Day Theatre Company has embraced.

The Field Day Theatre Company was formed in 1980 by Brian Friel and the Belfast-born actor, Stephen Rea. It is based in Derry/Londonderry, and has expanded to include poets, writers and critics. It now produces not only plays but also pamphlets and anthologies. The particular perspectives of the company are considered in the context of Brian Friel's work. Of interest here is their 1986 production of Thomas Kilroy's new play, *Double Cross*, which was written especially for Field Day and directed for them by Jim Sheridan.

Double Cross is based on the real lives of two men who rejected and obscured their Irish birth and upbringing: Brendan Bracken and William Joyce. Kilroy has also written a radio play for BBC Radio 3 based on Brendan Bracken, who became Churchill's Minister of Information during the Second World War, and was elevated to the British peerage as Viscount Bracken of Christchurch. The programme was first transmitted in June 1986 under the title *That Man Bracken*, and rebroadcast six months later. In the stage play, *Double Cross*, Kilroy juxtaposes Bracken with William Joyce, better known in the British Isles as Lord Haw Haw: the man who broadcast from Berlin in English during the war on behalf of Hitler and the Nazis.

The first half of the play is about Bracken; the second part of the play is about Joyce. In each half, a huge image of the other man, the alternative ego, is projected on to a screen at the back of the stage; and his voice is heard over a radio, a stage property. The radio voice, as a broadcast, is integral to the action on the stage at that moment. In each half, the central figure on stage – Bracken in Part 1, Joyce in Part 2 – constructs his own separate world entirely by speaking about it.

Kilroy describes the play as being about 'doubleness' or 'doubling':

. . . to surrender to a vision of doubleness is to see most human behaviour (including one's own, of course) within a field of irony.   (programme note)

59

Another way of saying this is to see commitment, as it becomes more intense, generating within a person the potentiality of its opposite. Thus, in Graham Reid's *Remembrance*, Victor's commitment to upholding law and order can become a commitment to lawlessness and disorder. Hence, his ironical utterances. What *Double Cross* more deliberately explores are the deeper levels of irony in British and Irish prejudice. For instance, the idealist in the play is the Fascist Joyce, not Bracken, who, although seemingly on the side of the angels, is portrayed as affectedly prejudiced and racist, and with a suffocating British arrogance which is all the more objectionable because it is assumed. Bracken, however, is paradoxically more perceptive than Joyce.

Joyce and Bracken attack each other over the radio. It is a personal fight beneath their official tasks in the midst of a global war. They seem to recognise from each other's voice a deeper sign of Irishness which feeds a loathing of their own Irish engendering.

In this mutual recognition is a further desperate need to define themselves as the opposite of the other. However, the play is not about the Irish: the ending of the play is intended to confront both British and Irish audiences with the sense of an unrecognised partiality of the Britishers' sense of their own history. The moment of Britain's victory over Hitler in 1945 heralds the end of the *British* imperium and the beginning of Britain's incipient decline and social disintegration. When Joyce is tried, executed and buried in quicklime, a woman journalist covering the event describes how the young Fascist English followers of Joyce wept for him and for the destruction of England. Bracken, who is present at this ceremony, appears, paradoxically, to be the more compromised and venal 'English' figure.

Ultimately, the betrayal, the treachery, was not by

Joyce only; nor was his a betrayal of England, really. Both men betrayed their Irishness: Bracken by suppressing all information concerning his origins, Joyce by actually fighting on the side of the British against the Irish in the Civil War in the 1920s. By cutting themselves loose from Ireland they had cut themselves off from reality. These men, in their respective 'Englishness', saw Churchill's England and Hitler's Germany as preposterous alternatives to their own perception of being 'English'. Both saw their own commitment as the appropriate way to ensure the continuation of the British imperium. It was doomed anyway, and not for reasons which either man could understand. Both men chose the wrong side of their own history. If we set MacIntyre's play, *The Great Hunger*, in its Abbey production, alongside Kilroy's characterisation of these two historical figures, we can see what they hated but could not understand in the bleakness of the lives of the Irish peasantry during the Second World War.

The economic and cultural legacy of British colonialism in the Irish Free State is most effectively summed up by the intellectual perceptions offered by these two plays. In writing his play for the Field Day Theatre Company, Kilroy comments that it is the most important movement of its kind in Ireland since the beginning of the century:

It has provided a platform for the life of the mind, of whatever persuasion, at a time when mindlessness threatens to engulf us all.   (programme note)

I think the mindlessness which Kilroy refers to is specific neither to Ireland nor to Britain. It refers instead to a collective sense of impending global collapse: of economies, moralities, sensibilities. This sense is shared by a number of Irish playwrights whose work has already been discussed. Some of their work has been developed collectively, together with the audiences which various among them have nurtured. A constant refining of dramatic structures in performance strives to create a sense or meaning which is not yet complete, and which can only be completed in the imaginations of the audience. It is as though the playwright is begging his audience to help him or her – and them – understand things more clearly.

For playwrights such as Kilroy, Murphy and Friel the dramatic vision comes as much from the West of Ireland as it does from Dublin and Belfast. For these playwrights, the dominant drama discourse has changed from being complete into being open-ended. This is in the structure of the drama as much as in its 'message': neither the narrative nor the idea can, any longer, be complete in itself. Because there are no answers, the meaning for the audience must inevitably be found within their imagination, outside the written text.

Specifically, many Irish dramatists now perceive that 'Irishness' defines itself in relation to a wider Superpower hegemony and the attendant suffering in the Third World. The next chapters analyse how Irish playwrights, actors, directors explore the potential of this new Irish drama.

2
The Theatre in the West

The development of theatre in Ireland in the second half of the twentieth century has differed from the development of theatre in mainland Britain in one crucial respect. New British and English drama (the terms are used interchangeably even by sensitive English commentators) has, since 1957, regarded the process of defining what it is to be 'British' (= English) as both necessary and awkward: an embarrassing duty within the dominant hegemony. By contrast, new Irish theatre has found the process of defining what it is to be 'Irish' creative and stimulating: a challenge to colonial stereotyping. This does not imply that Irish playwrights are more chauvinistic, or that English playwrights are more self-critical.

'Britishness' or 'Englishness' is predicated upon the loss of economic and political international muscle whilst still retaining the institutions, populations and ideas of former greatness. 'Irishness' is predicated upon actually managing to survive colonial occupation and find new state institutions and ideas. If pragmatism is the mark of the former, then a certain idealism is the mark of the latter. Some Irish playwrights are fiercely critical of the present Irish state and what they see as the cultural and intellectual aridity of its *petit bourgeois* mentality: a Catholic middle-class occupying the gap left by the departing Protestant Ascendancy. However, the constricting vision of this new ruling class is seen by some to contradict, rather than embody, Irish nationalism, even though the middle class may use the idea of nationalism to justify its materialist ambitions.

British and English nationalism seemingly cannot exist as separate in any way from the British state – that is to say, as represented by the monarchy, Parliament and the legal institutions of the Crown. A radical English nationalism has yet to emerge out of the resolution of the contradictions in its institutions, diminished economy and cultural pluralism. On the other hand, Irish theatre is finding itself increasingly liberated from the lack of self-awareness which has marked the dominant English culture. It is particularly in the contemporary theatre in the West of Ireland that we see depicted the idea of being Irish as a positive resistance to colonialism, transcending colonial stereotyping and generating independent thought and new ideas.

The dramatic expression of this reaches a peak in the work of Brian Friel and Tom Murphy. Specifically, their work synthesises the formal artistic commitment to economic and social change of the urban theatre of Dublin and Belfast, with the unique experience of the West of Ireland which effectively resisted English cultural imperialism. In order to begin to understand fully their achievement and their separate and complementary poetic vision, the context of drama in the West of Ireland needs to be appreciated. And drama in the West of Ireland needs to be seen in the wider context of its social production, before audiences.

Drama and theatre are more than the published play texts. The performance text is perhaps even more important. But theatre in live performance is the most ephemeral of all the arts. This is perhaps why the published text becomes so important for the critics and academics in establishing the meaning of a play. The resulting dominance of the written text unfortunately diminishes the importance of the 'reading' of a performance by an audience. The realisation of the performance before an audience is what is meant by the term the social production of dramatic art. This is not simply staging a play. It involves the training and unionising of all those professionally involved: actors, playwrights, stage-hands, technicians, directors, producers, and so on. It involves the provision of performance spaces; of subsidies, grants and patronage; of Oscars, competitions and rewards; the cumulative development of dramatic conventions between audiences and actors; the publication of scripts; and the role and function of the critic.

The social production of dramatic art in Ireland today is specific to late bourgeois Western society and for the people involved it necessitates both recognising and changing the meanings of such notions as 'professional', 'amateur', 'subsidised', 'commercial', 'popular', 'High Art', 'traditional art'. The need for both recognition and change is reflected in the ambiguous attitudes towards the audience. The marketing of theatre sees audiences as 'bums-on-seats'; the development of the art of theatre sees the creative imagination of audiences in the generation of meaning.

In many ways, the theatre in the West of Ireland actually anticipates changes in the urban Irish theatre, north and south of the Border. A number of drama and theatre initiatives already taken can be conceived of as opposing or contradictory tendencies. Margaretta D'Arcy points to a division among earning playwrights between those who belong to the trade union of playwrights, the Society of Irish Playwrights, and those who do not. The latter tend to be those who have international reputations and whose writing attracts state subsidies for the professional performances of their plays.

Theatre production is also marked by a division between amateur and professional performers: in Galway there is an amateur *Gaeltacht* theatre, *An Taidhbhearc* (pronounced 'an Tie-vee-argh') and a fully professional theatre, the Druid Theatre Company. Both have their own theatre buildings in Galway city. *An Taidhbhearc* performs plays in Gaelic; the Druid does plays in English or Irish English. The Druid has used actors from *An Taidhbhearc*, some of whom then go on to develop their professional acting careers in the English-language theatre in Dublin and on television. This points to the complex language division, between Irish plays written and performed in Gaelic, Irish plays written and performed in Irish English and English, and plays written in other languages and translated into English, Irish English, or Gaelic. Finally, there is a division within the content of the drama, between traditional folk art and 'modern' or 'contemporary' drama. *Siamsa Tire* is committed to a revival of the *context* of traditional performance, within, paradoxically, the modern theatre.

Ironically, the expected correlations among these divisions do not occur. There is not, for instance, a correlation between *Gaeltacht* theatre and the revival of traditional performance art. Some Gaelic theatre – for example, the work of Siobhan ni Suilleabhan – is highly

66

contemporary and often more critical of traditionalism than drama in Irish English. It certainly does not see traditionalism as an inherent part of a Gaelic theatre aesthetic.

Neither is there an automatic correlation between Gaelic playwrights and amateur Gaelic theatre, like *An Taidhbhearc*; and there are further paradoxes here between professionals and amateurs. The unionisation of Irish playwrights in the Society of Irish playwrights aims to raise payments for their scripts. Some union members not only allow – and charge – amateurs to perform their scripts, they actually prefer to work with non-professionals. Other ununionised playwrights will only work within the professional theatre. Often, Arts Council and other subsidies will support the most literary Irish drama in fully professional productions, while completely professional playwrights will be performed in fully commercial amateur productions.

Two playwrights, John B. Keane, from County Kerry, and M. J. Molloy, from the border of County Galway and County Mayo, have, in 30 years of playwriting, shaped the sensibilities of a West of Ireland experience since the Second World War into a body of plays known in performance by appreciative audiences there. They are part of a wider dramatic tradition: the work of the National Folk Theatre of Ireland, *Siamsa Tire* (pronounced 'she-am-sah tee-er') based in Tralee, County Kerry; the *Gaeltacht* theatre and the *Gaeltacht* playwrights such as Siobhan ni Suilleabhan (Shivaun O'Sullivan); innovative community drama work like that undertaken with working-class and rural farming women by Margaretta D'Arcy; the internationally-acclaimed Druid Theatre Company of Galway City, and the creative work of its founding director, Garry Hynes.

Siamsa Tire

Siamsa (meaning entertainment and socialising – 'plays' and 'playing' in the broadest sense – in each other's homes during the evenings) was started in 1968 by Fr Pat Ahern, who wished to recreate the pattern of old rural entertainment which he remembered from his north Kerry upbringing. In the entertainment which he developed he linked traditional songs and dances to the seasonal round of work and play in a traditional rural Kerry farmyard. His company of performers was initially *Siamsoiri na Riochta* (pronounced 'Sha-sho-ree nah Ree-agh-sta' – 'Players of the Kingdom', since County Kerry is known as the Kingdom of Kerry). The original six performers have remained with the company as professional soloists while it expanded and became *Siamsa Tire*. The company incorporated itself as the National Folk Theatre of Ireland.

Siamsa Tire has toured in Europe and America and performed in London. In 1974 the company won the European Prize for Folk-Art. Over the past 10 years it has sustained both its clerical support and its original pastoral idyll. In its publicity, Siamsa describes itself as a 'theatrical recreation in mime, music and dance of what life was like for a rural family in Gaelic-speaking Ireland many years ago'. The rural past of the West of Ireland was a Golden Age:

> there was tea in the meadows, with grasshoppers chirping and seeds blowing into white, blue-rimmed enamel mugs. Thick swards, new mown, were turned by tall men in the shadows of ancient pagan dolmens, monuments to dead warriors.

The traditional songs and dances are revived, rehearsed

and performed as a theatrical metaphor for this pastoral idyll. The performance as a whole is meant to suggest the conviviality and communality of a pre-materialist society. This is folk art which promotes a vanished rural idealism. It sets itself up deliberately in opposition to the values and artefacts of a mass-producing materialist culture while using some of the technology of that materialism.

The performances are simply nostalgic. Fr Patrick Ahern's company has extended the process of realising a performance into a movement offering local children and young people training in the songs and dances; and then incorporating these young performers into the narrative structure of the dramatised scenes for the summer performances in different parts of Kerry. The children are introduced to a specific sort of dramatic creativity incorporating folk dances and songs; and they are made aware of a specific performance context. They enjoy the dramatic extension into narrative-acting of the skills they have learned in traditional dances and songs. The performances have a guaranteed audience in the summer of local parents and tourists, many of the latter being Irish-American, for whom this type of theatre is an extension of their own dream of Ireland.

Ultimately, the *Siamsa* enterprise is inhibited by its nostalgia. Its aesthetic derives from the museum rather than from the social realities of peasant farming life, then or now. It is a dream of 'Irishness' which is always in the past.

John B. Keane

John B. Keane was born, the son of a teacher, in County Kerry in 1928. He worked at a variety of jobs in England

and Ireland, writing in digs, encouraged by landladies and his mates. He eventually came back to Ireland, married, bought a pub and started to write successfully. He continues to run the pub in Listowel, the town in which he was born.

John B. Keane is a popular writer, not only of plays, many of which continue to be successfully performed in amateur and professional productions, but also of short stories and humorous books, such as *Letters from an Irish Parish Priest* and *Letters of a Successful T.D.* (a Member of the Irish Parliament). In these books Keane creates a character who is self-consciously defining himself in a series of letters, but who in the unconscious subtext is ironically defining himself far more accurately. His work fuses together two strands of Irish writing which have been kept separate: the eighteenth-century pamphleteering of Jonathan Swift and the nineteenth-century farce of Dion Boucicault.

Keane's successful plays are marked by three key elements: a strong narrative line; a Humanist morality; and an absence of authorial judgement on the central characters he creates. Each of these needs a further explanation.

Keane resolutely believes in entertaining his audiences and that the roots of an entertaining performance lie in a powerful story, a strong narrative line. This is achieved by starting with an intriguing situation, which leads one or more of the characters in it to state an entrenched position, a deliberate projection of their behaviour into the future with a provocative confidence. The characters then precipitate a development which changes the situation. The play's narrative focuses on the working-out of those entrenched attitudes. The appeal of the narrative, therefore, lies in the play of ironies within the dramatic structure. For Keane, people change as the situation changes; and they are capable of all manner of unpredictable behaviour.

Secondly, Keane's humanism makes him depict characters who are quite capable of charting a moral course through conflicting familial and sexual relationships. Our basic biological and emotional needs are explicitly stated by characters as they move through the moral minefield which the play's narrative has staked out. At least one person in the play will indicate that it is necessary to work out the moral position for oneself. Keane's most original plays all demonstrate this moral autonomy: *The Year of the Hiker*; *The Field*; *The Crazy Wall*; *Big Maggie*.

This moral autonomy could be undermined by Keane the playwright in the way he structures the drama. Inevitably, precisely because the plays are constructed by an author, the characters are presented to the audience in a structure which offers a narrative conclusion. The audience is not being allowed to conclude the play itself (as happens in some Third World popular theatre) which would allow the process of moral decision-making by the characters to be far more autonomous, outside the authorial dramatic structure. Nevertheless, Keane does manage to suggest to his audiences that the central characters remain unjudged by him – even though he has written the play. The exception to this is always the character who exhibits strong materialist self-interest. This is usually a self-centred young person on the make. In the course of the play, Keane usually dumps such a character outside the circle of understanding and self-awareness into which the central characters are able to move.

This is clearly seen in a much-liked early play, *The Year of the Hiker*, first produced by the Southern Theatre Group in Cork, in 1963. It was directed by Dan Donovan, who successfully realised a number of Keane's scripts on the stage. It is about a father/husband who is a compulsive hiker and who has, quite literally, walked out on his family 20 years before. His wife has grown old and his children have grown up with a resentment towards him, his memory and his reputation. For, paradoxically, he has achieved an admiring folk-loric reputation for his ability to walk immense distances, suddenly setting off on an unexplained whim.

His family consists of his wife and her unmarried sister, Freda; his daughter Mary who is to marry a young doctor – ironically on the day her father chooses to return – and his two sons, Joe and Simon. As the family prepares for the wedding, the absence of their father intrudes into all their conversations; and they are provoked into saying what they will do if he returns. The rest of the play is about their very different behaviour when confronted by his unexcused presence again in their lives. He humbly accepts his guilt; but he does not explain it.

Paradoxically, his family, in coming to terms with him now, have to come to terms with themselves, and to rediscover the roots of their relationship with him. Joe, an adult and running the farm, intuits his love for him. It is a slow and painful process which climaxes in a statement of the real hurt of his absence:

> Why didn't you take me with you? I wouldn't have given a damn if we starved together. I'd have followed you to hell because you were my father and I loved you. (p. 85)

Freda is the opposite. Her resentment is the greatest and her antagonism knows no restraint. She has a sudden epiphany, however, and realises her own guilt in his departure 20 years before:

> Oh what a terrible mess we made of it all! O Merciful Holy Mother, forgive me! (*weeping*) O, Lovely Son of God, take the hurt and the hatred out of me and soften my heart!   (p. 80)

The Hiker has struggled to bring her to this self-realisation: when he asked her sister – and not her – to marry him, she imposed her spinsterhood on their relationship out of revenge.

The Hiker's other son, Simey, now qualified as a vet, is meanly materialistic and aspiring towards upward social mobility. He is quite literally cast out of the play, judged unredeemable. Simey is the one character who seems to me to be overdeveloped, overwritten. The others seem to be underwritten – even Freda – in order that they may be completed in the audience's own imagination, as they make their tentative decisions and move towards a deeper moral understanding of themselves.

Keane explores the interstices of familial and sexual relationships, searching for a language, in dramatic image and dialogue, to express the complex dilemmas that we make for ourselves. Such relationships occur in a number of his plays. In *The Year of the Hiker*, the relationship between father and son, between the Hiker and his elder son Joe, intersects with the relationship between the Hiker and his wife Kate. The really powerfully-drawn love is between father and Joe, which is further emphasised by the sour distance which Simey puts between himself and his returned father. The relationship between Kate and her sons is ignored.

In a much later play, *The Crazy Wall*, this intersecting of the relationships between father and son on the one hand and husband and wife on the other is treated more extensively and without the narrative and emotional device of the returned husband/father after a long absence. *The Crazy Wall* was premiered by the Theatre of the South in Waterford and Cork in 1973, with Dan Donovan in the leading role of the father and husband Michael Barnett. This central character is a National Teacher and is conscious not only of his responsibilities in this public role but also, more privately, in the rearing of his four sons, Tony, Lelum, Tom and Paddy. The way he brings them up is liberal (in Ireland in 1973) and is based on a great love for them. He allows them to make their own mistakes; and it is this which their more conservative mother finds so disconcerting.

The climax of the play is her showdown with her husband, in front of the sons, when she discovers that the second youngest son, Tom, has made the young female servant in the house pregnant, and that the older boys are also sexually experienced. In her mind, male sexuality becomes linked to a lack of discipline: men discipline their wives but not themselves. In Michael Barnett's case, as far as his wife Mary is concerned, this is parallelled by Michael's love and concern for his boys at the expense of his relationship with Mary. Michael's 'liberal' attitudes are nothing more than an indulgence of male sexuality, and they do not extend to the behaviour of wives or daughters. Mary accuses him of a lack of self-awareness:

I started out our life in love with you but it died slowly slowly, slowly, day after day, month after month, year after year. It died under your very eyes and you saw it die. You watched it die and you were content to do

74

nothing about it. . . . You dodged the reality of it
like you dodged everything. . . . I never failed you,
remember that. There was no escape for me. You had
your pub and you had your fantasies and you had me
silent, obedient and dutiful.   (p. 97)

Michael begins to see himself with his wife's eyes, and he
is appalled. The portrayal of these conflicting relationships
is creatively open-ended.

There are other textual elements which give the play an
historical specificity. The framing device of the sons
gathering together, years later, at Michael's funeral, and
the historical setting of the main action of the play in the
1940s locate this domestic crisis within a particular social
malaise. The wall which Michael is building in his garden,
and which he passionately knocks down when he
understands its significance within his psychological make-
up, suggests a futile male productivity within this malaise.

I am not sure that these alternative gender perspectives
surface during a performance, either in the dramatic
structure or in the dialogue. In a way, the sensibilities of
the play require corresponding sensibilities within the
audience for the richness of the play's meaning to be fully
apparent. Tom Murphy's play, *A Whistle in the Dark*,
which is concerned with a similar matrix of macho
relationships but in the context of the Irish working class
in England, locked into an incipient awareness among
Irish and English audiences. Keane's play, however,
anticipates the development of female gender insights,
and, I suppose, it still awaits its Irish audience.

The father–son relationship, which conflicts with the
alternative sexual relationship which men pursue, occurs
in most of Keane's plays, and especially in the most
visionary of all his plays, *The Field*.

This was premiered by Gemini Productions and directed by Barry Cassin at the Olympia Theatre in Dublin in 1965. The pivot of the play is an acute antithesis between the father–son relationship of 'The Bull' McCabe and his son Tadhg (pronounced 'Taig'), both peasant farmers, and the mother–son relationship of Maimie Flanagan and her son Leamy. Maimie is the wife and Leamy the son of the local auctioneer and publican. During the action of the play the mother–son relationship is sundered, and Maimie and Leamy both crack up as a result of a murder committed by 'The Bull' and Tadhg – a murder which has nothing to do with them, but about which they, like the rest of the community, must keep quiet, intimidated as they all are by the McCabes.

The play does not judge 'The Bull'. The focus of the play is an evaluation of the received notions of morality which, the play suggests, are class-based. The story is about a 4-acre field which a poor widow who owns it asks Flanagan to auction for her. 'The Bull' McCabe has grazing rights and is determined to acquire it. A businessman, born locally but who now lives in England, hears about the auction and wants to acquire the field in order to manufacture concrete blocks. He can afford to pay a lot more than McCabe and is determined to do so. 'The Bull' and Tadhg want to frighten him off by roughing him up; but they actually kill him by accident. The villagers are forced into silence, or forced to connive with the McCabes out of fear of them.

Priest, Bishop and Gardai (pronounced 'Gor-thee' – the police) all fulminate against the conspiracy of silence and seek to break it by overwhelming moral pressure. The young Leamy, who is characterised in the play quite deliberately as a 'mother's boy' cannot cope with the cowardice of everyone, including his macho father and abused mother. She sends him away to England. She discovers she is pregnant again by her husband and by the end of the play is fast losing her grip on reality. The play is deeply sympathetic to her plight. However, in an extraordinary last scene, 'The Bull' and his son are positively drawn, seemingly unrepentant and publicly determined to sustain their control on the situation. They express an alternative moral position, based on the overriding importance of the land to peasant farmers:

> BULL: When you'll be gone, Father, to be a Canon somewhere, and the Sergeant gets a wallet of notes and is going to be a Superintendent, Tadhg's children will be milkin' cows and keepin' donkeys away from ditches. That's what we have to think about and if there's no grass, there's the end of me and mine.
>
> FR MURPHY: God will ask you questions about this murder one day.
>
> BULL: And I'll ask God questions! . . . Why did God make me one way and you another?
>
> SERGEANT: Let's go, Father, before I throw up!
>
> (p. 76)

Bull realises that he is the only person now who will remember the murdered man for the rest of his life. The punishment is in this life. But they need the grass of that field to survive.

John B. Keane's plays are important because of their consistent expression of the dual commitment of the peasant farmer: to his son and to his land. We find the father–son relationship in a very large number of Irish plays; but the linking of this relationship to the land is usually absent, as it is in Hugh Leonard's *Da*. The interrelationship of the ties of blood and land find their best dramatic expression in the problematic but necessary love between fathers and sons. In Keane's plays this is pre-Freudian: it offers a quite different, earth-bound, explanation of our troubled sexual relationships to Freud's Oedipus complex. The one Oedipal character in *The Field* is Leamy, who has a morality unrelated to his community and he is shipped off to England.

Siobhan O Suilleabhain

Of the playwrights of the *Gaeltacht* (the Gaelic-speaking areas of the West of Ireland) the work of Siobhan O Suilleabhain provides a comparison with the work of John B. Keane. Keane is from North Kerry; O Suilleabhain is from West Kerry, from Ballyferriter. She writes in Gaelic for Irish radio and television, and for amateur theatre groups who perform in the *Gaeltacht*. She is a member of the Society of Irish Playwrights; and through the union she campaigns for better fees for all playwrights, but especially for playwrights writing in Gaelic.

There is a double problem. The first part of the problem is how the Gaelic writer contributes to the development of a drama discourse which is generally conducted in Irish English. The second part of the problem is how the Gaelic playwright can earn a living.

To take the aesthetic part of the problem first. It is through critical reaction and comment to both performance and printed texts that the dramatic discourse in Gaelic can be developed; and by this means the Gaelic playwright can avoid being marginalised. Siobhan O Suilleabhain's commitment is to writing in Gaelic, her first language: the language of her West Kerry upbringing and her creative inspiration. Writing dramatic dialogue in

Gaelic is particularly rewarding because of the past and present strength of the oral traditions in the language. It is an excellent language for drama because it is still robustly metaphoric and extensively vocalised. However, even as the creative vision of a new play possesses her and she begins to find compelling dramatic form within the Gaelic dialogue, O Suilleabhain's creative excitement is contradicted by nagging doubts about where the play might be performed, where it might be published, and who will read what she has written.

This leads in to the second part of the problem. Amateur theatre companies who perform new plays in Gaelic obviously cannot pay commercial performance rights. Even well-established theatre companies, like *An Taidhbhearc* in Galway City which has a semi-professional cast and an established and regular audience, cannot contemplate a run for a new Gaelic play which will pay the playwright anything like the rights a professional playwright can expect when his or her new play in English or Irish English is premiered at the Abbey Theatre. *An Taidhbhearc* was founded in 1928 by Professor Liam O Briain and some of his friends (including the actors Hilton Edwards and Michael MacLiammoir). It manages to stage about nine productions in Gaelic each year; and some of these are bound to be plays already in the repertoire, as well as some others which are translations from the Irish English, or English, in which they were originally written. The scope for the production of new work in Gaelic is, obviously, very limited.

The main source of performance income for a Gaelic playwright is RTE, Irish radio and television. In fact, the rights for a play may well be bought by RTE, who then seem unable to make a further financial investment and actually produce it. This is a most patronising patronage:

to feel obliged to buy a writer's Gaelic script, merely because it is in Gaelic, but then not feel obliged to produce it.

Neither can the Gaelic playwright look to the publication of playscripts, which could both stimulate performances and subsidise performance rights. Priority is given to the more 'literary' genres of poetry, prose fiction and essays. Indeed, the texts printed are usually the classic Gaelic texts; new work is not going to appear on the school syllabuses for a while.

O Suilleabhain feels that her playwriting in English is not fired by the same love for the words she is making into dramatic speech. Her problem as a Gaelic playwright is acute. Talented *Gaeltacht* playwrights will not be able to channel their creative energies into the development of a drama discourse without a responsive audience and, today, without a readership as well. There will be neither audience nor readership if the language in which that creativity occurs is dying. The Gaelic playwright's creative insight can be there and yet not there, because the language which generates that creativity is in the process of being lost. O Suilleabhain's creativity and her vision as a playwright are evidenced by the television and radio drama awards which she has won – and then contradicted by the lack of production and publication.

The agony of experiencing the death of her language is strongly contrasted by the deftness of her handling of the contemporary content of her plays. It is the actual language which she loves, and not a nostalgia for the Celtic Twilight or the pastoral idyll of *Siamsa Tire*. For instance, in a series of four plays for radio, *Meaisin Liom leat* ('A machine which is mine which is yours'), she dramatises what happens when four households on a housing estate share a fully automatic washing-machine.

She got the idea for this series from hearing a man on 'Woman's Hour' on the radio complaining that domestic washing-machines lie idle for most of the day. He was advocating that women should stop complaining about the lack of laundrette facilities and club together to share a washing-machine. Her four little plays show the tension and fights which result when four women whose households and needs are very different from each other share the same washing-machine. The four episodes are told from the differing perspectives of each of the women. It seems like a good idea at the start and everyone is enthusiastic about it. The dramatic fiction carries the listeners into the actuality of the idea. The plays move inventively and with wit to the point at which the women put forward their own solution to the problem.

Siobhan O Suilleabhain believes that the origin of drama lies in story-telling. Everything else falls into place once the story is worked out. She shares this emphasis on narrative in dramatic creativity with John B. Keane, as well as the over-riding commitment to plays that entertain. The purpose of the story itself and the wit displayed in its dramatisation is to bring in the audience. It allows a rural audience great sensibilities; and recognises that the people in the audience know of the harsh economic and ethical realities in their lives, as well as in the lives of others in other circumstances. The problems are not solved by making an audience see them in a play. Answers are more likely to be found through wit and wisdom, and the positive outlook which these qualities within a play can reinforce in members of the audience.

O Suilleabhain's play, *Citi* ('Kitty'), which won the Irish Life Award in 1974, was inspired by the media accounts of the filming of *Ryan's Daughter* in Kerry in the Dingle Peninsula. The play is fictional beyond this point. It is

about a Dingle girl, Citi, who falls desperately in love with
an English member of the film crew. The Englishman,
however, falls in love with Ireland and the Dingle. In
loving him, Citi wants to leave the Dingle; in responding
to her love, he wants an excuse to stay. In a skilful way
the play deals with two common and opposite obsessions:
a foreign romanticisation of the West of Ireland and native
emigration from the place. The play does not seek to
provide any solution to either of these obsessions.

Other stories from her plays come from her Ballyferriter
childhood. She suggests that everything has happened to
us by the time we are 20, and that the rest of our lives are
an imaginative reprocessing of that initial discovery of the
world. The significance of this becomes apparent in, for
example, her radio series *A Dubh ina Gheal* ('Black into
White') which describes what happens when a black priest
is sent to a rural Irish parish: the strangeness of the place
and the people for the black priest is approached through
an imaginative recall of those years of vivid discovery
of the people and places surrounding her during her
childhood.

Her one play written in English, *A Place Apart*, which
was submitted to the BBC in Northern Ireland, tells of a
Catholic woman and some Belfast Protestant women in
the ante-natal ward of a Belfast hospital on 12 July (the
day Protestants in Northern Ireland commemorate the
victory of William of Orange at the Battle of the Boyne).

Margaretta D'Arcy

The dramatic vision of Margaretta D'Arcy, whose drama
work with John Arden is dealt with in Chapter 5, has
shifted in her separate work to a commitment to enable

oppressed women in the West of Ireland to find their own voice through drama and drama-related activities. Instead of creating audiences for her plays, D'Arcy's enterprise now is to make women, whose lives are mired in anxieties, poverty and brutal assault, at one and the same time authors and audiences of their own dramas.

This is a development away from her own play, *A Pinprick of History*, which has a measure of actor-improvisation in the context of structured audience participation. It is also a development away from the audience participation in D'Arcy's and John Arden's two-hander show *The Menace of Ireland*. It is D'Arcy's response to her internment in Armagh gaol in 1980 and her involvement in the 'H'-Block campaign. She is now committed to alleviating the oppression of working-class women, and works specifically with women in Galway city and the rural West of Ireland. She has emphasised that she has changed her perspective since being in gaol: there is now a perceived need to work only with women in small groups, over a much longer period of time. Even the sort of improvisation work which she and Arden developed in Ireland in the 1970s she considers to be no longer appropriate.

The purpose now is to enable the women themselves to find words to describe the nature of their oppression. Gaining confidence in articulating the truth of their own understanding of their situations is a necessary first stage towards discovering strategies to counteract their oppression. D'Arcy works with about 11 women in Galway, and has done so since 1982. They are beginning to make links with other women's groups in the West of Ireland.

As professionals, both O Suilleabhain and D'Arcy are working with a similar awareness of the forces governing the social production of their creative work. Both are working towards a similar goal as well, though superficially it may not seem so: to make the languages of drama express new concepts which are outside the conventional drama and outside the conventional patterns of thought. When O Suilleabhain talks about 'telling the truth' in a created piece of drama, she is not referring solely to her own created piece, but to the reception of it by rural audiences – their 'reading' of a performance. Furthermore, these audiences remain undefined by intellectual economic and political analysis, even though they may be so defined by others. In expressing the truth about their own lives, the women D'Arcy works with are rejecting the established male analysis of their situation. The irony is that the truth of our lives can be discovered in the process of making fictions out of them. It is the development of language which lies at the heart of both the creativity and the politics of these drama projects.

Garry Hynes and the Druid Theatre Company

Garry Hynes founded the Druid Theatre Company in Galway City, with Mary Mullen and Mick Lally, in 1975. Mick Lally was a teacher and outstanding amateur actor with *An Taidhbhearc*. During the next 10 years, the Druid revived established Irish plays, such as *Playboy of the Western World* (of which they have done three productions), newer Irish plays, such as M. J. Molloy's *The Wood of the Whispering* and Tom Murphy's *Famine* and *Conversations on a Homecoming*, premieres of Irish plays, and classics of the European theatre.

Druid's production of Garry Hynes's own play, *Island Protected By A Bridge of Glass* (1980), which she developed into a performance text through rehearsal with both the company and the professional musicians, De Danaan, won a Fringe First Award at the Edinburgh Festival. It was generally acclaimed and forced the professional theatre Establishment in Dublin to take notice of this dynamic theatre in the West from which they had previously remained aloof. The company made Tom Murphy Writer-in-Association with the Druid in 1984; and they have also encouraged little-known playwrights such as Geraldine Aron, giving premieres and successful runs of three of her plays: *Bar and Ger* (1978), *A Galway Girl* (1979), and *Same Old Moon* (1984).

One of the most significant achievements of the Druid is the way they have built up their audiences both in Galway and in remote areas. They have had ridiculously small State and commercial subsidies. They have much more directly involved their audiences both in the intellectual process and in the social production of theatre art in Galway. The success of the Druid in establishing a theatre discourse within the professional theatre in Ireland reflects their belief in, and commitment to, their growing Galway audiences, and their origins in the intellectual amateur theatre of the university and the Gaelic *An Taidhbhearc*. Opportunities have been created for young theatre directors and stage designers to develop their talents in the professional Irish theatre; and for Irish playwrights writing in Irish English to develop their work. Opportunities have also been made for *Gaeltacht* actors from the amateur theatre to develop their own professional careers in the English-language theatre.

In a way, the success of the Druid defines the limits of both the amateur theatre and theatre in Gaelic. In the bourgeois state in the second half of the twentieth century it is the 'High Art' of the Great Tradition which both secures and is secured by professional theatrical performance. It is this which attracts subsidy – eventually – and box-office success and subsequent publication. This is a dramatic enterprise which establishes one kind of drama discourse. This is not the same discourse which is set up by the drama projects of Margaretta D'Arcy, neither does it touch on the deep dilemma, exemplified by the playwriting career of Siobhan O Suilleabhain, which creating drama in Gaelic provokes.

M. J. Molloy

The shadow of M. J. Molloy lies behind the work of some younger Irish playwrights, especially Tom Murphy, on whom he has been a major influence. Molloy was born in 1917, in Tuam on the border between County Mayo and County Galway. His vision of the West of Ireland today is influenced by the history of these communities as it is perceived through oral tradition by the people themselves. Molloy has developed this vision over the past 40 years in plays for the theatre, television and radio. His drama has interacted with their history to become a shared understanding. His voice as an Irish playwright is original and significant.

Molloy is a member of the Society of Irish Playwrights. His work continues to be performed by amateur theatre groups. A number of his plays have been given professional productions at the Abbey, and, in 1983, *The Wood of the Whispering* was revived by the Druid in a professional production which received critical acclaim. It was toured around the West where it was rapturously received by rural audiences. He has published some of his plays in America.

Molloy's creative achievement has received some critical

analysis and recognition, notably from Robert Hogan and
D. E. S. Maxwell. Nevertheless, his importance as a
playwright of international stature has been overlooked.
His dramatic achievement has been compared with J. M.
Synge's – a playwright of the West of Ireland whom Molloy
greatly admires and whose aesthetic he has consciously
and successfully developed. Like George Fitzmaurice, the
Kerry playwright of the 1930s whose excellent drama is
now almost entirely overlooked, Molloy is ignored outside
Ireland. Irish and English scholarship focused solely upon
Synge as the voice of the rural West; and in the 1960s
attention was turned to playwrights such as Brendan
Behan (who, if he were still alive, would be four years
older than Molloy, although he is still thought of as a
'young' Irish playwright) and to the urban agnostic
aesthetic of Dublin. Irish drama now had to be
sophisticated and street-wise, rather than explore the
contradictions of brutality and gentleness in rural
understanding.

In the 1990s, the insights of Molloy, and of Murphy
after him, may strike a more contemporary note than the
quaint debauchery of the 1960s. This will be likely as
Western Irish sensibilities become increasingly aware,
through world news coverage, of the scale and complexities
of peasant suffering in the Third World. There is a further
specifically political significance in this West of Ireland
perspective. In John B. Keane's autobiography of 1964,
Self-portrait, Keane describes how, as a young Irish
labourer in London, he was invited to join a Communist
Labour Club in the factory in Birmingham in which he
was working. The young Irishman who was the party
operative in the trade union had passed his Leaving
Certificate and, Keane comments, like other Irish
Communist Party members in the Labour Club,

they were all semi-educated and self-educated. There
was not one of what, for my purpose, I will call the
peasant class. The British and the Irish Communist
Parties, like the Russian, are fairly exclusive – even
snobbish.   (p. 53)

In the Third World now, Marxist–Leninist groups
struggling to liberate their peoples from neo-colonialism
are themselves not free from similar accusations of an
urban rationalist rejection of the peasants on whose behalf
they claim to fight. These committed revolutionaries are
then baffled by the lack of support by peasant-farmers for
'their' revolution, and by these peasants' alternative and
self-debilitating support for counter-revolutionary
movements. Within the Republican struggle in Ireland –
particularly in terms of the unwavering support for that
struggle this century in the West of Ireland – there has
been a tension between the urban Marxist factions located
in Dublin and Belfast and the rural culturalist factions of
the *Gaeltacht*.

   Molloy's plays show, on one level, an historical class
analysis of Irish society in the late eighteenth and early
nineteenth centuries, when industrial capital was actually
*under*developing Ireland. What is much more radical in
his plays is his depiction of the Irish peasant sensibilities
vis-à-vis their class oppression. He shows, over and over
again, the contradictory knowledge which the more
assiduous landless farmers had of the injustice and
oppression of the landlords towards them and of their
residual feudal bonds with those landlords. There is in the
plays a passionate humanism which shows, through the
characterisation, a sharpening of the imagination in the
face of extraordinary injustice. We find a significant

morality in the words and deeds of those from whom we
least expect it.

John B. Keane and Tom Murphy are the inheritors of
Molloy's humanism. Keane finds it in his own experience
of late industrial capitalism in the second half of the
twentieth century. He describes the Irish peasants from
the West who are forced to go to England to find work as
labourers in the 1950s:

> I met and made friends with some wonderful Irishmen
> during this time. These were a proud, resilient kind of
> men who had taken the knocks of the world in their
> stride and came up, smiling, for more. . . . They were
> rarely married and they had not seen Ireland for
> years. Many of them could hardly read, but they were
> knowledgeable men and fit for any company. . . . They
> had their own poets and their own rules about behaviour.
>
> (p. 64)

Molloy's political perspective reveals hidden
contradictions: the debilitation of the oppressor through
his own compulsive injustice; the inconsistent violence
and passivity in the peasant response; a paradoxical
exhaustion from passivity, and the flow of adrenaline from
a flash of violence: the former largely the experience of
women; the latter, the experience of the men.

For M. J. Molloy, whose historical focus tends to be
the end of the eighteenth century, the tensions for peasants
then who tried to find an effective response to the injustice
and oppression resulted in a reaffirmation of human
resilience. Their resilience is seen, quite deliberately,
to be a product of their vigorous and fruitful peasant
imaginations. Molloy is precise in his depiction of this: it

is the *imaginations* of his characters which define their strategies and their continually inventive moral ordering of their de-structured communities. The landlords are themselves a part of the fracturing which they cause.

The imaginations of the characters also define the subsensible worlds of the fairies and of their late usurpers, the persecuted and scattered Catholic clergy. Far from religion and mysticism being the opium of the people, both are, in Molloy's dramatic vision, active tools of the inventive imagination of people forced to live in the very eye of contradiction. The radical inspiration of Molloy's plays is the transcendental quality of the peasant imagination, which he sees as creating the reality of their lives. It is this which defines their humanism, rather than any sluggish attempt by them to come to terms with an extant moral world, already ordered in a particular way.

This analysis, as well as that of the four plays which follows, is a regrettable intellectualisation of the creativity of positive non-intellectualism. Ironically, my descriptions diminish what I am seeking to define. Unfortunately, I know of no other way of showing in this written form Molloy's aesthetic and artistic enterprise, which was to find a dramatic language for the ways in which the Irish peasants survived British colonialism and Western industrial expansion. He wanted to show the following contradictions: the depiction of brutality at the centre of relationships of love; the excitement of violence as the seam in the rockface of passivity which splits the rock; the human delimitation of the supernatural and the divine. These contradictions make up the passionate, human context of the underdevelopment of Ireland as the United Kingdom rose to imperial and industrial greatness on the backs of the Irish and assumed moral leadership of the 'civilised' world.

The Theatre in the West

Molloy's large oeuvre is all evenly accomplished: from *The Old Road*, of 1943, through *The Visiting House*, 1946, and *The Paddy Pedlar*, first produced by the Balina Players in 1952, then produced at the Abbey in 1953, to *Petticoat Loose*, produced at the Abbey in 1979, and published in 1982. *The Wood of the Whispering*, produced at the Abbey in 1953, was brilliantly revived at the Druid Theatre in 1983. His most extraordinary play is, however, *The King of Friday's Men*, first produced in 1948 and first published in 1949.

The King of Friday's Men

In *The King of Friday's Men* Molloy offers new insights into the relationship between the passions and the economic conditions which determine our social behaviour. The play is about the feudal *droit du seigneur*, the aristocrat's right to have sex with any of his female serfs, which was translated in the eighteenth century into the landlord's right to sleep with any of the virgin daughters of his tenants.

For Molloy, the dominant contradiction within the system of *droit du seigneur*, known in the West of Ireland as 'His Honour's tallywoman', which he expresses in this play, is mythic and psychological rather than economic. Molloy is like Homer, no less, in linking the life-force of passionate love with fighting. Despite their contradiction of each other, both are seen as ennobling, both denying self. While one is confirmed in marriage and the other is confirmed in war, both are confirmed in sport: practice for the real thing. A code of sporting conduct underlines a system of morality in love and war.

Molloy's starting point is an unfeigned acceptance of an ideal of monogamous marriage: it ennobles both partners in the first flowering of their love, rewards them with a deep friendship in old age, and provides them with children who will see them decently into their graves. This ideal of marriage is contradicted by class and specifically by the pattern of relationships within late feudal landlordism. Marriages are economic contracts for both landlords and tenants – the former further abusing the contractual obligations which they have forced on the latter. It is easy to see how love becomes debilitating rather than ennobling under these circumstances. It is not quite so easy to see how fighting becomes debilitating as well, because it is difficult to see how it could ever be seen as ennobling in the first place. The paradoxical interaction of the passions, and their deeper contradiction by social forces, is the task Molloy has given himself.

The first paradox is that the ideal of the love match for life, which late-eighteenth century Irish society denies, is kept alive at the peasant level by a preferred bachelorhood. Some of these bachelors dream of an ideal love and of achieving a marriage which has been made in heaven, and instead become great shillelagh fighters, leading their communities in the shillelagh contests between the villages at the various religious *pattens* (processional feast-days in the Roman Catholic Church). Love for a woman and great fighting strength – both perceived as virtues – can be generated at the base of an oppressive society and eventually challenge the oppressors' moral hegemony. The recognition, by the landlords, of these powerful sensibilities among the peasantry, necessitates their destruction by that dominant class. However, frenzied suppression only confirms the peasants' moral worth in the process of social disintegration. This is the view of late feudal society which Molloy offers his audiences in a performance of *The King of Friday's Men*.

Like most of the drama of the West of Ireland, the

dynamic of this play is its narrative structure: the audience watches the story unfolding, its twists and turns, its sudden reversals, disjunctions and subsequent illuminations. The audience watch characters making decisions – right in terms of what they know but wrong in terms of our further privileged knowledge – but are powerless in their fascination to alter the ironic progression of the story.

The play is set in 1787, two years before the French Revolution. It tells the story of the peasants and servants of Caesar French, their landlord. He is the last of the line of an old Norman-French family, a representative of the Old Aristocracy of the West of Ireland who hailed from the eleventh-century Conquest of England.

He is deliberately provoked by his current tallywoman, Maura Pender, and throws her out. One of the stories which the play tells is hers: she tries to find a peasant husband who will accept her for what she is, who will love her and care for her in her old age. Oddly, Caesar French really loved her; but his peers and society could never allow him any other liaison with her than as 'His Honour's tallywoman' – and there is no future for her in such a relationship. Another tallywoman must, of course, be found immediately for his honour, by the bailiff, Boorla. This leads us into the story of Una, or Oona. She is about to become the virgin bride of Owen Fenigan, a 19-year-old tenant of Caesar French. They are passionately in love with each other.

The first task of the play's structure is to intersect these two stories in a precise way. Maura's brave and positive action in leaving Caesar French, in an attempt to find a real marriage, immediately contradicts the possibility of Oona finding happiness in her love of, and proposed marriage to, Owen.

The action of the first act takes place in the bedroom

of Oona's uncle's cottage. He is Gaisceen Brehony (pronounced 'Gosh-keen'): huntsman and gillie to Caesar French; poteen-maker, smuggler and ageing lively bachelor. The stage direction describes him as 'one of Nature's gentlemen'. The local people are all gathered in the adjoining kitchen for a dance. To this dance comes Maura Pender, looking for a husband; Owen and Oona announce their engagement at the dance; and immediately after this, Boorla, French's bailiff, arrives at the dance, with his henchmen armed with their shillelaghs, to seize a new tallywoman for Caesar French.

In Gaisceen's bedroom, sleeping in Gaisceen's incongruous four-poster bed, is Bartley Dowd, a shillelagh fighter of great repute who has been brought in by Gaisceen from a distant landlord's lands, for the annual St Brigid's Patten when, for sport, after the mass and the procession, the men of two neighbouring communities beat the daylights out of each other with their shillelaghs. Bartley has great strength and is renowned throughout the region; but his face is smashed up through all the sporting fights in which he has found glory for his own community. His brother was killed in a fight and so he has spent 13 years minding the widow's farm and bringing up her brood. He is chaste; and he longs now for his own marriage to brighten with love what he sees as his empty life. His experience over the next few days is the third story which the play tells.

Maura wonders if he will have a tallywoman; but Oona's sudden prospect of losing her true-love Owen for Caesar French is more pressing. Gaisceen thinks up a strategy. Oona is persuaded to tell Bartley that she will marry and cherish him if he will take on Boorla and his six armed henchmen. He is fired by love for her; is inspired to even greater strength than ever before and routs French's men.

The fight takes place in the kitchen. In the adjoining bedroom, the various protagonists assess the new situation. Oona is now committed to Bartley – for the moment at least – and she and he flee into hiding beyond French's lands. Owen, however, is taken captive by Boorla as a hostage.

Act II is set outside the cabin off the French lands to which Bartley and Oona have fled. They are now waiting for the St Brigid Day's fight. During this act, Oona becomes aware of a new love growing within her, for Bartley. Her dilemma is acute, for she still loves Owen. Not only does she love both, she now has a duty to marry both, because Owen is being held by Caesar French on her account. Her situation seems impossible. However, as in *The Paddy Pedlar*, it is resolved by a great leap of the imagination. Oona and Bartley are surprised by the sudden appearance of a strange wild character – *a man less favoured by nature and fortune one could hardly imagine, yet his whole aspect and behaviour is one of the wildest, most touchy and arrogant pride* (p. 50). He is Rory Commons, son of the Chief Composer of Ireland, Blind Cormac Commons. Rory, after a lifetime of caring for his father, is now waiting for him to die. His father has promised that he will inherit the gift of poetic and musical composition. The discontented son of a brilliant story-teller and composer, Rory's intrusion into the story of the play is a wild disjunction.

Quite arbitrarily he informs Oona that he knows her story, it is a well-known story in Ireland, and her duty towards Owen is for her to marry Bartley. Owen will be released by Caesar French once Oona is no longer going to be his bride. From the audience's point of view this is a satisfying conclusion to the play. But immediately Rory leaves them, the waters of the narrative are muddied –

again by Maura Pender, who ironically is trying to do Oona some good. She has nearly given up all hope for Bartley Dowd herself. She has bribed one of French's serving men, a lout named Murty, to release Owen, who will come for Oona. Well, says Oona, I'll tell him I'm going to marry Bartley. But Murty shows more loyalty to Caesar than to his own class, and Oona is tricked and abducted while Bartley is winning honours for the peasant community he is championing.

Act III is in Caesar French's drawing room. Caesar is carefully described in the stage directions. So is his drawing room, which is presented as an extension of his personal character as well as of his wealth and inheritance. He is Bartley's true antagonist. His sport is fighting, as is Bartley's. Caesar's sport is debased, however, by his class obsession with making other men and beasts fight for him while he gambles on the outcome.

Caesar, like Bartley, is unmarried in middle age; and although he is not chaste – perhaps *because* he is not chaste – he now has the same hankering for a life-long partnership with a woman. He loved Maura his tallywoman as far as he was able. But the two women he wants, Maura and Oona – both of whom he can have simply by taking them – both love Bartley Dowd. His power and wealth have trapped him emotionally, as much as they have economically circumscribed and curtailed the freedom of men like Bartley. Caesar's desire for Maura and Oona is sterile, for him as much as for them; whereas Bartley's desire for Oona is fired by an unfettered imagination which reveals a new emotional potential for both of them. The stage direction sums up Caesar thus:

The bold cynicism of his youth has developed into pessimism; and the most striking thing about the man is

1. *The Freedom of the City*, Royal Court Theatre, London, 1973.

2. *Translations.* Field Day Theatre Company, 1980, Ann Hasson as Sarah, Mick Lally as Manus.

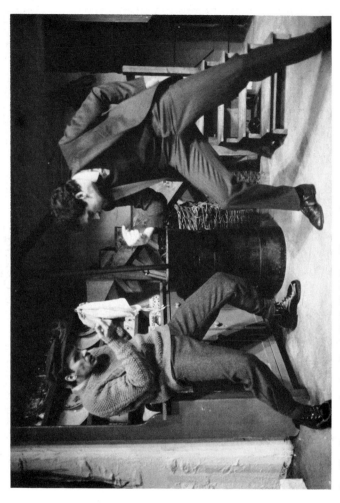

3. *The Communication Cord*, 1982. Field Day Theatre Company.

4. *The Communication Cord*, 1982. Field Day Theatre Company.

5. *Double Cross*, 1986. Field Day Theatre Company. Stephen Rea as William Joyce.

6. *Double Cross*, 1986. Royal Court Theatre, London. Kate O'Toole and Stephen Rea.

7. *The Great Hunger*, 1986. Almeida Theatre, London. Dermod Moore, Vincent O'Neill, Conal Kearney, Tom Hickey.

8. *Observe the Sons of Ulster*, Hampstead Theatre, London, 1986. John Bowe.

9. The Field Day Theatre Company in 1986. Richard Howard, Lisa
   Stifler, Douglas Laing, Ursula McAllister, Julie Barber, Joe
   McGrath, Kate O'Toole, Consolata Boyle, Fiona Macmillan, Jim
   Sheridan, Stephen Rea, Jane Perrott, Brian Friel.

his air of fierce gloom and disillusion. But its very
intensity and genuineness almost enobles him; at least it
redeems him from commonplace arrogance and brutality.
(p. 73)

This heavily particularised characterisation of the man
signifies that he is not just Bartley's class enemy (and
the 'baddie' of a nineteenth-century melodrama) but a
significant adversary: a *potentiality*, in different economic
circumstances, within Bartley's own personality. Caesar's
pessimism increases as he begins to perceive Bartley's
optimism. For the audience, watching the unfolding of the
narrative, there are a number of possible solutions; and
the outcome could not be more uncertain.

In Molloy's poetic vision the 'life of the drama' pushes
Caesar to destroy Bartley's faith in women, to undercut
his love for Oona, to reduce Bartley's imagination and
break his optimism, and to bring him down to his own
disillusioned level.

Caesar perceives a strategy. He first lies to Oona: if she
will say to Bartley, who is bearing down on the French
mansion to rescue the woman he passionately loves, that
all along she lied to him and never had any intention of
marrying him instead of Owen, then Caesar will not kill
Bartley. Oona and Owen can then leave his lands. It is
true he will not kill Bartley. But he intends to recapture
Oona to rape her. There is deep irony here: Oona by now
loves Bartley so much she will lie about it in order to save
his life. The audience then watch her doing this. It is an
unbearable scene.

After she and Owen have gone, Bartley says bitterly,

. . . My curse upon her, and the curse of my people
and the curse of God, moreover.

97

CAESAR: (*with grim satisfaction*) That is spoken more like a man. That is the way to deal with women – curse them into hell, and out of your mind, then drink yourself back into good humour. (p. 89)

Gaisceen privately manages to moderate Bartley's hurt. When the recapture of Oona and Owen is botched by Boorla, and Bartley hears her screams, he again leaps to her defence. He crashes through the casement window, followed by Caesar with a drawn sword. Bartley first clubs him to death; then goes off in pursuit of the bailiff Boorla. Rory Commons comes into the French drawing room: his father has at last died – but has taken the gift of creativity with him. The narrative veers into farce as Rory tips French's body off the table-cum-bier and lies down in his place, seeking in vain to compose a lament for the fallen aristocrat, the story of his death.

When Bartley returns the view of everyone is that the gentry will hang him and he should make good his escape. Maura then begs him to have her, even though she is a tallywoman. She says she will take her chance with him, and he agrees. Oona has finally gone off with Owen, with what feelings we do not know. For us things seem to have worked out appropriately. However, Molloy does not allow us this satisfaction for long: Gaisceen points out that this is madness. A woman would only hinder Bartley's escape, and Maura accepts the over-riding logic in this. Rory wails about not being able to match the moment with a lament that will be sung all over Ireland. In fact, nothing has worked out for anybody. In the midst of this farce, the tone of which is precisely judged to convey the irresolution of the conflicts and desires in the telling of the story, Bartley suddenly understands who he is:

Rory, you have made the same mistake as me. 'Tisn't for good fortune God put our like in this world, but only to do odd jobs for Him. Yourself to give good minding to His composer that was blind, and myself to snatch a girl from the Pressgang, and to keep hunger from my sister-in-law and her orphans. We can no way complain. Himself gave His life for us of a Friday.

(p. 94)

So they are the King of Friday's men. Rory and he go off together, Bartley to look after Rory and Rory to teach him all Cormac's stories. There is only limited consolation in this moment of understanding:

Spare an odd prayer for Rory and myself. . . . Misfortune that strikes too long'd wear the rocks.

(p. 95)

The immanence of both pathos and comedy of this bizarre concluding scene is carefully controlled to convey precisely the sensibilities of the people in the scene. People may have special talents in order to accomplish only small and mediocre deeds. They can have great intellectual and physical gifts for quite unremarkable ends. Good fortune and success, within a pernicious social system, is usually at the expense of others. Using our wits to solve a problem can create new dilemmas for others. It is the same with a play: the extraordinary stories of Maura, Oona and Bartley have only modest conclusions. The imagination of the audience is not cheated; these perceptions outweigh the satisfaction to be derived solely from the narrative.

It is appropriate to look briefly at two of Molloy's plays in recent productions: *Petticoat Loose* and *The Wood of*

the Whispering. Petticoat Loose is set in the winter of 1822.
It is about the struggle for continuing influence between a
fairy doctor and a suspended priest. It was premiered at
the Abbey in 1979, directed by Thomas McAnna. The
published text of the play contains a Preface by Molloy in
which, giving the historical context for the subject-matter
of his play, he makes three crucial points:

(1) The conversion of Ireland to Christianity did not
    eliminate pagan beliefs and practices in the
    countryside. Nevertheless, the priests and
    schoolmasters threatened the continuing influence of
    the pagan priesthood.

(2) The conversion of England to Protestantism in 1534
    resulted in the proscription of Catholic priests under
    the Penal Laws, but not of pagan beliefs which were
    ignored. Fairy doctors, usually women with access to
    the Fairy Forts, were able to extend their influence in
    curing the sick, both people and animals. The biggest
    threat to the influence of these fairy doctors was the
    suspended priests who sold 'gospels' to people to cure
    their sick relatives. These 'gospels' were words written
    out by the priest from St John's Gospel on a bit of
    paper which was then sown into a piece of cloth and
    worn around the neck of the patient.

(3) At the beginning of the nineteenth century the Penal
    Laws were repealed. The Catholic Church began to
    claw back its influence within the rural communities;
    and this, together with the developments in medicine
    and veterinary services throughout the nineteenth
    century, saw the eventual disappearance of both fairy
    doctors and the asking for and giving of 'gospels'.

Molloy consciously refuses to pass judgement on peasant

beliefs and practices, and on the behaviour of fairy doctors and suspended priests. He is neither sceptic nor apologist. Nevertheless, he seems to be suggesting in his historical overview that there is a strange irony in a colonial Protestantism which attacked Catholicism for superstition while allowing paganism to continue unchecked. Within the play Molloy's sympathies lie with the humanist priest, Father Tarpey, disgraced and suspended for drinking, rather than with the ideologically intense fairy doctor, Biddy the Tosser (her soubriquet comes from her divination by throwing – 'tossing' – the bones). Fr Tarpey is a scholar, devoted to his books and longing only to become a hedge-schoolmaster in another part of Ireland, and to escape from his alcoholic past. Hunger and exhaustion initially drew him into selling 'gospels' to cure people; but he does have a further commitment to freeing the rural folk from a debilitating superstition.

As in the other plays, *Petticoat Loose* explores the ironies and contradictions in people's passionate behaviour within the specific social and economic conditions in which they were generated. Their passion, within the context of their mutual oppression, reveals the social contradiction. Confronted by seemingly insoluble dilemmas, the protagonists have to chart their own moral course, take their own decisions, and find within the community the resourcefulness necessary in order to keep going. This is accomplished, as in the other plays which we have considered, by an emphasis on narrative structure. It is the precise way in which the telling of the story is structured that the ironies and contradictions come into our understanding.

Apart from Biddy the Tosser and her antagonist, Fr Tarpey, there is a collection of other characters: Petticoat

Loose herself, who is described as 'a country-style semi-whore'; Peg Above All, a young girl described as 'a famine refugee'; Shawn Lally, a peasant who has now become a big freehold farmer and a 'half-sir'; his wife, who is barren; and one of his farmhands, Mullee, who cannot afford to marry and avails himself of the services of Petticoat Loose. All these people are caught up in their own sufferings and illnesses and disquiet. They project these onto the rivalry and animosity of the local rival folk-healers, Biddy and Tarpey.

These oppressions are consciously known by the characters. What they are not aware of is the wider process of British industrialisation in Europe and of the accompanying underdevelopment of Ireland in which Catholics are being emancipated – paradoxically – and the peasantry are being differentiated into landless wage-labourers and Irish small-farmers.

The narrative line is fairly complicated as everyone struggles for his or her own advantage, in the context of their superstitions and bet-hedging. The various strategies come together in getting Peg Above All to sleep with the priest, so that Honor ('half-sir' Shawn Lally's wife) can acquire the 'shift of a priest's wife' and fall pregnant, to conceive a son and heir for 'half-sir's' acquired lands. Act I which sets out these strategies moves along a ridge of dangerous comedy, becoming neither ludicrous nor indulgent. Molloy's brilliant Irish English dialogue and characterisation convey the paradox of the debilitating fear and creative wit that frames the lives of oppressed rural people. Act II contains two scenes, both in Tarpey's cabin, which depict the seduction of the priest. There is, however, a significant disjunction between the two scenes. The sexual union of Peg Above All and priest has transformed both of them. Love has been awakened in both of them and they have discovered physical and emotional fulfilment for themselves and for each other. This is a love-match which, it seems, was made in heaven; and they immediately plan to marry.

This positive, passionate result of the mean strategising of the others causes disquiet among the latter. A conventional morality, well-rehearsed and limiting, is suddenly confronted by a new positive humanism. The success of their strategy now threatens the community at large in a more comprehensive way. Indeed, at this point, no one is certain of the way forward, least of all Fr Tarpey. The suspended priest, who has now broken his vow of chastity, is cut adrift from his former certainties and weakened in his faith.

The play resolves the narrative in the following way: Tarpey will not marry Peg Above All: she will marry someone more suitable (someone whom the audience have hardly got to know); he will try to become a hedge-schoolmaster; he will try to regain a state of grace; he will not lose his faith.

There is a pulling-back here, by Molloy: an authorial intervention which rounds off the play in a satisfactory ideological manner, though away from the inventive thrust of the narrative and characterisation. In fact, the ending of the play shows that in reality Tarpey is trapped. His true love presents him with intolerable options. In this situation it paradoxically ennobles him yet presents him with demeaning alternatives. He tells Peg Above All:

A priest is the only man in all the world who can't do his day's work unless he is in a state of grace; because he can't say Mass unless he is in a state of grace. You grow to like being in a state of grace: you feel safe.

103

And you realize there can be no real happiness away
from God, our Creator.   (p. 73)

This faith is confident and is unlike the superstition of
Biddy the Tosser, whose long, morbid speech invoking
the spirits of the place to continue to support her closes
the play.

In between these two speeches, Petticoat Loose, the
person whose name gives the play its title, comes on with
her lover. She and he are more carefree than the rest.
Her song, much more than either Tarpey's or Biddy's
speeches, seems to sum up the tone of the play:

> While we can we'll live in Clover
> Because when we die, we'll die all over!

                                                    (p. 74)

The Wood of the Whispering is different: the narrative
structure is less connected with action and more with
reflection and conversation. The play is set in 1950;
nevertheless the colonial history of Ireland hangs over the
play in the atmosphere and in the sense of the past in the
present. The play's single set signifies this; it is a metaphor
for Ireland a generation after its people had shaken off
colonial rule. Outside the ceremonial gates of D'Arcy
Hall, seat of the old Norman-French family, now shut up
and vacated, is the impoverished camp of Sanbatch Daly.
He is an old bachelor-farmer whose farm has gone to
wrack. Around his little camp are the emblems of a way
of life in the West of Ireland which has been carried into
the present time.

The play is about dying communities in rural Ireland.
There are political and economic reasons for the
disintegration and demise of whole communities in the

West, and Molloy acknowledges them in a polemical Preface. The play, however, is not about this macro-analysis, valid though it is, but about the attitudes of old and young alike within one such dying community towards marriage and emigration to England. Economic pressures prevent the former and force the latter upon unwilling people who have lost their lands and their livelihoods.

Sanbatch Daly has a ragged, intense presence. He refuses to accept any sort of charity and is desperate to keep himself out of the poorhouse. Hence his camp. He has drifted sideways into this situation. It is within this self-imposed internal exile that he perceives his mission to save the community by bringing about marriages among young people. His strong charisma makes both young and old feel that some sort of solution might indeed be found.

As in *Petticoat Loose*, the tone of the play is that of dangerous comedy. The wit and repartee is on the edge of despair: talk of marriage is to postpone or avoid such a decision; conversation about their future within the community is to confirm their intention to emigrate. The older people have become 'characters'. Unable to face their own ageing and death in a dying community they have retreated into bizarre behaviour and self-parody. Molloy's characterisation of them is to show their heroism, beneath this odd exterior, which is beyond despair. They are the 'wonderful men' whom J. B. Keane praised. Unfortunately, dying communities do not need bachelors.

The play is an extraordinary *tour de force*. Its dramatic idiom is far ahead of 1952 when it was written – at the same time, for example, as Samuel Beckett was writing *Waiting for Godot*. Like that play, which may owe something to Molloy's special West-of-Ireland poetic vision, the comedy is deadly serious. The outcome, however, is positive in proportion to Beckett's negative tone. This is because of the political commitment which underpins Molloy's play. It is understated and yet dramatically accomplished: the playwright shows how economically deprived people in the rural areas in the impoverished West of Ireland can take responsibility for their own lives. The success of the Druid's revival in 1983 shows how perceptive the play is today. It is both a modest and a unique play; and, like the rest of Molloy's plays, it indicates the special quality of this dramatic vision which stands apart from other European drama in the twentieth century.

3
The Plays of Thomas Murphy

Tom Murphy is one of the most important playwrights in Ireland today. He was born in Tuam in County Mayo in the West of Ireland in 1935. He earns his living as a playwright, though even for an established writer like him it is difficult to continue to do so. His work is regarded by other playwrights – Thomas Kilroy, Brian Friel and Frank McGuinness especially – as being of great significance for the development of Irish theatre. Productions of his plays get Arts Council subsidies, as well as extensive notices and reviews; and his work as a whole is attracting academic critical analysis.

Comment is usually on the content of his work, and includes inquiry into what the plays are really about. There is also a wider discussion which relates his plays to political and ethical issues, and how drama as an art can effectively do this. In this sense, Murphy can be described as a playwright who is seriously concerned to develop Irish theatre aesthetics: in the last quarter of this century, drama needs to be able to communicate more about the human

107

condition, and to more people, than it has previously done, even under the influence of the founding members of the Abbey Theatre. Dramatic art – as opposed to other forms of artistic expression – must, above all, be about people communicating with each other.

Irish culture in the late nineteenth and twentieth centuries has returned to being a part of a highly literate – and literary – European culture. This occurred, ironically, as British culture was becoming more insular and divorced from Europe. Tom Murphy's plays exemplify this late culmination of European literary greatness. He is, above all else, a *European* Irish playwright (in a way that few of the notable English playwrights are today) and his creative vision draws on a breadth of nineteenth-century German and French literary references.

There is a paradox here of which I am sure he is aware: he wants his drama to communicate more to more people, and yet his references are not likely to be theirs. The paradox is resolved in his poetic vision of the ethical function today of, for example, Romanticism, or Goethe's *Faust*. Those sensibilities must be re-established, and the power of the idea must again be complete in itself. In this way it works on the sensibilities of the audience without them needing to recognise the source.

This leads to a further paradox. Murphy's plays are published because audiences find them compelling in performance. Once published, however, they are no longer performances. They begin to be judged by criteria applicable to written texts, that is to say, by literary rather than performance criteria. Indeed, the reader of what I write here is already, even without knowing it, locked into an appreciation of Murphy's work as literature. The audience side of the performance equation has disappeared. Even although Murphy's plays continue to receive professional productions, once the printed texts become available for students to study, the individual's response to the playwright's work changes: from the reception of the play in the company of others, to its reception as a solitary reader.

Ironically, this literary appraisal establishes Murphy not so much as a writer as a playwright. Also, Tom Murphy is much better known as a playwright than his fellow-townsman M. J. Molloy, very much because of the translation of Murphy's play-making skills, which are not any greater objectively than Molloy's, into printed texts.

Murphy's work owes a great deal to Molloy's breaking of new ground. Both dramatists draw on the European literary traditions. Before Murphy started writing, Molloy's plays were enriched by a sense of how people, and their history, are best described as continually in the 'process of Becoming', a dialectical resolution of opposing tendencies, which he derived from the German philosopher, G. W. F. Hegel (1770–1831). Both dramatists have been concerned to structure drama out of what has gone before, in terms of the way we structure our thinking, and what is derived from what might be called a specific West of Ireland sensibility.

Both playwrights confront what we might call mysticism in their dramatic representations of reality. Molloy approaches magic directly, as historical fact. It existed in so far as it was believed in. He does not see magic as a 'thing', objectively, but dialectically, that is to say, brought into existence by opposing systems of belief, which were politically based in Ireland's colonisation by England. 'Magic' was constantly in the process of becoming something else, as history forced new social relations upon people. This is a dynamic view of a people and their history.

These non-rational commitments, which he embodied in the characterisation within his plays, are endorsed by a sense of place. The Hegelian 'process of Becoming' is augmented by an attendant 'process of belonging'. Belonging to a place comes sharply into focus at the moment exile from it becomes a real possibility. Put another way, only those whose identity is defined by place can be forced into exile from it. Those who are forcing people into exile wish to destroy the identity of those people. The most interesting example of the mystical processes involved in exile and the related discovery of a specific rooted in place are the Rastafari of Jamaica. Their belief in Jah, in 'I and I' ('myself and God-in-me':'I-Jah-Man'), is indissolubly linked to the Ethiopia of Emperor Haile Selassie. This mystical expression of the African origins of the blacks in Jamaica relates to identity more than it does to place; but place – Ethiopia – is metaphysical, located in both the present and a past much more distant than the period of the European slave trade across the middle passage. For both Molloy and Murphy, place is similarly metaphysical: the West of Ireland as a nexus of ancient and later beliefs, of sexual and familiar relationships, of 'belonging' to it and 'becoming' fulfilled there.

It is the same colonialists who shipped the blacks to the 'New World' and forced the emigration of the Irish there over 200 years later. Today, it seems as though the colonialist has withdrawn his coercive hand, but he has distorted the minds of the people whom he colonised. Now, the moment of decision to emigrate is accompanied by alienation and a deep sexual ambiguity. For both Molloy and Murphy there is not just a Freudian link here but a metaphysical one as well, which is expressed either in dreams (actually enacted on the stage and not merely referred to) or in some ironical Romantic Quest of journey (= emigration) to discover the identity of the undivided Self by going away from the place which both defines and inhibits the psyche.

Molloy carefully structures the ambiguities of sexual choice at the moment of exile. In his special historical perspective, place is feudal and local; and so exile is not necessarily out of even the West of Ireland. Murphy's linking of sexual choice and emigration leads him to a different dramatic structuring of alienation: a vision of Irish people displaced today by modern materialism as well as by colonisation, in the last quarter of this violent century.

The Early Plays

Tom Murphy was a vocational schoolteacher from 1957 to 1962. In 1959, when he was 24 years old, he wrote a play in collaboration with Noel O'Donoghue, the State Solicitor for County Galway East, *On The Outside.* It is a short play, set outside a ballroom somewhere in the rural West of Ireland. It depicts two young men trying unsuccessfully to find 6 shillings in order to get into the dance which is in progress inside. The audience, like the two lads, Joe and Frank, are excluded from the ballroom. We observe the two young men closely, intimately: we are within their personalities, looking out. All the others in the play – the ones who have access to the pleasuring inside the ballroom – are observed by us the audience as being distanced from us by more than the stage. As audience, therefore, we identify with Joe's and Frank's exclusion, rather than with them as characters. An interesting alternative play was written by Murphy in 1974, *On The Inside*, which is set inside the ballroom.

A Whistle in the Dark

In 1962 Murphy retired from teaching and emigrated to
England to become a full-time writer. His first major play,
A Whistle in the Dark, which established him as a serious
playwright and made the career of writer a possibility, had
been staged by Joan Littlewood's Stratford East Theatre
Company in London in 1961. It had received considerable
critical acclaim. This was reinforced when it was staged in
Dublin in 1962; and also in New York in 1969. It has
subsequently been made into a film.

The play is set in Coventry, in England, and explores
the relationships between five Irish brothers, their father,
Dada, and Betty, the English wife of the eldest brother,
Michael. Michael tries unsuccessfully to change the mores
and attitudes of his violent, dispossessed brothers and
father. In the end, Betty walks out on the brothers
and ironically Michael unintentionally kills his youngest
brother, Des. He feels he has some rapport with Des, and
has a strong compulsion to save him from the corruption,
rhetoric and violence of the father and his immigrant sons.

The dramatic structure is less concerned with narrative
and character than with the structuring of relationships
and the need to express these in language. In analysing
the structure we can reach the play's meaning.

The play opens with the three brothers, Harry, Iggy
and Hugo, dressing themselves to go to the station to meet
their father and youngest brother off the Irish ferry train.
Betty is arranging beds and the sleeping arrangements for
the new guests. There is another character present: Mush,
an obliging fall-guy who toadies to the three big men.
The actions of the three brothers, their disconnected
conversations, and their mere presence, all convey a
vague and ill-defined threat which undercuts the seeming
jocularity of the occasion.

Everything about them is ambiguous: their relationship to Betty, to each other, to Mush, and above all to Michael who comes in just before they go off to the station. The relationship between Michael and Betty is low-key, Michael patiently but persistently avoiding the difficult questions Betty needs to ask him about his family taking over their home. Harry and Mush return ahead of the others from the station and this allows the central relationship of the play to be introduced to the audience: Harry and Michael. This is a brilliantly structured scene which starts and ends with a reference to 'Muslims'.

Harry uses Mush to put down his elder brother; but Michael ignores these provocations. Their conversation is about Englishmen and Irishmen: it is halfway to a discussion on class. Oppression, by a class of intellectuals and professionals, is strongly felt by Harry – but he needs Mush to express it for him in words. Harry intuits Michael's *petit bourgeois* aspirations. Although Michael cannot ever achieve these, merely by having them he fires Harry's resentment. Michael's only concern is for the youngest brother, Des, to remain uncompromised and, with the help of his brothers, become something they can now never be. This necessitates Des going straight back to Ireland.

Harry wants the opposite for Des: to stay and become 'one of them', a proper Carney – which, by implication, Michael is not. Des will be much-needed muscle in brawling with a rival pack of Irish brothers in Coventry, the Mulryans. And when the rest of the Carneys come in all of the chat is about fighting. Indeed, since getting off the train, Des has already been blooded in a brawl in a pub urinal. Other relationships are established: Harry's dislike of his eldest brother is exceeded by Dada's dislike of his eldest son, whom he senses is critical of his values and would like to take over his paternal role with regards to his brothers. Des enjoys being the centre of concern, and he is somewhat disingenuous. Michael's battle for his Irish 'soul' has already been lost.

When Harry and Mush go outside, Dada's attack on Michael reaches a peak of verbal violence and threatened physical violence:

> DADA: He wants to live with men and he hasn't a gut in his body. Worse, he wants to give the orders. You! You're like a mangy dog. The more it's kicked, the harder it sticks on. (p. 30)

Dada takes off his belt to beat his 35-year-old son, in front of Betty, in their home. He orders his other sons to help him. The stage direction indicates an arrangement on the stage that is echoed later in the play's ending:

> Iggy *and* Hugo *stand, one each side of* Dada. *The whole attitude is threatening.* Michael *shakes his hands, meaning calm down, and exits hall door.* Betty *follows.* Dada *hesitates, then laughs harshly after* Betty.
> DADA: Hah-haaa! . . . I showed him. He never changed a bit. Like old times. (*He throws his arms around* Hugo *and* Iggy.) But do ye know I was very lonely for ye at home. I'm glad I came. I'm glad. Yes. Aa, ye're great lads.
> (Des *seated, is looking up at them.*) (p. 31)

On stage are Iggy, Dada and Hugo in a threatening line, pulled into this line-up by Dada with his arms around his two sons, supporting him. Michael and then Betty retreat before it. Des remains a seated onlooker.

In this act Murphy has set up the patterns of familial

114

relationships which he then explores in a fugue-like way in the two following acts. The relationships appear ambiguous not only to the audience but also to the characters themselves. The deepening tensions result from a lack of understanding of their own and other's motivations, and eventually force them to express what they have been unable to before, because they have lacked the language to form their thoughts and reactions precisely. Murphy, quite deliberately, makes us share the frustration. Again, as members of the audience, we are not considering the characters as fixed personalities, but as people embodying contradictions and oppositions. Their relationships, marred by language, force them into conflict with each other.

Act Two starts with an awkward and ambiguous scene between Dada and Michael; and it ends with Michael being challenged by Betty – against everything she has said before – to go out and fight the Mulryans alongside his brothers. This support for Harry's position, against Michael's more principled stance, serves to make Harry's violent and articulate dislike for Betty even more ambiguous. During this act Dada and his sons go off to do battle with the Mulryans. We also learn of the significance of Harry's dark references to 'Muslims': Michael was about to be beaten up by four blacks and was saved only by the fortunate arrival of his three brothers, who eventually saw off the threat though Michael himself ran away and did not stay to help them. This keys into further macho discussion about the morality of violence and fighting.

With this knowledge about Michael we begin to find him a more compromised figure: can he criticise his brothers for fighting when he has been protected by their behaviour and reputations? His stand against Harry now seems more problematic. However, we learn, moments later, that Harry, Iggy and Hugo earn their money by pimping for English whores, and also by running a protection racket against black labourers. Michael himself is not against petty pilfering; but it is Dada who quite unequivocally praises the fast buck, crookedness and corruption. Again there is a half-expressed class position here: this is merely a mirror of capitalist relations. All Dada longs for is to become a *petit bourgeois* shop-owner: the legitimising goal for the graft he advocates.

At the end of the act the audience perhaps feels, along with Betty, that Michael should go and support his brothers – not because the fight itself is legitimate, but simply to improve relationships with his family who might then listen to him.

The fighting Carneys come out of the shillelagh fighters Molloy depicted in *The King of Friday's Men*. But this twentieth-century version is distorted by the strangely attenuated misogynist male world which seems to exclude all positive relationships with women. Iggy, easily the strongest of the brothers, refers to all younger men as 'she', 'her', not in any sense of abuse, but as a means of distancing himself from other men in a world in which there are no women. There is a discussion of the film star Hopalong Cassidy, who is approved of by the brothers because he never got involved with girls – except for kissing one who was dying once (the 'her' and 'she' refer to Hopalong, and not to the girl he kissed):

IGGY: I seen that one! And Hoppy – Well, she nearly
      started crying, and grinding her teeth, like that. Aw
      yes, she was the kiddie. Used like her.   (p. 42)

Even Michael's relationship with his wife Betty is severely

116

limited, torn as he is between his commitment to his brothers – or reforming them – and to her.

Act Three is after the fight. The Mulryans were, apparently, defeated. Dada did not make it – deliberately – but is drunk and celebrating 'his' victory nevertheless. The first scene is between a worried Betty – 'Where is Michael if he wasn't with you?' – and a maudlin Dada who keeps singing the Irish air 'I hear you calling me', while trying to engage Betty in fantasising 'big talk'. The brothers come in flushed with victory, and with Mush who is further inflating their egos.

There is an inspired use of song in this scene. Mush has composed a poem about Iggy which he recites to the assembled Carneys. It is truly appalling doggerel, lying for the sake of a clichéd rhyme – 'He was big and strong/and could sing a song' –

HUGO: Iggy can't sing!
IGGY: Shush!   (p. 60)

The dramatic purpose of the poem becomes apparent when Dada immediately follows it by singing the well-known Irish song 'The boys from County Mayo'. This song tells poignantly of enforced emigration during the bitter period of Ireland's colonisation. In this contemporary context, it is brought down to the level of Mush's doggerel, romanticising what is by now an Irish addiction to emigration, contributing to their own stereotyped 'Irish' identity.

The focus is now on Des, heady from his brawling experience and experimenting with his new persona as a fighter. He is prepared to fight anyone and everyone. He smashes into Mush – with his brothers' laughing approval, although moments before they had been applauding

Mush – then squares up to Hugo, and finally to Iggy who lashes him up against a wall, admonishing him.

Michael comes in. The subsequent scene depicts Harry's determination to communicate to Michael his objection to him, even if he cannot properly articulate it. He refuses to allow his father to appropriate and distort what he wants to say: he has a different view of Michael from his father's. He disciplines Dada into silence. He also hits Michael a couple of times; but he does finally manage, physically in body-language and verbally, to communicate his sense of being wronged by Michael.

Language is desperately important at this point in the play. Harry needs to pinpoint Michael's profoundly ambiguous attitude towards him. The only way he can do this is to keep his own words ambiguous. This is done brilliantly, by Murphy, in the following dialogue:

HARRY: . . . It's the other – the – the other things – the – the –

DADA: Implications, Henry.

HARRY: Things! He doesn't think that we can think straight. The things that's behind him. The things – where does he stand? Getting fed two sides, like. The sort of – the – the –

DADA: Implications.

HARRY: *Things!* (*He kicks a chair*)

DADA: I understand –

HARRY: No.

DADA: I –

HARRY: No.

DADA: Actions have roots. I can explain.

HARRY: No! Not to me. No explaining to me. Things are clear enough to me. There's been so many good intelligent blokes for so long explaining things to thick

118

lads. So many. So worried. All of them clever blokes,
cat smart, so worried about it all. (*Points at Michael*)
He's so big and bright, he talks about families and
home and all, and he's ashamed of us. See him
apologizing to Betty when he invited us here. Little
jokes for all so she could take us. And all the times
he doesn't know me outside. The preacher. Family.
Home. (*Harry is suppressing tears*) But I'm thick.
Thick lads don't feel, they can't be offended. . . .

DADA: Yes, yas, yas, that's him all right! That's –

HARRY: No! Not *you*! I'm talking now.   (pp. 68–9)

By insisting on the all-purpose word 'things', and resisting
his father's more 'intellectual' word 'implications', Harry
prevents Michael being accused of a *deliberate* hurt. Harry
sees his father's attitude towards Michael as being deeply
false. In shutting his father up, Harry communicates
to the audience Michael's unconsciously false attitude
towards his brothers, which is a result of Michael's
aspirations to transit out of his class, and out of his 'Irish'
identity.

In his very inarticulateness, Harry is made by Murphy,
to say clearly that Michael, too, is lost. There are no
deliberate implications; and Michael's ambiguous attitude
towards Harry is contradicted by Harry's consistent
attitude towards him. Neither of them can reason their
hurt to the other in verbal language. Both intuit their pain
in each other's *presence* in body-language: a physical meta-
language of blows and looks which is further mirrored in
the stage *gestus*, the grouping of the actors. Harry is now
between Iggy and Hugo, in the way Dada tried to be at
the end of Act One. Harry, not Michael, has become the
father of the family.

The last scene of the play shows Dada trying to claw

back his authority from Harry by instigating a childish, violent and pernicious attack on Michael, trying by these means to call his other sons to his side. Betty walks out on the household (to their cheers, including Des's). Des attacks Michael, goaded on by both Harry and Dada. Michael hits him with a bottle, killing him. The play ends with Dada, isolated, blathering on about it not being his fault.

The ending may be theatrically effective, but is not thematically convincing in terms of the play's focus on relationships. It is a melodramatic end for the sake of an Aristotelian catharsis. What would have happened, if Michael had merely knocked Des out? The whole thrust of the play seems to be towards inconclusiveness: a continuation of inarticulate non-communication which makes relationships corrosive and demeaning. Obviously, in this early play, Murphy felt that some tragic climax was conventionally appropriate. Few of his subsequent theatre plays have such finite endings.

The Fooleen/A Crucial Week in the Life of a Grocer's Assistant

It is interesting to compare the ending of *A Whistle in the Dark* with the upbeat and positive ending of another emigration play which Murphy wrote in the following year (1962), *The Fooleen*. He revised it some years later, in 1969, and it was given a professional Irish premiere in Dublin under the new title of *A Crucial Week in the Life of a Grocer's Assistant*. In this play, the grocer's assistant, John-Joe Moran, decides not to emigrate – either to England or America: the actual destination is clearly immaterial.

Apart from emigration, the play is different from *A Whistle in the Dark* in almost every other respect. It is as though Murphy wanted to write a play which was the mirror opposite of *A Whistle* . . ., not only in terms of the way characters think and relate to each other and reach conclusions, but also in terms of a theatre aesthetic. The pure Naturalism of *A Whistle* . . . is replaced by experimentation with non-Naturalistic theatrical illusion after the manner of Genet or the French Absurdists.

A Crucial Week . . . describes the choices made and decisions taken by 29-year-old John-Joe from one Monday morning to the next Monday morning: a beautiful week in the spring of 1958. At the beginning of the week he is an assistant to the village grocer, Mr Malachy Brown, and contemplating emigration. By the beginning of the following week he has been through considerable emotional turmoil. He has thrown up his job and his girlfriend during the course of the week, but decided not to emigrate.

The first 4 of the 12 scenes of the play concern the events of the first Monday. Scene 1 is about waking up in his parents' wee house in the centre of the village. Scene 2 is at his place of work. Scene 3 is back in the house in the evening; and Scene 4 is in a hay-shed with his girlfriend, Mona, later in the night. Scene 5 is on Tuesday: he throws up his job and decides to run off to America. Scene 6 is on Wednesday: the priest visits to try to dissuade him from going. Scenes 7 and 8 are on Thursday and Friday, and show his mother scheming to get him set up as heir to her ageing bachelor brother's store next door. John-Joe's emotional contours are redefined: sexually, spiritually and commercially. Scenes 9 and 10 are on Saturday: he breaks up with Mona at dawn in a hay-shed; and then in the afternoon witnesses the surprising departure of Agnes Smith who, out of the blue, is emigrating to Boston. Scene 11 is in the early hours of

Sunday morning: he comes to understand the choices he has and the decisions which he can take. Scene 12 is a surprising postscript, which takes place on Monday morning.

Although the narrative and the characters are not presented naturalistically, as they are in *A Whistle . . .*, nevertheless *A Crucial Week . . .* is very much about relationships: Mrs Moran and her son, John-Joe; Mrs and Mr Moran (though hardly any more a relationship between wife and husband); Mrs Moran and her bachelor brother; John-Joe and Mona. In the play the relationships are not seen as fixed: they have become what they are; they once intended some fulfilment, and they can still change again. This idea of a process of relating to people is underscored by other characters in the play who represent the opposite of any sort of relationship whatsoever. The cloying, depressing relationships – even non-relationships – within the family are counterpointed by the depiction of lonely people without families. This situation is shown to be worse, even though it may be without even these problematic emotional commitments.

For Murphy, opting out of the family, opting out of the ambiguous and conflicting ties of seed and blood, is not a way forward at all. Murphy drew Michael Carney and Harry as brothers who could not break away from each other, he shows them needing to communicate the ambiguity of their emotional commitment to each other. In the same way, John-Joe Moran discovers that the ties (which make him want to leave his home and yet stay) can be expressed and therefore better understood. When choices can be spoken, then better decisions can be made.

Within the play's story of a week in John-Joe's life, within the actual writing of the play by Murphy, and within the audience's actual presence at a performance, the essential discovery we all make is the connection between familial relationships and language. Relationships exist prior to and beyond verbal explanations of them; but they are ultimately defined by language. John-Joe finds himself in an emotional bind which is physical (sexual drives), moral (recognised obligations to his parents) and economic (a twentieth-century commitment to materialism). They all suggest to him one thing: emigration. For emigration to be a choice, however, rather than an imperative, John-Joe needs to be able to communicate, in some sort of language, this nexus of relationships. He needs to be able to translate his emotions into comprehending speech. The playwright is doing the same with writing the play.

John-Joe, in the climactic scene with his parents at 1.30 a.m., tells his mother that she drove his brother Frank away:

> JOHN-JOE: And Pakey Garvey didn't want to go. And it wasn't the money. It isn't a case of staying or going. Forced to stay or forced to go. Never the freedom to decide and make the choice for ourselves. And then we're half-men here, or half-men away, and how can we ever hope to do anything? (p. 80)

'Well,' says his father, who has hardly made any communication with anyone which has meant anything throughout the play, 'if you've finished talking you can make your free choice now.' This is brilliantly succinct. It can be set alongside Harry's communication breakthrough in the companion play when he turns to Des and says: 'You like my nouns and singulars? . . . you like the ways I talk? . . . I like the ways I talk too . . . I like the ways our Michael talks too . . . I think he should have been your daddy, I think he should have you then, 'cause he

wants to look after you so much, and you like him . . .'
Harry finds words to describe the relationship. This is
emphasised by the very opposite situation a moment later:
Dada, the father, is unable to find words to understand
the relationships he so consistently fouls up:

> DADA: . . . Now you listen to me and I'll tell you a thing
> or two. Now you listen when I talk. . . . Now, I want
> you all to hear, 'cause I have something to tell
> everyone. . . . I'll tell you about life . . . I'll tell you
> alright about it . . . I'll . . . I'm going to . . . I have
> something to tell you all . . . I . . . I . . . Boys. . . .
> Ah-haa!   (*A Whistle . . .*, p. 73)

These attempts to find a language to clarify the
emotional turmoil of problematic relationships are also
the playwright's attempts to structure the dialogue for his
characters. The dialogue which Murphy writes not only
creates and defines his fictional characters; he himself
experiments with the possible choices which he as a writer
of fiction has. Murphy writes the words, sentences, which
Harry struggles to put together – or rather, which the
actor playing Harry plays 'Harry-struggling-to-put-
together' each night in the theatre. What is so significant
about Tom Murphy's writing is that he builds into the
fabric of the play the crucial notion of the ambiguities of
language, the difficulty of making words carry meaning,
and then continue to carry meaning. Characters within
the play actually speak about their use of language,
conscious of the options which they have as Irish users of
the English language.

In *A Crucial Week . . .* the use of language is deliberately
disorientated further by using dream sequences which are
linguistically absurd. Within the surrealism of John-Joe's

dreams, acted out on the stage, everyone has a rather archaic, stagey utterance, reminiscent of Dion Boucicault's nineteenth-century farces and Brendan Behan's *The Hostage*. Murphy uses the established conventions of a stage-Irish-English language as a contrast to the more muscular dialogue of the other scenes. The achievement is all the more significant because this vigorous language comes out of the mouths of potentially stock stage-Irish stereotypes: the 'fooleen' himself, his suffocating mother and useless father, the lonely gossip, Peter Mullins, the 46-year-old drunk, Miko Feely, and the complacent priest, Fr Daly.

The development of the play's language presupposes the prior development of an appropriate dramatic construction within each scene in which the language can gain immediate resonances. The play oscillates between the public face of private relationships and the private face of public encounters. To do this the play is staged upon a multiple set: the villagers can interact with each other on the village street; the home is territory reserved. Within a single scene there can be a transition from the street into the house. Beyond this, the relationships can expand spacially within the drama sequences, using the whole set, and blurring the boundaries between public and private.

The last scene is optimistic and centres, surprisingly, on the relationship between John-Joe and his uncle, the bachelor Alec Brady. Earlier in the play, the relationship between them was shown as virtually non-existent; but there is an extraordinary exchange between them in Scene 7 which concludes with a lengthy speech by Brady, confiding in John-Joe:

> ALEC: Oh, sure, one time, they were making out I was one of the boys that goes after the boys. . . . Not that

I minded that. But the priest, Fr. Daly, he was only
a nipper at the time, came back to see me about the
rumour. I told him the truth 'I'm not,' I said, 'your
reverence. But I have all the same thoughts and
dreams and urges as any celibate in the country.' . . .
But I was too late in learning to speak out my mind
when it was needed. There was too many wheels
spinning round in my head; and when all I needed
was two: one to say yes, and one to say no.

(p. 60)

The rapport between Alec and John-Joe which ends the
play is entirely appropriate – they have both achieved
some sort of self-awareness of the sex, morality and
commerce of the relationships in which they find
themselves. And John-Joe's gentle teasing of his uncle lifts
the atmosphere, suggesting a confidence not in solutions –
which cannot be so easily found anyway – but in a new
way of thinking things through.

In these early plays, both of which are set in the present-
day world of Ireland and England, Murphy's sensibilities
reveal to his audiences a continuing legacy of the British
imperium in Ireland. Colonialism, which supposedly came
to an end when the British administrators withdrew,
has left a continuing psychological dependence which is
revealed in defining one's Irishness by emigrating from
Ireland. The English imposed upon the Irish not just the
English language but a particular sort of English which
most easily expressed the rhetoric of political domination.
The language that communicated the imperial might of
the British empire was undermined in its capacity to
express more complex sensibilities. It has taken colonised
foreigners whose first language became English to find the
ironical nuances and potentialities for paradoxes which

126

already have a *de facto* existence in their lives. Some of the greatest English dramatists today are the Irishmen Murphy and Brian Friel, and the Nigerian Wole Soyinka.

Famine

During the period Tom Murphy worked in England, writing television scripts and screen plays, he worked on his one specifically colonial play, *Famine*. It was premiered at the Peacock in Dublin in 1968, directed by Tomas MacAnna. Set in the autumn of 1846 and the spring of 1847, this powerful play is an exploration of moral and political understanding beyond utterance. The central character is John Connor, a village leader, a peasant whose forebears had once been powerful chieftains. He has limited education, and no knowledge of the economic forces at work in nineteenth-century imperial and industrial Britain. Yet he is looked to by the other peasants in the community for leadership and strategies – which we, the audience, know he cannot give. We know, with historical hindsight, that the problem of the famine years was much bigger than him, and bigger even than Ireland.

Through the play's depiction of pain and destruction of all relationships, this created character, Connor, is shown trying to steer a moral and political course that will ensure the eventual survival of his community. He perceives no contradiction between moral good and a political act; and for this reason, probably, he cannot give utterance to the reasons for the choices which he makes. Others, better educated and in positions of administrative, commercial and spiritual advantage over him, are able to utter explanations to him, to talk at length and to justify their decisions and convince him that he knows nothing. In reality, they too have only a partial understanding – at best – of what the famine means. Most of them are ignorant and unaware of the depth of it. Against their explanations, and against their possession of a vocabulary and syntax in which to formulate 'explanations', Murphy sets Connor's increasing silence and his increasingly unuttered sensibilities by which he continues to make his choices. He also faces the revolt of his fellow peasants and of his family; and in the end he loses everything.

What is significant in the overall conception of this play is Murphy's unequivocal rejection of fatalism, or a peasant retreat into their Catholic faith (which is very close to fatalism). No, Murphy, is saying: even without language – a vocabulary and syntax for 'explanations' – even without understanding, we still do have choices. John Connor relentlessly pursues the choices he has made and the decisions he has taken.

Famine is structured through 12 episodic scenes which build steadily towards a deeper understanding of hunger unto death, and the political, moral, economic and sexual relationships which motivate the characters beyond hunger.

Scene 11 is the climactic point. Connor is goaded by his starving wife and child into killing her and his son, into beating them to death with a stick. The woman is *in extremis*. She is relieved when he at last finds the courage to do it. The scene is emblematically arranged. On one side of the stage is Connor's inadequate shelter with himself and his daughter Maeve in front of it. On the other side of the stage is Dan O'Dea's inadequate shelter, in front of which Dan is grieving over the dead body of his wife. Mother, John Connor's wife, comes in with their son Donaill. She puts a crust of bread before her husband – for which she had walked for 14 miles, begging. Maeve snatches it away from her father. Mother is pushed over the edge of despair. She rails against her husband and against Christ.

John is silent almost throughout the scene; but Dan's rambling reminiscences are in counterpoint to Mother's final challenging words to her husband. In a stage direction Murphy refers to these utterances being spoken simultaneously as a trio. No printed version of the scene can even approximate to the aural and emblematic effect of the scene; but it is worth quoting Mother's words:

> MOTHER: . . . No rights or wrongs or raimeis talks, but bread bread, bread. From where, but myself – Not him (*her husband*), not You (*God*) – but always the slave, the slave of a slave, day after day to keep us alive, for another famine. . . . Jesus Christ above, what's wrong at all and all the clever persons in the world? Biteens of bread are needed only.

She fears he is not going to use the stick to beat her to death.

> Johnny, I've understood your defiance, the hope you have picked out of nowhere, I've understood all along but it's not of my kind, nor can it ever be. Now they have me prone, and I can only attack your strength to withhold myself a while longer from their last whim. But you will protect yourself. They gave me nothing but dependence. I've shed that lie. And in this moment of freedom you will look after my right and your children's right, as you promised, least they choose the time and have the victory. Take up the stick.
>
> (pp. 85, 86)

She is demanding that her husband, rather than the famine, should kill her. Previously, her harsh attack on his stubborn hope has been a way of keeping herself alive, but now she chooses death at his hand. This is her means of shaking off her dependence: on the British, on God, on her man. Her husband clubs her to death. Dan's keening speech, on the other side of the stage, which continues relentlessly throughout the sounds of John Connor's stick rising and falling, shows, in a ghastly tableau, the spirit still of a people *in extremis*.

> DAN: The auld is to be deserted, Daniel, said Mother. Yis, I said, and married herself that the Colonel had spoiled. Oh, we were both passed 'Collopy's Corner' and I had doubts I knock any rights out of her. And didn't. And didn't. No one to tend me now. As Jesus was noble and denied, he has long since been repaying the closed doors to him in Bethlehem! He has. And all the doors that's closed and black throughout today will have to be repayed. . . . Cait! Caiteen! Well, you're a divil like myself. (*He laughs*) Well you are! . . . . And she'll be first asked at wake or wedding to sing. Oh, I married the blackbird, boys. . . .
>
> (p. 86)

Dan's speech refers to the fact that his wife, whose corpse now lies in front of him, was tallywoman to the local landlord. For Dan, Jesus is also noble and vindictive. He, like the others, has reached out to alternative humanist values against a Christianity that breeds dependence. Dan, Mother and John Connor all represent a free will and a sloughing off of relations of dependence.

In the very short concluding Scene 12, which is set in the spring of the following year, Connor stands with the handout of a meal in the ruins of his home, his community, his land. The stage direction offers the reader a comment on him, and offers the actor a guide to the presentation of the character at this point:

> *He has a cake of bread in his hands. In his isolation he is beginning to sense what he has been through, and to understand that his family, his village, his army are gone.*
>
> (p. 87)

The hunchback, Mickleen O'Leary, is now a corpse at Maeve's feet. Mickleen's brother Malarky had pursued a violent personal campaign against the authorities – in defiance of Connor – and had killed the Justice of the Peace. Maeve had supported Malarky and had rejected her father's more passive moral stance. Her final statement is bleak:

> MAEVE: There's nothing of goodness or kindness in this world for anyone. But we'll be equal to it yet.
>
> (p. 87)

This is the voice of the exploited. The daughter's understanding of the situation makes Connor's own position throughout the play ambiguous. It harks back to the final ambiguity of the tentative, non-combative Michael Carney. Making these sorts of unremarkable and personally uncompromising choices, in pursuit of a sensible morality, often achieves contradictory results. Even in a post-colonial context, pacifism seems to achieve only a more pervasive violence. Colonising a peaceful people will in the end break their pacific sentiments. Colonisation calls forth a violence among the colonised, in order for the colonisers to justify their own brutality. The peaceful and moral John Connor clubs his wife and child to death: that 'proves' to the civilising (= colonising) English what 'all' the Irish are 'really' like.

This sort of imperialistic distortion succeeds finally when the colonised accept the colonisers' view of them. Murphy writes his play against this final defeat. People can still make choices. They can still be unsure of themselves, even as they act. We become aware of an outcome contradicting our intentions when we make a decision; we try to make a better decision.

The play was revived in a new production by the Druid Theatre company in February 1984. For this production, Druid hired a ballroom in Salthill for its Galway performances, rather than commit the staging of the play to the small Druid Lane Theatre. The large-scale production then toured rural areas and marked the beginning of Tom Murphy's writing collaboration with Druid.

The Return to Ireland

The Orphans and *Morning After Optimism*

Tom Murphy returned to Ireland in 1970, an established playwright and able to earn his living professionally as a script-writer. In 1968, his play *The Orphans*, which was set in England, had been staged at the Dublin Theatre Festival. It was published in America and subsequently in the *Journal of Irish Literature*. In 1971 the Abbey premiered another play, *Morning After Optimism*. The first play is set in an English country garden; the second in 'A Forest' in which the country (= a state) is not specified.

The two plays are contradictory explorations of a theme

which is generated by a particular dramatic structure. This structure is to create, within each play, two alternative sexual pairings. In each play, one pair is an idealisation of love and the other pair is a compromise and a convenience. The fulfilment of the former is, ultimately, its betrayal; the lack of fulfilment in the latter has some potentiality for deeper understanding. In each play, the sexual pairs are linked by one member of each pair being siblings: brother and sister in *Orphans*, two brothers in *Optimism*. The structure of each play has further similarities. A situation has been brought about by one of the characters which causes the two pairs to interact with each other in ways they have not done before, and which forces a reassessment of the values which underlie both relationships.

In the earlier English play the setting is the Victorian country house, inherited by the sister, but now incredibly difficult to maintain, and the idyll further marred by an insistently close motorway. The later play takes us further into the country: into the wild wood. It is not really the ancient wilderness: we are not even in the world of Shakespeare's Forest of Arden, in *As You Like It*, but definitely in the world of today, of bottled gas and end-of-the-pier pimping. The forest is ambiguous, as is the English country garden. Both, in the respective plays, have different connotations for each of the pairs. The *mise en scène* in *Orphans* is deliberately Naturalistic; the *mise en scène* of *Morning After Optimism* is absurd, deliberately the opposite. The playwright shows that the same idea can be worked out in either convention. This overarching idea is that different values and moral attitudes can exist between siblings without destroying the bonds between them and the familial ties of blood. Sexual relations are much more tenuous, whether they be idealised or compromised, and are threatened by an alternative set of values.

Ironically, the relations of sex succeed over the ties of blood. In the Naturalistic *Orphans* the compromised brother and his pregnant skittish wife in the end flee from the brother's morally self-assured sister and her Irish ex-priest lover. In the Absurdist *Morning After Optimism* the compromised pair kill the morally self-assured: the pimping brother stabs his idealised brother in the back, and the pimp's prostitute girlfriend kills off the virginally pure heroine. Pimp and prostitute exit crying, saying they might be back in a minute laughing. The endings of both plays are enigmatic – they are hardly solutions – but they yield insights into the contradictory nature of sex and blood relationships.

During the 1970s Murphy's dramatic vision explored the North American connections of Irish familial, sexual and economic relationships in *The White House* (written in 1972/3 and reworked in 1984 for a production by Druid with the new title *Conversations on a Homecoming*); *The J. Arthur Maginnis Story* (1974), *The Blue Macushla* (production at the Abbey in 1980). In addition, he adapted two plays by Oliver Goldsmith: *She Stoops to Conquer* and *School for Scandal*, prising that Irish playwright away from two centuries of anglicised production; and he also adapted *The Informer* for the stage from a novella by Liam O'Flaherty. These plays have had mixed critical reactions.

The Sanctuary Lamp of 1973, however, is a major play, an important preparatory text for *The Gigli Concert* of 10 years later, which has undoubtedly secured his recognition as one of the leading playwrights in the English language in the last quarter of this century.

The Plays of Thomas Murphy

The Sanctuary Lamp

A play which seeks to depict ambiguity can least afford to be ambiguous itself. Most of Tom Murphy's plays have honed in on ambiguities: in relationships and language especially. His achievement as a playwright is how he has been able to deepen our understanding of the human condition through these ambiguities. In *The Sanctuary Lamp* the central ambiguity in Irish society today is shown to be the vestiges of the Christian faith.

At the beginning of the play, the protagonist, Francisco, interrupts the Mass with a diatribe against Christianity:

> FRANCISCO: A pox, clap, double-clap, crabs on Christianity and all its choirs and ministers.
>
> *(The Sanctuary Lamp*, p. 16)

We do not see Francisco until the very end of this act. At the beginning of Act Two he tells the waif Maudie that God is dead:

> FRANCISCO: God made the world, right? And fair play to him. What has he done since? Tell me. Right, I tell you. Evaporated himself. When they painted his toenails and turned him into a church, he lost his ambition, gave up learning, stagnated for a while, then gave up even that, said fuck it, forget it, and became a vague pain in his own and everyone else's arse. (p. 46)

Jesus gets shorter shrift; only the Holy Spirit has some potential for staying the course: 'No, as an experienced punter, in the three horse race of the Trinity, I'm inclined to give my vote to your man, the Holy Spirit.'

At the end of the act, which is also the end of the play, when Francisco is lying in a horizontal confessional box, with Harry and Maud lying on either side of him, he has the following exchange with his antagonist, Harry, about God:

> FRANCISCO: You're praying to a dying horse here, Har.
> HARRY: . . . And what – what are you doing? Kicking him?
> FRANCISCO: Not bad. . . . But you agree the horse is dying?
> HARRY: No. I don't agree with you.   (p. 74)

Francisco's antagonist, Harry, was once the strong man in the circus, and is still a physically powerful man. He understands himself to be in an emotional, moral and economic crisis. He is seeking some solution to his confused sense of guilt and injustice literally inside the Church, from Jesus, whose eternal presence there he is prepared to believe is signified by the burning sanctuary lamp. Harry is, therefore, a man of faith; he has temporarily escaped from his friend Francisco who has no faith and whom he believes to be the cause of the immorality and injustice in his life. It seems, from the elliptical references each makes, that Francisco slept with Harry's wife, Olga, who – consequently? – did not care for their child, Teresa, who died.

The very first image in the play is Harry, in a single spotlight, trying to do a little dance, his great bulk repudiating his child-like ballet. He makes this same physical movement at other moments in the play, as he attempts to recapture a fleeting image of expressive happiness he once saw his little daughter spontaneously accomplish.

With a measure of inconsequentiality, a 16-year-old girl, Maudie, follows him into the church and they are later drawn into a sort of confessional friendship: a moment of communication of a mutual accusatory guilt, and a vague, paradoxical need for both justice and forgiveness. Maud sleeps in the church at night, in an upright confessional box. Harry, with his brute strength, lays it horizontal for her so that she – and he – may sleep more comfortably, in a chaste arrangement.

When they have established some rapport, Maudie begins to tell him about her circumstances, living as an unwanted orphan with her grandparents, and about her mother who kept 'visiting' her after she had died in pain and suffering, until she had achieved 'forgiveness' and became content. Harry is excited at this evidence of forgiveness. He says to the sanctuary lamp: 'That was very successful'. He feels he has achieved some contact not only with Maudie but through her 'confession' with Jesus. Things will now start going right for him.

A bit later, when Maudie is obviously wanting to confess something more personal to him, he actually prevents it – so caught up is he in what he believes is his epiphany. He does not want her to spoil it by an excess of confession on her part. He feels this moderate moment is the key to his own redemption, and addresses the sanctuary lamp again:

> HARRY: I think it was no simple stroke of luck that led my faltering footsteps here, Jesus? Everything is alright now. (*To Maudie*) And starting tomorrow I'm going to recommence my exercises. I'll soon be back in shape. . . . And starting tomorrow I might do a lap or two of this place morning and night. 'Did you come here to die?' 'No, I came here yester-die!' (*They*

laugh) The way talking can build you up: it's better
than food: it's worth ten pounds. (p. 40)

Unfortunately, this epiphany through language, this
building himself up through 'talking' words, is immediately
contradicted by the 'real' world, represented by
Monseigneur, the scholar-priest in charge of this church,
a man, incidently, who has virtually lost his own faith.
Monseigneur, who has returned late in the night to check
up on his new verger Harry, cannot let him turn his church
into a doss house and sleep in an upturned confessional
box with whoever strays in. For all that most moderate
priest's scholarly liberalism, Harry is led out of the church;
but unnoticed by Monseigneur, Francisco slips in and
immediately makes contact with the hiding Maudie.
Maudie 'confesses' to Francisco what she was not allowed
to tell Harry: the account of her giving birth to her
illegitimate child, which then died.

There is a major disjuncture in the play at this point.
Francisco has finally caught up with Harry, who has now
returned to the church. The friendship between these two
men is underscored by a latent violence towards each
other, and their meeting seems to be full of threat. The
reason for Francisco's resolute pursuit of Harry, we
eventually deduce, is that Francisco has to tell Harry that
Olga his wife has died and that he has buried her. He
does this by way of an account of the last performance of
their circus act – one which Harry had, apparently, walked
out on. Their act is hired out to the Dublin rich to 'grace'
their parties, and on these occasions Olga offers her sexual
favours to whomever. Harry now seems to be far more
compromised than from his own account of himself,
through his 'confession'. Harry's faith, his morality and

his epiphany are in the end only words: they represent nothing which has actually happened to him.

But then, Murphy makes sure we do not write Harry off; he makes Harry suddenly find a way of telling Francisco something significant:

HARRY: Silhouettes.

FRANCISCO: Yeh?

HARRY: The soul – y'know – like a silhouette. And when you die it moves out into . . . slow-moving mists of space and time. And it moves out from the world to take its place in the silent outer wall of eternity. . . .
. . . Stack them, softly like clouds, in a corner of space, where they must wait for a time. Until they are needed. . . . And if a hole comes in one of the silhouettes already in that outer wall, a new one is called for, and implanted on the damaged one. And whose silhouette is the new one? The father's. The father of the damaged one. Or the mother's sometimes. Or a brother's, or a sweetheart's. Loved ones. . . . The merging . . . of the silhouettes is true union.   (p. 76)

It turns out, in the downbeat ending of the play, that Francisco is not against spirituality but against what Christianity has become; and that his antagonist, Harry, is not showing faith in Christ but in the endurance of relationships beyond mortality. There is nothing of the reforming zeal of Luther or Calvin in Francisco either. Instead, his attack on Christianity has its origins in the late Romanticism of the German Philosopher, Friedrich Nietzsche, who also proclaimed the death of God; as well as, perhaps, in the Fraticelli of the fourteenth century –

followers of St Francis of Assisi – who waged, and lost, a fierce fight against the wealth of the Papacy and the Church. The metaphysics of Christianity oppose materialism. Today, however, materialism and the Christian religion are even more closely allied against spirituality; and both Harry and Francisco have achieved an awareness of this.

There is a final paradoxical image of this awareness: the confessional has been lain out horizontally again by Harry. Maudie is fast asleep in the one booth; Francisco is lying in the central booth, the priest's booth; Harry is in the third booth. They have achieved self-awareness, and are now calm in each other's company. Francisco yawns and tries to say an act of contrition:

> FRANCISCO: We'll go together, right? (*Harry nods*)
> (*Sleepily*) It's quite an adventure though. It isn't half bad down here. . . . (*Yawns*) Oh my God I am heartily sorry for having offended thee and I . . . . See? I can't remember. I've beaten them. Goodnight, Har. (*Pause*)
> HARRY: Y'know? (p. 78)

Lying in the upturned confessional Francisco's mind is no longer cramped by the confessional's treacherous symbolism: Francisco feels that he has finally shaken off the influence of the Jesuits who educated him. They had moulded his mind in the words of the act of contrition. Now, at last, these words have been dislodged, together with their malign influence. However, Harry's final 'Y'know?', after a pause, suggests that he is still sceptical – his own short-lived epiphany earlier suggests that they should all beware of purely verbal resolutions to their problems.

The Gigli Concert
MAN: Of what use is beauty, Mr King?
                              (*The Gigli Concert*, p. 56)

This play (1983) follows on from *The Sanctuary Lamp*, though as much as 8 years separate the two plays. Both plays are, at one and the same time, a response to Nietzschean Romanticism and yet firmly located in the Dublin of here and now. The Nietzschean death of God and Derrida's death of the European imagination are elided in a Dublin which, in its paradoxes of Church and materialism, reflects the European psyche *in extremis*.

The Gigli Concert depicts the interaction of two men who, before the play begins, are unknown to each other. This is unusual for Murphy whose plays are generally concerned with people already enmeshed in relationships which are very strong but which lack articulation and verbal explanations. Understanding comes to these people through the acquisition of a language adequate enough to describe the potential of these relationships. But in *The Gigli Concert* the two men have never met before. The one, an upper-middle-class Englishman, J. P. W. King, is a quack. He calls himself a 'Dynamatologist', which is a mixture of psychology, scientology and Norman Vincent Peale's *The Power of Positive Thinking*. The other man has no name. He is a self-made Irish property developer. He is in a deep emotional crisis: he wants to be able to sing like Beniamino Gigli, the popular Italian tenor whose fame coincided with the development of gramophone recordings. In response to J. P. W. King's sign outside his flat, this Irish property developer wanders into the Dynamatologist's sleazy consulting room, seeking, or half-seeking, help.

There is a third character: a positive and unconventional

married woman who seeks a sexually fulfilling but emotionally undemanding relationship with J. P. W. It turns out that she is probably dying of cancer. This is Mona; and although she seems to be peripheral to the central duo of the two men, she is central to the overall conception of the play.

The play refers to Goethe's *Faust*; and more especially to the German writer Thomas Mann's great novel *Doctor Faustus* (1947). This tells the (fictional) story of the brilliant music composer Adrian Leverkuhn: the book's intention is to link the themes of genius and sanity, beauty and purpose, with the historically-specific period of the Nazis' rise to power and the Second World War. There is another version of the Faust legend which Murphy may have been familiar with: a play by the Belgium playwright Michel de Ghelderode, *La Mort du Docteur Faust* (1925; and note especially the characterisation of Mephisto in Ghelderode's character Diamotoruscant). Mann's novel and Ghelderode's play derive from Goethe's *Faust* which was concerned to unite the Romantic hero's search for the idealised Self with the bourgeois notion of the divine discontent of productive man, endlessly yearning to extend human potential to the very limits of scientific and materialist rationality.

I do not think that *The Gigli Concert* relates schematically to any of these versions: J. P. W. King is not the devil – although he has a number of Goethe's Mephisto's characteristics: the wry wit, an awareness of others and of their psychological limitations, world-weary, yet knowing this world is his only sphere of influence. The Irish Man with no name is not the equivalent of Faust, although there is an obvious reference to that figure in his productive success as a property developer and in his attendant neurotic dissatisfaction. His present psychotic state is an overwhelming desire to sing like the Italian opera singer Beniamino Gigli.

This ambition seems bizarre to J. P. W. King; but paradoxically it is he and not the Irish Man who finally captures Gigli's voice. The latter is content merely to purge himself of his obsession. In the process he manages to articulate to J. P. W. the ambiguous and traumatic relationship with his violent brothers during his youth and in particular with Mick, the eldest, who runs the family after the father's early death. (The obsessions of *A Whistle in the Dark* recur again and again.) Having achieved this catharsis, he does not develop new, creative insights, but retreats back into a defence of a narrow and arid *petit bourgeois* Irish chauvinism. J. P. W., the Englishman, is consistently more honest. He risks the total disintegration of his persona, is prepared to cast himself into the abyss, the chthonic realm, primordial chaos, in order to discover a wholeness in his fractured humanity. In the process, recourse to a previous rhetoric – in the manner of the Irish Man – is self-defeating.

The play is called *The Gigli Concert* and it is in one sense a concert of Gigli on gramophone records. The arias, sextets, trios and so on, which Gigli sings on record are precisely specified by Tom Murphy in elaborate stage-directions. Any reading through of the play without listening to the particular extracts from the operas will inevitably limit the reader's response to the text. In any performance of the play, the arias and songs are played through, sometimes without the characters speaking, sometimes in relation to their talk. Often the songs are deliberately repeated. The music is romantic: J. P. W. King makes a specific reference to this sort of ordinary romanticism – 'But this practical man [the Irish Man] is declaring that the romantic Kingdom is of this world,' he tells Mona (p. 33). The cadences, the timbre of Gigli's voice, the lyrical quality of the nineteenth-century operas are all part of the heroic bourgeois world which has continued into this century and which has been inherited by the Irish Man.

Like him, and like J. P. W., we as an audience immediately respond to the songs played on the records. Gigli's records are a deliberate overscoring of the love affairs which are talked about by the two men – J. P. W.'s endless and unsatisfactory telephone conversations with whoever 'Helen' is (a further reference to *Faust*) and the Man's account of his abuse of his wife. There is an element of male romanticisation of self in all this, a need to create fictions; and, together with the Gigli songs, it is in sharp contrast to the enacted love scenes with Mona, which represent an overwhelming female reality. Murphy is juxtaposing the European world of Art and Beauty – male creations of the 'Other' – with a reality (probably female) which is beyond this imagination. Of course, the whole – 'Art', 'Beauty', 'reality' – is Murphy's creation in a piece of fiction, a 'play'.

The climax and conclusion is a demonstration of this. Murphy's dramatic art creates an awareness in his audience of a more accurate depiction of 'reality' on the stage, than we are normally aware of in the theatre. 'Slice-of-life' Naturalism is a betrayal – just as Harry's own 'talked-up' epiphany in *The Sanctuary Lamp* proves to be mistaken words, mistaken feelings – as is any 'playing' on our emotions. Murphy wants us, instead, to become aware of the creative potentiality of the process as a whole: (1) we, as audience, sitting together, making one mind with the actors through the play being created, through the very words building into sentences realising fictions; (2) actors, director, designer and technicians, rehearsing together and with the playwright, hoping that what they are doing is going to make meaning: the social production of drama; and (3) the writer, historically-specific in the solo task of initially trying to imagine a deeper reality – which can still only be realised by actors and audiences together, using words. Realising that nothing is fixed, neither words nor any reality which they might signify, the dramatist struggles to find dramatic structures which will make us realise the same thing. We become alive to the *potentiality* of this whole creative process.

This potentiality is evident in the moment of climax in this play. J. P. W. is suddenly on his own. Mona has gone out of his life unexpectedly. She has cancer: unaccommodated pain, irrelevant tragedy. The Man has smugly left him, though not without a conciliatory acknowledgement of the help which J. P. W. has actually given him. J. P. W. perceives his potential for 'real' help within 'real' human relationships at the very moment that this potential is aborted – by Art. His 'real' way forward is through a parody of literary creation: the Romantic paradigm. The sacrifice of the Self here is through an overdose of Mandrax washed down by Vodka and sundry other drugs. Suddenly, he sings like Gigli. He has unplugged the record player so there can be no mistake about this moment of supernatural and superhuman achievement. His fevered talk, at the very moment he is about to sing, is a precise and deliberate parody of High Romanticism:

> J. P. W.: Stops taking alcohol, purity of potion, contentment in abstinence, care of personal appearance. Diminishing fears of unknown future. . . . Resolution fixed in mind for possibilizing it. Increase in control to achieve it. . . . Abyss sighted!

All my worldly goods I leave to nuns. Leeeep! (*Leap*)
Pluhunnge! (*Plunge*) . . . (*Sigh of relief*) Aaah!
Rebirth of ideals, return of self-esteem, future known.

(p. 75)

He sings. *He* is singing; but it is the voice of Gigli, as on a
record, although the record-player has been switched off.
Art and reality have merged – in Art. As the song fades
he is left frightened in the dark. Again there is a Romantic
motif: 'J.P.W.: Mama! Mama! don't leave me in this dark.'

Renewal is through womankind: the echoes are of the
final salvation of Goethe's Faust by The Mothers –
representing a purpose in the universe beyond God – and
by his first love, Gretchen. There is also an echo of Ibsen's
Peer Gynt who finally discovers his true self in Solveig who
has waited for him all her life and who now merges with
the figure of his mother. The stage direction is revealing:
'*Some resilience within pulling himself up*'. More than the
Irish Man, he has purged himself: of Art as much as of
guilt. Both Art and guilt are cloying; European, and male-
imagined. He packs up and clears out, leaving the Gigli
record to play out over the Dublin street, on endless
repeat. The parody of Romanticism is precisely judged.
It is ironical and not crass.

> J.P.W.: Do not mind the pig-sty, Beniamino . . . mankind
> still has a delicate ear . . . that's it . . . that's it . . .
> sing on for ever . . . that's it.

4
The Plays of Brian Friel

Brian Friel is one of the most accomplished playwrights writing in English today. His work is developed around a central poetic vision which has found, and enhanced, a language of theatre to communicate difficult ideas. This language of drama works through wider poetic sensibilities we actually share with the playwright but which we have lost sight of. Brian Friel sharpens our perceptions and makes us able to understand our human condition, and the deepening ironies and contradictions of our age. This is his poetic vision.

In pre-literate societies the organising principle of a poetic vision is through mnemonics (patterns, rhythms, rhymes: forms of remembering). The oral culture is essentially communal, small-scale. It is writing which makes the State: a literate culture enhances the status of the individual and is essentially civic. In literate societies the organising principle of the poetic vision is the individual imagination. This is not just in literature but in the plastic and performing arts as well: their wider comprehension is ordered by written critiques of the work. The developed cultures of the East and the West are entering a new state of post-literacy. Writing is now only one of a number of sign systems; speech is only one kind of communicating language; and a hierarchy between writing and speech, either way, has now been abandoned. This has cancelled out the significance of verbal language as a means of creative communication. We now know we are 'used' by words and sentences; we no longer 'use' them – at least not creatively and originally – in the way we thought we did. Today, the provisional organising principle of a poetic vision in the so-called First World is actually a *reflexive deconstruction* of that very poetic vision.

Like the double helix in genetics, 'reflexive deconstruction' is no longer an elusive or difficult concept. Our sensibilities import a meaning to those words; we have an inkling of what they mean. In one sense, it means the undermining of a particular moment of powerful communication: the possibility of a deep lack of understanding at the point of understanding. If art can help us understand this failure of communication at the moment of communication then perhaps we can glimpse the nature of other failures beyond communication which language is trying to accommodate. The poetic vision of Brian Friel uses the theatre to explore failure: in language and in society.

Audiences, not only in Ireland or amongst Irish immigrant communities in Britain and the United States, understand what Friel is saying. He has struck a chord. He has been able to communicate a failure of communication which is a metaphor for a social failure.

There are two excellent short analyses of Friel's work by Seamus Deane: one is the Introduction to the collection of his plays, *Selected Plays of Brian Friel*; and the other is 'Brian Friel: the Double Stage' in Deane's own collection of essays, *Celtic Revivals*. In the latter, Deane conceptualises Friel's oeuvre as follows. Each play has a secret story at its centre. This is a 'kernal', a '"magic circle", a place into which the audience is being given a privileged insight' (p. 168). This secret story is surrounded by a public exhibition of self and society. The whole play is a fiction: a creative accomplishment in writing by the playwright/in speech by the actors. Within the play, the characters/actors create contradictory fictions: the fiction of the kernal, the secret story, shows a failure of communication; the fiction of the public exhibition of self shows an ironic 'reality' – the supposedly real world in which communication constantly fails. The interpenetration of these contradictory fictions is purely theatrical. There is no ultimate reality to which the play as a whole refers; but, Deane claims, the 'truth' lies at the hidden centre of what the playwright/actor is doing with the characters:

> The central failure is one of feeling and, proceeding from that, a failure of self-realization and, deriving from that, the seeking of refuge in words or work, silence or idiocy, in exile or in a deliberate stifling of unrequitable desire . . . every fiction is generated out of the fear of the truth. But the truth is nevertheless there, hidden in the story which lies at the centre of the play . . .
>
> (*Celtic Revivals*, p. 167)

This analysis helps us to explore the relationship of the social aspects of Friel's poetic vision to the way he experiments *formally* with theatre as a medium of communication. The process of structuring drama is for Friel a formal exercise as much as a writing-out of his social commitment.

I am especially concerned with his work for the live theatre where the audience are physically in the presence of the 'acted out' 'text' of the play. He has adapted some of his plays for radio, and written radio plays as well. There is a television adaptation of his early play, *The Enemy Within*, and a film adaptation of *Philadelphia, Here I Come!* He has also published stories, which exist only as written texts. His plays now exist as written published texts, and this confirms his authorial status. Students of his drama will now read versions of his plays which are printed signs upon the pages of a book. They will read these on their own, silently, as individuals. In so far as there is any 'performance' it is an imaginary one, taking place inside the silent reader's mind. This is very different from a live performance of the play which employs a much greater range of theatrical sign systems: speech, music, movement, light and darkness, spacial and temporal emblems. These are created communally, and they are 'read' communally by the audience. The more experimental a play is with theatre languages the less likely is a silent reader able to sustain the performance-in-the-mind. The words on the page, not just the stage directions and tone directions, but the disjunctures in languages, constantly refer the reader away from the signifieds to the signifiers: the reader never becomes more than a prosaic reader-of-words.

The Early Plays: 'The Enemy Within'; 'Philadelphia, Here I Come!'; 'The Loves of Cass McGuire'

This framework for analysis can offer insights into three plays of the 1960s: *The Enemy Within* (1962), *Philadelphia Here I Come!* (1964), and *The Loves of Cass McGuire*

(1966). Deane accuses the last of having an unsatisfactory, sentimental ending. The play is a development, thematically, on the other two. It exhibits Friel's concern to explore failure as an inability to communicate. Here, the return from exile/emigration is a confirmation of failure (of the individual, of Ireland). In this context, even if the conclusion is not entirely satisfactory, it nevertheless lays the ground for future mastery of the theatrical form to point to the inaccessibility of any *a priori* reality outside the play.

The Loves of Cass McGuire followed upon the success of *Philadelphia, Here I Come!* in productions in Dublin, in New York and in London. The situations presented in the two plays are at either end of the parabola of the lifetime of an Irish emigrant to America. *Philadelphia . . .* is at the point of departure in youth; *Cass McGuire* is at the point of return, aged. In the earlier play, Gar O'Donnell leaves his father and his father's grocery shop for a job in an hotel in Philadelphia. This has been made possible by his dead mother's sister, Lizzy, who emigrated to America and spent a lifetime in a fairly affluent but childless marriage there. The (non-)relationship of Gar and his father lies at the heart of this play.

In the other play, Cass, aged 70, comes home from New York to her successful younger brother's home. What lies at the heart of this play is the (non-)remembering of her life. Cass is the product of a rougher emigrant experience than Lizzy had in the other play; but they are a similar characterisation of an Irish woman who has been Americanised to the point of caricature. It seems as though they have turned themselves inside out: they have externalised their emotions and sensibilities, and now brashly publicise that which they had in their former Irish selves. The American Dream offers individuals opportunities for the realisation of one's potential. But this potential Self is separated from his or her Irish engendering. This new, public self is divorced from the ambiguous reality of emotional ties which were both broken and not broken.

Gar confronts this breaking-of-ties, which, in remembering to break them, are not broken. He is making a break. But at the moment of departure he is consciously remembering everything. He is trying to frame his remembrance of the place – in order to be able to forget it. He needs to be able to remember what he wants to forget. There is a wider import in all this: in wanting to emigrate and escape from the 'reality' of Ireland, it becomes impossible to know what is this Irish reality.

The reality of Ireland is substantial and unquestioned in the earliest of the three plays, *The Enemy Within*. The subject of this play is a fictional exploration of the later life of the sixth-century Irish monk and saint, Columba (521–597). St Columba, or St Columcille, established monasteries in Ireland as well as the monastery at Iona in Scotland. The enemy within is Columba's love of Ireland, his family lands in Tirconaill, in today's West Ulster, and his commitment to his family. He is haunted by the memory of his childhood, among them, there:

But the inner man – the soul – chained irrevocably to the earth, to the green wooded earth of Ireland!

(p. 21)

The play makes the point that the monk's duty to forget his homelands and his love of that earth is not just a problem for Columba. Other young novices in Tirconaill spend their last night before emigration sleeping on the 'Flag of Columba' which is a great cold slab of rock there.

By doing this they are supposed to cure themselves of their homesickness. Columba hears of this with ironical disbelief: as if he himself was free from homesickness! (This sleeping on St Columba's Flag is very much what Gar O'Donnell is doing 1400 years later, in more or less the same homelands: remembering to forget them.) The dramatic structure of the play makes the sixth-century universe of the play so convincing that we are able to identify with the 66-year-old Columba and dread him giving in again to his selfish family who constantly seek him out in Iona to fight in their clannish feuds and tribal wars in Ireland.

In the climactic moment of the play, Columba resists his brother Eoghan who curses him, white with fury at losing this religio-magical support. Columba makes the following emotional appeal, not only to Eoghan, but also to Ireland, whom Eoghan only partly represents:

> Go back to those damned mountains and seductive hills that have robbed me of my Christ! You soaked my sweat! You sucked my blood! You stole my manhood, my best years! What more do you demand of me, damned Ireland? My soul? My immortal soul? Damned, damned, damned Ireland! (*His voice breaks*) Soft, green Ireland – beautiful green Ireland – my lovely green Ireland. O my Ireland. (p. 70)

Written out here, the speech and its tone direction seems melodramatic; but in the intense all-male communality which is the play's space – within the monastery, on the very edge of the wilderness – it achieves the paradox of setting the seductive physical reality of Ireland against the Church.

This paradox is quite deliberately structured. Friel

includes a spiritual intervention at the moment of the climax. The play seems to be about faith, but actually it is about the complex relationship between simple ideological answers and the sheer physicality of our emotions, of belonging to people and places. Columba tells the monk, Grillaan:

> I cannot feel my sixty-six years, Grillaan. I am burdened with this strong, active body that responds to the whistle of movement, the fight of the sail, the swing of the axe, the warm breath of the horse beneath it, the challenge of a new territory.   (p. 46)

The effect of this is to set Christian faith against a physical, humanistic Irish reality. The play seems to be enlisting our (willing) support for the Christian monks and the purity of their communal life. But the problem of Ireland's reality remains, particularly for so complete a man as Columba.

For Columba Ireland was the physical place: unchanging in its natural beauty. For Gar O'Donnell about to leave for the States and for Cass McGuire who has just returned, the reality of Ireland is anything but unchanging. The wooded wilderness has given way, fourteen centuries later, to the *petit bourgeois* Catholic polity of the modern Irish state. By the mid-1960s, Ireland was riding on the back of the boom years of post-industrial Western capitalism. Cass had sent 'home' $10 each month for 50 years, remembering the 'reality' of her family's divided home and the genteel poverty of her mother. The money had been sent to help Harry, her brother. He does not need it at all, as he is making his way inexorably up the economic ladder. He saves it all up for her: she will have her economic independence. The Church affirms the new economic reality of Ireland: one of Harry's sons has become a priest. He did not like the Seculars and moved to the Jays (Jesuits); and his mother is convinced that he has the administrative flair to become a bishop.

Cass's own life in New York was anything but affluent materialism – though she clearly thought that her American experience was a materialistic one in contradiction to the deeper metaphysical values of (Catholic) Ireland. Ireland ultimately is 'home', the anchor of her sensibilities. That the opposite is the case strikes her like the slap of a wet fish across her face. She retreats into fantasy: Deane's 'failure of feeling' becoming a 'failure of self-realisation'.

Dramatic structure: *The Enemy Within*
The Enemy Within is a fiction. Friel includes an apologia to historians of the period in his Preface to the printed text of the play: geography and language are both different; characters are speculative. Friel's fictional universe which he establishes within the drama is intended to extend beyond the particular parameters of the sixth-century Celtic Christian world. The style of the play is Naturalism. There is a single set – Columba's cell – which, together with the props and costumes, aims to create period authenticity *in the theatre*. The audience's belief in the sixth-century Celtic Christian world must be established by the end of the play in order to achieve the antithesis between the physicality of Ireland and the Christian faith which is the play's climax. The spiritual triumph of *Saint* Columba, the securing of his sanctity and salvation, is a failure of Ireland: his triumph is over his physical and emotional commitment to what he perceives to be the reality of Ireland within himself. It is a rejection of a passion and violence, associated with a place that makes him human, in favour of holiness. The problem of Ireland's

identity is not resolved within this play because the holiness of the monks is still a legitimate ideal; their lives are uncritically drawn.

Dramatic structure: *Philadelphia, Here I Come!*

Philadelphia, Here I Come! still has a tendency towards Naturalism, although Friel is now beginning to puncture naturalistic conventions with contradictory theatre forms. Most significant is the characterisation of the central figure, Gar, as two presences on the stage, played by two actors. Friel calls them 'Public' Gar and 'Private' Gar. The latter is unseen and unheard by any of the other characters. He is unseen by Public Gar, though, of course, he is heard by him. A stage direction insists that Public Gar never looks at Private Gar.

The play's *mise en scène* arranges more than one locality within the performance space: Gar's bedroom and the kitchen in the O'Donnell house, both of which remain set throughout the play, and an empty space in front of these which can be used for short scenes outside the O'Donnell house, or for flashbacks. This additional space is used rather timidly, however, and the characters tend to remain in their more naturalistically realised settings. This composite setting exploits the potential of the dual presence of a public Gar who interacts with other characters on the stage, and a private Gar who comments on all of this. The private Gar can continue to occupy the spaces in the house even when the public Gar has gone out. This can work both ways: Gar can remember the rooms, continue to feel physically present in them; while the others can appear to be mindless of his continuing 'presence'.

This is an effective theatrical way of emphasising the play's depiction of the failure of relationships as a failure

of feeling or of sensibilities *in a particular place: a milieu.*
Friel repeatedly shows the central character in his plays
imagining that the source of alienation can be discovered
in the memory of Ireland. So Ireland must be remembered
in order to sustain this negative imagining. This holding
of opposite notions simultaneously has the quality of a
dream.

Through the characterisation of Gar the audience can
become aware of the attenuated feelings of those around
him. The dramatic conception of the whole play culminates
in a final scene in which both Madge, the housekeeper,
and S. B. O'Donnell, Gar's father, make an attempt at
expressing their sense of failure at the moment of Gar's
going. S. B. and Gar in the end fail to communicate with
each other, although both do try. S. B. manages to say to
Madge what he failed to say to his son. Father and son
each remember a different moment of fulfilment in each
other's company. However, the real achievement of this
scene is to hint that what father and son are each
remembering is not reality at all: Gar's memory of a happy
outing with his dad, fishing on the lake, is factually
discounted by S. B. (there was never a blue boat; S. B.
never knew that song); and S. B.'s memory of his pride
the day Gar left school to join him in the grocery shop is
factually discounted by Madge (Gar never had a sailor
suit). The details which are the crutch of memory betray
us. Madge's little soliloquy just before the play closes
communicates an awareness of people changing
themselves, precisely because of this lack of self-
awareness:

When the boss [S. B.] was [Gar's] age, he was the very
same as him: lepping and eejitin' about and actin' the
clown; as like as two peas. And when [Gar's] the age

157

the boss is now, he'll turn out just the same. . . .
. . . . That's people for you – they'd put you astray in
the head if you thought long enough about them.

(p. 109)

If people change into their opposite and memory goes on
false crutches, what ultimate reality is there? The play
hints at the question but does not tackle it.

Friel suggests, instead, that in the transience of memory
there is a paradoxical undertow of unchanging
conservatism in the rural Irish society. Gar says, over and
over again, 'It is now sixteen or seventeen years since I saw
the Queen of France, then the Dauphiness, at Versailles.'
This, as Seamus Deane reminds us in his Introduction to
the *Selected Plays*, is a quote by Gar from Edmund Burke,
the eighteenth-century British (Irish) statesman and
philosopher. Elsewhere, Deane shows how relevant a
re-reading of Burke's writings on Ireland are to our
understanding of Ireland's relationship with England
(= Britain) today. (See Seamus Deane, *A Short History
of Irish Literature*, London, Hutchinson, 1986: pp. 49–57.
It offers an illuminating summary of the relationship of
Burke's analysis of Ireland to his wider political
commentary.)

In particular, Burke provides a view, of his time, of the
intellectual links between politics and feeling. Those
familiar with the writings of Edmund Burke might find it
appropriate that Gar should quote the opening of Burke's
Reflections on the Revolution in France. This was a defence
of the *ancien régime*: perhaps Gar is being ironical
over his own 'rebellion' against conservative Ireland.
Unfortunately, an audience unfamiliar with Burke would
need this reiteration (of not having seen the Dauphiness
for 17 years) to work on a non-literary, dramatic level. I

am not convinced that it does work outside its literary context.

What does work is Friel's brief attack on the Christianity of conservative rural Ireland. Private Gar intrudes on a game of draughts his father is playing with Canon Mick O'Byrne. Public Gar is lying on his bed in his room. 'Unseen' by S. B. and Fr O'Byrne, Private Gar leans on the draughts table and speaks into their faces. He tells the Canon:

> You could translate this loneliness, this groping, this dreadful bloody buffoonery in Christian terms that will make life bearable for us all. And yet you don't say a word. Why, Canon? Why, arid Canon? Isn't this your job to translate? Why don't you speak then? Prudence arid Canon? Prudence be damned! Christianity isn't prudent – it's insane! (p. 96)

This little scene is as illogical as Gar quoting Burke, but within the overall theatrical inventiveness of the play this works for an audience. It creates a frisson, and so widens the play's implications.

Dramatic structure: *The Loves of Cass McGuire*
The Loves of Cass McGuire carries theatrical experimentation much further. It explores the use of disjunctions within a performance of the text, a rupturing of audiences' expectations. The play begins naturalistically: seemingly a drawing-room set, the 'fourth wall' missing, the audience peeping into the private lives of the rich. But just as soon as the scene is established the first disjunction occurs. Cass enters through the audience and literally stops the play. She acknowledges the audience – the stage direction says '*they are her friends,*

her intimates'. Harry, Cass's brother, in whose drawing-room the naturalistic action of the play was taking place, follows Cass's entrance with a further rupture: he tells Cass that their story is being told appropriately. Thus, her 'theatrical' intrusion is absorbed into the more pervasive naturalism. It is as though the characters themselves are carrying on a debate about theatrical form as they try to tell their present trauma: let's talk to each other in as 'real' a way as we can; no, let's talk directly to the audience. This is my drawing-room; no, it's the workhouse you dumped me in. Cass seems to win the first round of the argument:

> What's this goddam play called? *The Loves of Cass McGuire*. Who's Cass McGuire? Me! Me! And they'll see what happens in the order *I* want them to see it; and there will be no going back into the past.   (p. 14)

This last statement reveals the purpose of these disjunctions: memory, the act of remembering, is being translated into theatrical form. This is not merely to express it, but actually to be it. Our 'willing suspension of disbelief', as members of an audience, must constantly be ruptured in order to dislocate remembering the past. Logical syntactical thought, the domination of words and sentence structures, is a deep betrayal of feeling. Harry and his family go off, leaving Cass with the collective ear of the audience and in possession of the stage. This has now become Eden House, the old people's home – Cass's 'workhouse' – into which she has been 'dumped'. It is no longer Harry's drawing-room. As he goes out Harry tells her:

160

You may think you can seal off your mind like this, but you can't. The past will keep coming back to you.

(p. 14)

And it does so, more or less immediately. Harry, moments later, visits her in Eden House, and despite herself, Cass lapses into a memory of a few days earlier, in his drawing-room. She fights hard to resist it. We have now moved back into the (modified) world of the drama of their lives; and this soon veers back into a semblance of naturalistic presentation, this time within the institution. And in a little while the scene is actually drawn back to where it was at the point of its first rupture: in Harry's drawing-room. The stage direction, '*Cass cannot fight it any longer*' (p. 21), indicates that we are back in the first scene when the decision is taken by Harry to put his sister into a home because he and his family cannot cope with the trauma of her failed expectations of Ireland.

Once Harry's decision is uttered, Cass turns back to addressing the audience:

Hell, this is no fun for you, huh? No way to make friends and influence people. *The Loves of Cass McGuire* – huh! Where did he get that title from anyways? (*Rising to her feet as if confused*) Where have all the real people gone? (p. 23)

This is very controlled dramatic writing for the theatre. The 'real' people are now the people in the old people's home. Her family are, at this moment, figments of her memory, the memory she is trying to blot out. So we are not, in fact, back in the opening scene.

Furthermore, the collusion of Cass and ourselves (the audience) against all the other characters also extends to

161

the playwright. This sort of reflexivity – the playwright writing himself into the writing of the play – is peculiarly theatrical. It can only work in the theatre, and more especially it can only work through good acting: the sort of acting which can draw the audience into the fabric of the play. The actress must convince us that the text is her own and not the writer's – a more complex suspension of our disbelief. In fact, this signals another disjunction in the text. Two of the residents in the home are Trilbe Costello, an ageing elocution teacher who never quite qualified, and Meurice Ingram, a retired organist. We, like Cass, find them bizarre.

Ingram is reading out aloud the libretto of Wagner's opera, *Tristan and Isolde*. Unlike the literary reference to Burke in *Philadelphia, Here I Come!*, this reference is precisely explained to the audience, and the giving of the explanation is an integral part of the theatrical form. The 'real people' are telling a very unreal story of kings and princes, queens and princesses, magic potions and miraculous coincidence. The situation of them telling the Wagnerian story is framed by Cass's collusion with the audience – 'Abbott and Costello again! Maybe they'll give us a laugh' – and counterpointed by her New York Skid Row philistinism – 'That guy [Tristan] should ov bought hisself accident insurance!' This comment in fact is the one which precipitates the rupture. Trilbe asks Cass: 'M'dear, who *are* you addressing?'

Cass says she is having an odd word 'with the folks out there' – us. Trilbe peers into the auditorium, but she does not see us. Then she tells her:

TRILBE: Catherine, m'dear, we are your only world now. We have the truth for you.
CASS: Yeah?

TRILBE: Join with us, Catherine, for we have the truth.
CASS: Sure . . . sure. . . .
TRILBE: We know what is real, Catherine.   (p. 25)

Trilbe goes and sits in the winged armchair which is downstage right and has been conspicuous and unused up to this point. The stage lighting changes; Wagnerian music is introduced and Trilbe rhapsodises about her life as the gilded and exotic existence she once had, and tells us a story of true love. Ingram knows the story, feeds her the lines and enjoys her telling it again. She ends by quoting, formally, W. B. Yeats:

> But I, being poor, have only my dreams
> I have spread my dreams under your feet
> Tread softly because you tread on my dreams.
> Ingram repeats: 'Our truth'.   (p. 27)

As they exit, the stage direction indicates Cass's '*naked astonishment*'. Is what Trilbe has just spoken really the truth? Is Cass to take it literally? Memory intrudes and she recalls her own life story: her 'arrangement' with Jeff in New York, and before that her affair with Con Crowley which was one reason why she emigrated from Ireland. Friel, in a Preface to the printed text of the play, indicates a similarity between Cass's own (real) story and the fiction of the love story of Tristan and Isolde. She discovers from another resident, Pat Quin, that Trilbe's story couldn't be further from the actuality of her life. Later, Ingram tells his own idealised love story, a rhapsody as he sits in the armchair. However, we have learned the lesser reality of this love affair even before he tells it.

All these love stories, including Cass's, in their (non-remembered) actuality, are instances of a failure of a crucial relationship. They are all translated into a (remembered) idealism, a deliberate mythologising of the past. They perceive 'truth' in their attempts to salvage their sensibilities, their feelings, out of a certain self-awareness in failure. Cass begins to perceive that she needs the mythologising truth which Trilbe is offering her.

In the final act, the affluence and well-being of Harry and his wife, Alice, also becomes a disintegrating reality. There is a deeper – and unexplored – failure of relationships here. Cass finds herself drifting away from them: her failure can no longer be defined by her brother's success, for it now is evidently as hollow as her lack of material success. She also finds the audience drifting away from her appealing gaze. She is drawn towards the rhapsodic reality of the winged armchair. Eventually she gives up reality for its mythologising truth.

The play offers us a final disjunction: a new arrival comes to the old people's home, another aged woman who demonstrates the same collusion with the audience and the same antagonism to the other inmates, as Cass did. However, this woman is unknown to us, the audience, and so we do not collude with her. We have in fact come to understand a deeper truth in the behaviour of these people and their apparent self-deceptions. This new arrival at Eden House is talking into space. We pity her perhaps, but only momentarily. We are watching Cass disappear into the fabric of the play, into the mythology of her life: a retelling of *Tristan and Isolde* in the naturalistically-established home for the elderly, *The Loves of Cass McGuire*: Friel's own dramatic fiction.

The Plays of Brian Friel

After 1969: 'The Freedom of the City'; 'Living Quarters'

Since 1969 the British Army have occupied Northern Ireland, and military, police and sectarian violence have remorselessly increased. There has been a sense of fatalism in the inexorability of the conflict and an apparent reinforcement of the British view of the Irish as violent and irrational: 'barbarians' needing to be 'civilised'. That fatalism is now cracking and the prevailing British view of Ireland is being challenged by Irish intellectual initiatives, of which the setting up of the Field Day Theatre Company by Brian Friel and Stephen Rae in 1980 is one of the more significant. The development of Friel's drama through the traumatic decade of the 1970s is a significant preparation for this development in the relationship between art and politics.

The drama Friel created through theatrical experimentation in the 1960s was politically comfortable. Failure was the responsibility of individuals, interacting psychologically or metaphysically with Ireland as a place. The politics of the characters were the politics of the intellectual bourgeois audiences deeply aware of the ambiguities of their rootlessness and growing affluence. The violence after 1969 was a direct challenge to Friel's poetic vision and to his dramatic abilities. Yeats and his friends at the Abbey Theatre, 55 years earlier, has been confronted by the challenge of their own failure to change Irish history through their drama. With the eruption of violence after 1969 the marginalisation of the committed Irish playwright was complete.

Friel's response was to overturn his 'comfortable' drama, and find dramatic structures for the failure of the intellectual *petit bourgeoisie*, including himself and us, his comfortable audience: our need to discover our historical failure *as a class*, rather than as individuals. It is perhaps a measure of the success of his endeavour that the plays to come out of this had a hostile reception and so 'failed'. He has been influenced by Chekhov's plays; he and his fellow-playwright, Thomas Kilroy, have recently produced Irish transpositions of Chekhov's *The Three Sisters* (Friel) and *The Seagull* (Kilroy). There are Chekhovian overtones in four of the plays Friel wrote and staged during the 1970s: *The Freedom of the City* (1973), *Living Quarters* (1977), *Aristocrats* (1979) and *The Faith Healer* (1979).

The dramatic starting point for both *The Freedom of the City* and *Living Quarters* is the tragic drama of fifth-century BC Athens and the development of dramatic structures of plays, by Sophocles and Euripides especially, which explored the ambiguities of a fatalistic world view. The dramatic structure of *The Freedom of the City* is grounded in dramatic irony, which Sophocles developed in his play, *Oedipus Tyrannus*; and *Living Quarters* explores the same ambiguities between humanism and reason on the one hand, and destiny and the Gods on the other, which Sophocles showed in that play and which Euripides explored so perceptively across his extant oeuvre. *Living Quarters* is also based narratively on Euripides' early play *Hippolytus*. In both of Friel's plays people try to find a meaning in what has happened to them. But this thought, this talking logically, in words and sentences, cannot change what happened/what is going to happen, no matter how much we 'talk' about it. Put crudely, there is today a realisation of the severe rupture between actions and reasons; and for Friel this is prefigured in the ancient Greek dichotomy between 'destiny' and 'logic'.

The Freedom of the City

The Freedom of the City opens with a powerful dramatic image of the moment of death. Three ordinary citizens of Derry/Londonderry have been shot by the British Army. A moment of history: people shot by soldiers. It is not an isolated action, but one which is the outcome of certain events. As an action it is at one and the same time unjust, inevitable and unnecessary. In the seconds after the play opens, a photographer photographs the corpses; the priest gives them a final blessing. In these seconds, raw history starts giving way to myth. The language of the photographs, and the language of the priest's gestures and mumbled incantations, this mythic quality, which is laid upon this event, come out of the collective *oral* (= non-literary) culture. It can now be given a name: 'Fate', 'destiny'. It was 'ordained' thus: in its communality, its injustice, and inevitability.

It has become the oracle of Apollo at Delphi, which decreed that the baby Oedipus was cursed: he will grow up to kill his father and marry his mother. From that moment, Oedipus' rational avoidance of the curse, throughout his life, brings him unknowingly to an ironic fulfilment of it. Sophocles' play is about the last few hours before Oedipus discovers that his reason and humanity have been undermined.

In *The Freedom of the City* we are given the historical event which becomes myth. A Civil Rights march which is planned for Derry is banned by the Security Forces but goes ahead nonetheless and is broken up by water cannon and plastic bullets. In the *mêlée*, three people – two young men and a middle-aged woman – take refuge in a building in order to recover from the effects of CS gas. The place they have stumbled into turns out to be the Guildhall, and the room they find themselves in is the Mayor's Parlour, the *de facto* and symbolic centre of British administration in the city. They are unemployed, Irish Catholic working class, and are immediately aware of the irony of their accidental 'haven'. The Security Forces assume that they are IRA and their action has been deliberate. They surround the building and shoot dead the amazed three as they emerge from the building. We are given the first few moments after this fatal outcome in the opening image of the play.

The rest of the play is about the movement towards this moment of death, and away from reason and justice. Like Sophocles' Athenian audience at a performance of *Oedipus*, we know the outcome of this 'occupation' of the Guildhall in Londonderry. We are in possession of knowledge about people and the onrush of events involving them of which they themselves are ignorant. The dramatic triumph of Sophocles' play is that the audience do not, cannot, intervene in the play because they believe that they cannot change the myth. They know what is going to happen. They know it is unjust, yet they also know that they cannot intervene: the so-called truth of the drama for an audience is caught up in their unquestioning behaviour as an audience towards it in performance. This is the peculiar impact of the dramatic structure of dramatic irony: the attractive paradox of its injustice and inevitability persuades us not to intervene; and our non-intervention ensures both. Our behaviour as an intelligent audience becomes a metaphor for our behaviour as intellectuals within society, except that we are unaware of the implication.

The Freedom of the City offers us privileged knowledge on two levels: three innocent people are going to be gunned down by the forces of law and order; and the official versions of the truth about what happened are lies. On both sides, the versions of the myth are false. Yet still we do not intervene. It is here, Friel is suggesting, lies the failure of our logical thinking in words and sentences. It is almost unbearable to watch the development of the framing lie around the tragic deaths of three luckless people, yet we 'serious' people do nothing about it but marvel at the play's dramatic power. The play is about a 'real' situation in Northern Ireland and about State violence, but it is also about our compulsive engagement with the myth rather than the originating reality. The play, at a deeper level, is about us watching tragedy, to talk about it.

We need to look at the text in some of its detail. The three who are shot are Adrian Casimir Fitzgerald (= Skinner); Elizabeth Doherty (Lily) and Michael Hegarty (Michael). Lily is a char: 43 years old, the mother of 11 children, married to an invalid consumptive. The two men are young: Michael is 22, Skinner is 21. He was orphaned as a baby; intelligent, but turned out of the grammar school. He has lived off his wits. He bets on the horses. Friel sees nothing inconsistent in giving this 'guttie' Skinner an intellectually fluent English register and making him quote from Kipling and Shakespeare: his characterisation within the structure of the play needs him to be able to articulate the central statement of the commitment of the playwright which occurs in the interior climax of the play (i.e. not the climactic moment of their deaths). It is a moment of communication between himself and Lily, and between the playwright and the audience. Skinner asks Lily why she marches for Civil Rights. She has a reason but she is unable to put it in words, which Skinner does for her:

Because you live with eleven kids and a sick husband in two rooms that aren't fit for animals. Because you exist on a state subsistence that's about enough to keep you alive, but too small to fire your guts. Because you know your children are caught in the same morass. Because . . . you grumbled and someone else grumbled and someone else, and you heard each other and became aware that there were hundreds, thousands, millions of us all over the world, and in a vague groping way you were outraged. That's what it's all about, Lily. It has nothing to do with doctors and accountants and teachers and dignity and boy-scout honour. It's about us – the poor – the majority – stirring in our sleep. And if that's not what it is all about, then it has nothing to do with us.   (p. 154)

The doctors, teachers, accountants are us, the theatre-going audience. Skinner is spelling out our exclusion from the march of history in our own language – when would a 'guttie' like Skinner use a word like 'morass'? He has come into the fabric of the drama from right outside it, as it were, and he has a privileged register of linguistic communication within it. His characterisation contradicts Michael's who is working-class, unemployed and committed to the political processes which have been laid down for him by the middle class. Indeed, he is struggling to move out of his class, into the *petit bourgeoisie* via a job with the Gas Board; Skinner refers to him as Lord Michael of Gas. Friel makes Michael dominate the commentary in the early part of the play, and the *petit bourgeois* audience can recognise the language they have taught him:

Some bastard must have done something to rattle them –

170

shouted something, thrown a stone, burned something –
some bloody hooligan! Someone like you, Skinner! For
it's bastards like you, bloody vandals that's keeping us
all on our bloody knees!   (p. 147)

He is excluded from the interior climax. Lily is a foil to
Skinner. She accepts him for what he is. She recognises
he has *nous*, a street credibility, and responds warmly to
his wit. His eloquence encourages her to be articulate:

I told you a lie about our Declan. . . . He's a mongol.
And it's for him I go on all the Civil Rights marches.
Isn't that stupid? You and him [Michael] and everybody
else marching and protesting about sensible things like
politics and stuff and me in the middle of you all,
marching for Declan. Isn't that the stupidest thing you
ever heard? Sure I could march and protest from here
to Dublin and sure what good would it do Declan?
Stupid and all as I am I know that much. But I still
march – every Saturday.   (p. 155)

Lily's problem is not being able to say what she thinks
and feels. At the beginning of Act Two, the opening image
of the play is recreated – except that now Michael, Lily
and Skinner stand quite still by their fallen positions. They
express their thoughts at the moment of death. Friel
allows them whatever register of language is necessary to
communicate that final moment of being. There is no
change, really, in Michael's insight: he has actually nothing
more to communicate than his previous limited
understanding – 'My mouth kept forming the word
mistake – mistake – mistake. And this is how I died – in
disbelief, in astonishment, in shock.' Friel makes him utter
the limited scope of his understanding – 'It was a foolish
way for a man to die.'

Lily expresses her regret that life had somehow eluded her:

> And in the silence before my body disintegrated in a purple convulsion, I thought I glimpsed a tiny truth: that life had eluded me because never once in my forty-three years had an experience, an event, even a small unimportant happening, been isolated, and assessed and articulated. And the fact that this, my last experience, was defined by this perception, this was the culmination of my sorrow. (p. 150)

It is Skinner, however, who expresses the real Frielian *Angst*:

> two thoughts raced through my mind: how seriously they took us and how unpardonably casual we were about them; and that to match their seriousness would demand a total dedication, a solemnity as formal as theirs. (p. 150)

This is the same sentiment that St Columba expressed about his enjoyment of his physicality and his earth-bound delight – and that he must feel guilty for this: it must be given up for a Christian seriousness. Ireland is an Eden that, like Eden, makes us feel guilty for having conceived of words to describe it.

Friel softens us up for Skinner's statement by the speeches of the character of the American Sociologist Dodds. This figure and what he says is an important element in the overall structure of the play. It would be wrong, I think, to equate him with the other public voices, especially the Judge and the Priest, although together they are providing an intellectual/legal/spiritual basis on which to construct a myth about what happened. Judge and Priest start with rigid ideological constructs on opposite sides of the sectarian divide; but at a deeper level they are on the same side against the potential of the mind and sensibilities of the class of people represented by Skinner. Dodds on the other hand is not bound by ideology. He is telling us, magisterially, what Skinner's potential is. Dodds is standing outside the play and speaking directly to the audience:

> Middle class people – with deference, people like you and me – we tend to concentrate on the negative aspects of the culture of poverty. (p. 135)

His speech repays close reading. Immediately he has finished telling us about our intellectual limitations, Skinner comes out of the robing room dressed up as the mayor – quoting from Shakespeare: '"You are much deceived; in nothing am I changed/But in my garments"', a *coup de théâtre* dense with meaning, clinching our understanding of complex issues.

The staging of this text requires the resources of the modern technical theatre. The space-time continuum has been subverted: a continuous present has been established which is poised on the point of death, extending into a mythologising past and future only by words. Stage lighting and a complex sound-track expand the play's arena. The very theatricality of the play enhances the dramatic structure and conceals it. The audience are made to confront their own passivity.

Living Quarters

The exact opposite is the case in *Living Quarters*. On a purely technical level the play needs very little by way of lighting, sound-track and other staging devices. Much more significant is the way in which Friel has turned the actual dramatic construction of the play inside-out. Like those examples of Post-Modernist architecture today which show exactly how the buildings have been constructed, *Living Quarters* shows us how the dramatic structure works. In doing so Friel advances the dramatic analysis of the destiny-logic dichotomy. Once again, he is concerned with the relationship between dramatic structures and audience passivity – especially in terms of our dramatic inheritance from the ancient Greeks.

Living Quarters is concerned with a single event – an unpremeditated suicide – and the prior action which led to that unjust and inevitable tragedy. In *Living Quarters* the event is not a major public one, but private and domestic. Nevertheless, within its reduced scale the same process occurs, of translating that prior action into logical sentences – i.e. thinking about it – and this becomes the focus of the play.

The event is the suicide of Frank Butler, commandant in the Irish Army, who has just been decorated and promoted to Lieutenant Colonel for his bravery in rescuing his troops while under seige, during a United Nations peace-keeping operation in which the Irish Republic has a contingent. The action which led to his suicide was the confession by his young, second wife that she has had an affair with his son by his first wife while he was away on active duty. His first wife bore him 4 children – 3 girls and a boy – and died from chronic arthritis. The youngest girl, Tina, is now 18. Anna is the new wife; Ben the son; his other sisters are Miriam (married) and Helen (deserted by her husband). On the periphery of the tragedy is Miriam's husband Charlie. More closely involved is the Army Chaplain, the priest Fr Tom Cartey, who is a close family friend. The action of the play takes place in their home which is in the living quarters of the regiment based in Ballybeg in Donegal. Ballybeg is the fictional place in Donegal in which Friel situates many of his plays: in Gaelic the name means small townland, or small home.

The play is subtitled '*after Hippolytus*'. Euripides' play has generated many subsequent versions in different languages, cultures and civilisations: most notable, perhaps, are the version by the Roman Stoic playwright, Seneca, *Phaedra*, and the version by the seventeenth-century Jansenist playwright, Racine, *Phèdre*. There has been a twentieth-century British version by the Northern English poet and playwright, Tony Harrison, *Phaedra Britannicus*, which sets the action of the play in British India at the time of the Indian Mutiny. It is interesting that Friel takes us back to the original play by Euripides.

The story comes from Greek myth. Phaedra, Theseus' second wife, is made to fall desperately in love with her stepson Hippolytus by Aphrodite, Goddess of Love, whom Hippolytus has slighted. Phaedra is morally repulsed by her passion but cannot control it. The young man, who has abjured all sexual contact with women, is nauseated by his stepmother's desperate protestation of love. Theseus fondly considered by Phaedra to be dead, returns. Phaedra, gripped by passion for Hippolytus but smarting at his scornful rejection of her, lies to her husband and claims that Hippolytus tried to seduce her. In a rage, Theseus summons Poseidon, God of the Oceans, to avenge him and kill Hippolytus. He does. Aphrodite is avenged; but Artemis, Goddess of the Chase and Chastity, has been slighted, because Hippolytus was her devotee. So Hippolytus' innocence is proved: Phaedra commits suicide. Theseus is left to ponder on his intemperate action.

In Friel's play, the ending is inverted: the Theseus

figure, Frank Butler, commits suicide; the others remain
alive, living a thwarted future, marked by endless 'thinking
about' that fatal day. The question which now controls
their limited and limiting lives is: How could that event
not have happened? In fact, the continual reliving, in their
thoughts, their actions and that event cannot change
either. To that extent only it was their destiny. It is this
sense of the finality of a culminating action, coupled
with our uncontrollable passions, which is essentially
Euripidean. Euripides is the most Humanist of all the
fifth-century BC Athenian tragedians: he is highly critical
of the Greek gods in his plays, and suggests that they have
been created by human beings in order to explain the
fundamental contradictions in human behaviour.
Hippolytus begins with the rival goddesses, Aphrodite and
Artemis, on either side of the stage, making unequivocal
statements about the fate of the characters, in a formal
emblematic opening which is ironic.

In *Living Quarters* the characters have created a similar
embodiment of their fate: the figure of 'Sir'. He, like
Artemis and Aphrodite, opens the play. He sits on a stool,
on one side of the set with a ledger on his knee. He sets
the scene, factually:

> the people who were involved in the events of that day
> . . . every so often, in sudden moments of privacy, of
> isolation of panic . . . remember that day, and in their
> imagination they reconvene here to reconstruct it – what
> was said, what was not said, what was done, what was
> not done, what might have been said, what might have
> been done; endlessly raking over the dead episodes that
> can't be left in peace.   (p. 177)

They have conceived in their imagination both a written

account of it, and of Sir, out of 'a deep psychic necessity'. They create these as some sort of ultimate truth – but then they try to get around Sir (whom they conceive of as the ultimate verification of what happened = God). Sir now establishes (re-establishes?) an informal relationship with the people who created him, and with us, too, who are witnessing the re-enactments:

> So on this occasion – with your co-operation, of course – what I would like to do is organize those recollections for you, impose a structure on them, just to give them a form of sorts.   (p. 178)

Sir is also the playwright. He is without and within the play. We, the audience, are quite outside the play. Before the play 'begins' – of course, it has 'begun' already with Sir's monologue – Fr Tom Cartey comes on to the stage: he begs Sir to tell him how he is described in the ledger. He does not like what he is told: that he is a cliché, and also that he embraces the role, for it 'allows him to witness the pain of the family but absolves him from experiencing it'. He is totally inadequate; however, he too 'out of his psychic necessity' has created Sir and the ledger, as an ultimate verification beyond his priestly office. He too needs arbitration beyond organised Christianity. Friel is making a similar point to the one he made in *Philadelphia, Here I Come!* in the character of Canon Mick O'Byrne: the inadequacy of the priest is matched by the inadequacy of Christianity. Fr Cartey is being pointed out as culpable, even before the play gets under way.

Thus far the audience have been able to observe how a drama can begin: the need for a structuring of the raw material, for example, we will start at this point in the ledger, rather than earlier. The characters are introduced and the dialogue has commenced. Throughout the play, Sir reveals this structuring of the drama to the audience. Shortly after the play has started, Helen, who was estranged from her mother because she married beneath her station – her father's batman, only to be deserted by him after they had got to London – is helped by Sir to articulate her very mixed emotions. Sir also indicates the subtext of the play, when Helen challenges the way the re-enactment is going:

> HELEN: The whole atmosphere – three sisters, relaxed, happy, chatting in their father's garden on a sunny afternoon. There was unease – I *remember* – there were shadows – we've got to acknowledge them!
> SIR: Why?
> HELEN: Because they were part of it.
> SIR: Don't you think they're aware of them? They're thinking the very same thing themselves (*Helen looks at her sisters*) Believe me – *it's exactly right.* (*Pause*) Go on – join them. (pp. 188–9)

Then, with the audience suitably alerted, the subtext of Chekhovian 'shadows' and 'unease' hovers across the seemingly relaxed atmosphere.

Sir later allows Anna, on her first entrance, to try to subvert the re-enactment, to cut it short. This enables us to see how that other important structural element in Greek tragedy – dramatic irony – actually works. Fr Tom is taking a photograph of the Commandant and his daughters. There is great excitement and conviviality. Anna rushes into the scene and stands facing the group. They do not 'see' her; but their ebullient comments and reactions to each other now have a deeply ironical, inverted significance:

ANNA: I had an affair with your son, Ben – with your brother, Ben! . . .

FR TOM: Even closer together.

MIRIAM: Thanks be to God Charlie isn't watching this caper.

ANNA: An affair, d'you hear – out of loneliness, out of despair, out of hate! And everybody in the camp knows – everybody except the Butlers!

(*Tina can control her laughter no longer – she explodes*)

(p. 202)

Everyone joins in the laughter. The audience, however, does not. The subtext has now expanded into an all-encompassing irony. The audience can only imagine the reactions of the Butler family when they learn the 'truth'. Furthermore, Anna has changed nothing; and she admits that what she has just said is a falsification anyway: she did not do it out of loneliness, or hatred or despair. So we see how the whole ironical process works to increase our tension.

Sir then indicates the ending of a scene by simply stopping the action and calling all the characters together. He wants to move on a bit to the point at which some of them had thought they might have been able to do something different. When he raises an alternative, however, they still reject it. Faced again with all the emotional contours of a moment when alternatives were possible, their reaction is to defend the actions they took:

SIR: And Ben, at this point you still had time to join your friends in the salmon boat.

BEN: Am I complaining? Am I?

SIR: But the thought did occur to you. And they didn't set out for – what? – another hour at least. So if you would like to explore that area of –

BEN: Just stick to the facts.

SIR: But this is a fact. And every time you get drunk it is the one thing you keep talking about.

BEN: What happened, happened. (pp. 206–7)

Sir moves them on to the scene in which Ben tries to tell Helen what has happened, but Helen is caught up in her own hurt – in which Ben was a culpable agent. Sir allows this act to end with the dark Oedipal areas in Ben's mother-fixated personality only hinted at. Sir then says they have broken the back of their task, and announces an interval to the audience. The actors, however, are still taking their break after the audience return for the second 'Act'. They are sitting around the set, waiting for Sir. They are unexpectedly relaxed and happy. They are cobbling together those remembered areas of relationships and family occasions when things still seemed positive and life held out prospects for them. Charlie, Miriam's husband, actually expresses our own amazement at the gaiety in the scene. Sir explains:

> I'm afraid some of it is wishful thinking of lonely people in lonely apartments. But they're always being true to themselves. And even if they juggled the time a bit, they're doing no harm. (p. 225)

Sir is showing us the relaxed mood which is needed to start the second act of a tragedy, after the interval: the possibility of hope.

Just before the scene begins, Ben tries desperately to say something loving and positive to his father – like the climactic moment in *Philadelphia* . . ., when Gar wants his father to recall that happiness on the lake – but neither Sir nor Frank allow him to say it. After the tragedy Ben refers again to this failed attempt at communicating his love for his father:

> and what I was going to say to him was that ever since I was a child I always loved him and always hated her [his mother] – he was always my hero. And even though it wouldn't have been the truth it wouldn't have been a lie either: no, no; no lie. (p. 245)

But Sir is really not accepting this sort of self-excusing. He stonewalls Ben, who does not persist in it when he recognises it for what it is. However, Sir is unsparing of the priest, especially in the moment of climax.

The structuring of the moment of climax is opened out for our close inspection to see how it works. At the moment of revelation, when Anna confesses what she confessed unheard in Act One, Frank makes a speech within the action. Then, before he commits suicide, he steps outside the action and tells Sir that he has been unjustly treated – 'it does seem spiteful that these fulfilments should be snatched away from me – and in a particularly wounding manner'. The affable Fr Tom is at this crisis point blind drunk and incapable of offering support when his friend Frank asks him for it. So when Tom steps out of the action, after Frank's brief appeal, trying to get the others to prevent the shot, Sir is merciless: 'You had your opportunities and you squandered them. . . . We'll have none of your spurious concern now that it's all over. So sit down and shut up.'

This spreading of the moment of climax allows the family, the actors in the drama, to retreat into their own private thoughts – to fall silent and become still on the stage, as Chekhov's characters do in *The Cherry Orchard*.

Sir concludes the play by reading out from the ledger

the factual details of the subsequent lives of each of the characters, as they drift off the stage. Anna remains on the stage with Sir. She seems to feel that there ought to be more about her in the ledger. A somewhat enigmatic exchange with Sir hints that she is coming out of her need for him, liberating herself from her guilt.

1979: 'The Faith Healer'; 'Aristocrats'

Seamus Deane offers us a reading of *The Faith Healer* which gives us great insight into Friel's whole oeuvre. It is Friel's most poetic work; and Deane draws our attention to what he calls the play's metonomy (the use of the name of one object or concept for another to which it is related), in this instance the naming of the creative artist in society today as the faith healer of the title. His name is Frank Hardy, whose

> capacity to heal others, in other countries, and his incapacity to heal himself except by coming back to his own country, dying back into the place out of which his healing came in the first place, is a strange metonym for the gift in exile, the artist abroad.
>
> (*Celtic Revivals*, p. 173)

Elsewhere, Deane describes *The Faith Healer* as being a profound revision of Friel's early work which was concerned with the relationship of Irish people to Ireland, and the relationship of creativity and eloquence to violence. *The Faith Healer*, Deane claims, is Friel's

> most triumphant rewriting of his early work and stands in a peculiarly ironic, almost parodic, relationship to

> *Philadelphia, Here I Come!*, of which it is both the
> subversion and fulfilment.   (*Selected Plays*, p. 20)

Here, though not in the *Celtic Revivals* essay, Deane sees
a connection between art and politics: the violent farmers
who kill Francis Hardy have the obverse 'gift': a violence,
which comes from the intensity of elation and despair over
which they have no control: Ireland is both Eden before
the Fall and mired in the hell of colonialism and civil wars.

The Faith Healer and *Aristocrats* were premiered in the
same year, 1979: *Aristocrats* in Dublin, at the Abbey, and
The Faith Healer in New York at the Longacre Theatre.
If *The Faith Healer* has a parodic relationship with the
earlier *Philadelphia . . .*, it seems to me to have a much
closer connection with the simultaneous *Aristocrats*.
Indeed, they could be thought of as the same play: a
fictional continuum that surfaces as discrete performance
segments on either side of the Atlantic, in places that
are different (but the same, modern European, theatre
building) and before different (but the same middle-class)
audiences.

Together, the plays extend the architectural metaphor
I used to describe the way *Living Quarters* externalised
the dramatic structure: *Aristocrats* is the normal and
conventional way we think about our homes: as having an
inside and an outside, both of which are permeated by a
particular atmosphere which makes each house unique
and inspires particular emotions in us. In *The Faith Healer*
that outside and inside has been transformed into a single
continuous space: the home is no longer a house, but a
van that endlessly travels the roads of rural Britain.

The architectural metaphor is appropriate for the setting
of the two plays. *Aristocrats* is staged on a composite set
which is part pleasure garden and part study of the

conventional 'Big House', mansion of the Catholic aristocracy of Ballybeg. Inside and outside are created naturalistically as 'one' space on the stage. This 'Big House' is on the point of destruction.

The Faith Healer initially has nothing on the stage but three rows of empty chairs, an 'audience' at right-angles to the audience, and a poster at the back. The poster remains for the next two 'scenes' but the chairs go and instead there is a small table and chair. The chair is changed between these two scenes. In the fourth scene, Part 4, the poster has gone and there is only one chair on the stage. It is obvious that this is the very antithesis of the *mise en scène* in *Aristocrats*. The 'Big House' of that play has given way to the rootlessness of the other. Frank, or Francis, Hardy and his wife Grace, and his Cockney fixer, Teddy, live on the road, in a battered van. Frank heals people (sometimes) in village or church halls in rural Wales and Scotland. The names of these villages are recited by all three as a sort of litany or sacred chant. There is a powerful antithesis between these two plays, calling forth, in architectural symbolism, all our cultural and emotional responses to a declining aristocracy and their fatalistic alter egos, the gypsies, the 'travelling people'.

A deliberate, contradictory, structural relationship does not make them the same play. What links them together is the signifying figure of the Judge: the character of Father in *Aristocrats*, whose voice intervenes in the action at odd moments and whose death in front of our eyes is the climactic moment of the play; and, in *The Faith Healer*, Grace's father, whom she refers to at length in her monologue. In both plays the Judge is Catholic, of the old Irish Aristocracy, a figure of senility, ending his days in the aftermath of a stroke.

The Judge is involved in a particular relationship which occurs in both plays, expressed in the same set of three dramatic images. The relationship is between him and his radical daughter (Grace in *The Faith Healer*, Judith in *Aristocrats*). The first of the images is of the daughter, returning from self-exile, taking her father's white face, or white hands, into her own, with a great wave of love and compassion flowing from the daughter to her father. This love is repulsed, even beyond the senility of the man. The second image is of the Judge speaking bitterly of the betrayal of the family by the daughter (Grace/Judith). This also stretches beyond the father's senility, though its formulation comes out of it. The third image is of the Judge hectoring a defendant: easy cadences of admonition.

Lying behind these quite specific images is the more shadowy contextualising image of the Judge in his domestic setting: in *The Faith Healer* in his formal and extravagant Japanese gardens; in *Aristocrats*, of course, the 'Big House', whose former glories are recreated by his 'peculiar' son Casimir: throughout the play, Casimir remembers not only his youth there but also the (burdensome) literary history of the house.

In terms of the two plays' fictions, this Judge figure is not the same man; 'Grace' is not 'Judith' by another name. But in the drama's enactment, his relationship with his daughter is the same trope; and he himself is the same metaphorical – or metonymic – figure of a ruptured culture. As such he links the two plays, deepening the significance of their structural antipathies. Together, these two plays continue the scrutiny of language in drama as the means by which we 'remember': 'think about', 'talk about', and so 'understand'.

These intellectual activities do not occur uncontextualised as 'philosophy' (as they do in Beckett's plays, for instance); but, since 1969, Friel has written them out within a specific political context in which the actors, directors, audiences and readers are of a particular social class: educated, intellectual and (at least in terms of the Third World now) materialist – as is Friel himself.

The specificity of who we are who write, act in, watch and read these plays is matched by another kind of specificity in which the plays scrutinise language as the means of 'remembering' 'Ireland'. Defeated, occupied, colonised, neo-colonised: language *continues* to enhance this debilitating history.

The characters of *Aristocrats* are alive in the space and time of the drama: in *The Faith Healer* Grace and Frank Hardy are already dead when they speak to us. Initially we do not realise that they are beyond the space and time of the drama which they create for us through their four monologues and into which they have inserted themselves. We assume throughout Frank's first monologue that he is still alive. We learn from the next monologue, Grace's, that he was killed in Donegal. We assume that Grace herself is alive, until we learn from the next monologue, Teddy's, that she too is dead, having committed suicide in London in the wake of Frank's death.

With Frank's second monologue, Part 4 in the play, we have to some extent got our bearings, as it were, and we now accept the non-corporeality of everything upon the stage: an *absence* of what minimal set there is; and an *absence* of Frank himself already – even though he is still 'talking about' the moment of his death. In *The Freedom of the City* there is, in the characters, a moment of heightened awareness and communicable insights: the moment of death. This has become the whole basis of this play, in a way that is similar to the psychic need of the characters in *Living Quarters* to 'talk about' that fatal moment of death. Friel now seems to feel sufficiently confident in structuring death as a moment of linguistic intensity, as to need no psychic explanation of incorporeality.

Friel's dramatic accomplishment is extraordinarily powerful. For instance, in the climax of the play, Frank creates the strong corporeality of the place of his death – only to dissolve it the moment before his death. Indeed, following the consistency of the architectural inversion within the two plays, Frank deliberately describes the architectural form and material substance of the yard of the inn:

> The yard was a perfect square enclosed by the back of the building and three high walls. And the wall facing me as I walked out was breached by an arch entrance.
>
> (p. 375)

He describes the smooth cobbles, the trailer in the yard, the four implements lying against it which will be used to kill him. He also describes the four young farmers, yesterday's wedding-guests, white faces, white carnations in dark suits, in a line with the cripple whom he knows he is not going to cure. These young farmers are going to be his assassins. As he walks towards them, he tells us:

> I became possessed of a strange and trembling intimation: that the whole corporeal world – the cobbles, the trees, the sky, those four malign implements, somehow they had shed their physical reality and had become mere imaginings, and that in all existence there was only myself and the wedding-guests. (p. 376)

This is not merely rhetoric, within a piece of naturalistic drama. Frank is already dead. From the conflicting information which the other two characters have given us it is not really possible to assume that anything he tells us has a point of reference, a significance, in the real world ('our' world). The only thing that exists in what Frank says is the language he uses to say it. Frank's only reality is the *language* of his story. Frank's creation and dissolution of the yard is Friel's creation and dissolution of Frank himself. In the closing moments of Grace's monologue, earlier in the play, she describes herself as one of Frank's fictions – she has said how Frank endlessly remade everyone as fictions in stories including himself – 'but I need him to sustain me in that existence' (p. 353). The testimony of the Cockney fixer, Teddy, is to some extent corroborative. It confirms the two 'events' that might exist in an objectively real context outside their own memory and governing subjective fictions:

(1) the burial of the stillborn baby of Frank and Grace in a field in Kinlochbervie, which is a real place in Scotland (and in reality it is exactly as it is described in the play);
(2) Frank's assassination, or murder, in Ballybeg – not a real place – in Donegal, Ireland.

Teddy gives a third event: Grace's suicide in London.

The Naturalism and concrete physicality of *Aristocrats* is markedly different. Every bizarre element in the story is carefully explained. Nothing can disrupt the play's logical materialism. For instance, the amplification of Father's voice, and his overbearing presence in the early part of the play (and, symbolically, in the lives of his children) is shown being arranged in a sequence in which Willie Driver instals a 'baby-alarm' in the study, so that Judith who is nursing him in his senility does not have to keep going upstairs to check on him. This contrivance is on a par with the naturalistic detail of the composite set, as is the other 'voice from the past': Anna's the Judge's beloved daughter now a nun and missionary in Africa – which is elaborately 'explained' by Casimir: he plays a tape which she had sent him.

All the eccentricities of this remnant of the Irish Catholic Aristocracy are given psychological and symbolic explanations. Casimir is allowed a lengthy speech of explanation of his childhood to his brother-in-law Eamonn, in which he gives psychological reasons for his 'peculiarities'. Casimir, now in his 30s, lives in Germany, is married to a German woman, has three sons and works in a sausage factory. His aristocratic flamboyance and eccentricity is deliberately contradicted by his prosaic *petit bourgeois* existence. Even Uncle George, brother of the Judge, who never talks, eventually agrees to go to London with Alice and her husband Eamonn: he is transformed, by them, out of their psychic need, into a living symbol of the 'Big House's' residual presence in their lives.

We are given an enormous amount of detail about the lives and personalities of the characters, beyond the edges of the present drama. There are enough characters in the drama for this sort of personal information to be confirmed or challenged so that the audience can readily differentiate between 'fantasy' and a referential historical reality beyond the play. We should not allow ourselves to be taken in by this insistent logical historicism. The one non-Irish character in the play, Tom Hoffnung, an American academic researching for a book he is writing on the 'Catholic Big House in Ireland', is the key to the exact nature of an objective historical 'reality': all the evidence is *written* evidence: documents, PhD theses, biographies, histories, literature.

Written knowledge is today regarded as the only suitable evidence of the past. It is quite specifically not an oral tradition of knowledge. Tom Hoffnung wants family reminiscences, and Casimir generously obliges with an avalanche of personal anecdotes of celebrities who have been hosted in the house: Yeats, Chesterton, Cardinal Newman, Gerard Manley Hopkins. The trouble with Casimir's account is that he always inserts himself into the picture.

Hoffnung, a bastion of bourgeois academic knowledge, pedantically checks the chronology and finds that Casimir was not even born in most of the instances. He is compelled to tell Casimir, casting suspicion on the reliability of his 'memory'. Casimir is humiliated; and Hoffnung decides not to use this 'unreliable' material. However, although Casimir's chronology is inventive rather than prosaically precise, his received memory of all those occasions, from oral sources within the family, is faultless. His vivid imagination, which gets the dates wrong, gets the atmosphere, the contours of feeling, absolutely right. We are told that Casimir does not like books. His references are deeply-felt emotions: he is closer to the oral culture. Hoffnung is being given privileged access to an immediate and vivid account of the family – which he foolishly rejects in favour of his own predetermined thesis. This thesis, incidently, is succinctly and eloquently rubbished by Eamonn. Eamonn later reassures Casimir:

> There are certain things, certain truths, Casimir, that are beyond Tom's kind of scrutiny. (p. 310)

Eamonn, who comes from the servant class – his grandmother, who brought him up, was a servant at the Big House – summarises the problem of the relationship of knowledge to people:

EAMONN: They were good times, Professor.
HOFFNUNG: What were?
EAMONN: Plebian times past. Before we were educated
    out of our emotions. (p. 288)

Actuality – within this play as well as with an objective
reference to a reality outside it – is the life of the emotions
within the characters. The family is described as reticent
by Eamonn, who is eloquently the opposite, and indeed
they do not use words and sentences very much to each
other. Claire and Casimir communicate as sister and
brother with a special feeling for each other as fellow-
artists through Claire's brilliant playing of Chopin (the
piano is logically and usefully in another room which is
off-stage). All of the siblings sing songs together, their
memories carried forward by the remembered music
cadences and the rhyming words. After his father has
died, Casimir recalls Reid's poem, 'My Father Dying', in
his conversation with Eamonn. Through all of this, the
siblings are accepting that the rest of their adult lives will
be an inevitable contraction of the history into which
they were bred. Claire, for example, destined to be an
international concert pianist, is marrying 56-year-old Jerry
who

    runs a successful greengrocer's business and he has a
    great white lorry with an enormous banana on top of
    the cab. (p. 269)

The only one who seems to have failed to come to terms
with the ending of their Romantic aristocratic world in a
more insistent *petit bourgeois* one is Anna, Father's
favourite, now a nun and missionary in Africa. Like Friel's
other divines she is mercilessly caricatured. Even though

there are only a few moments of her voice on a tape, everything she utters to her family shows her to be lacking in understanding and sensibility, her 'work' in Africa a mask for her ignorance and a continuing expression of it.

The play leads us into siding with Tom Hoffnung; but then ironically leaves us out in the cold, as we realise progressively that this declining class, seeing its scion and progenitor in senile dementia, has acquired an oddly accurate assessment of their emotional geography. This is a different sort of knowledge to ours, which is out of books. Friel is not romanticising this class or apologising for the remnants of it who now make the bourgeoisie 'legitimate'. Hoffnung in his ignorance is doing both of these things. Friel is using their self-awareness to show us the limitations of ours.

The Faith Healer completes *Aristocrats*. Friel leaves the family of the Big House to their marital arrangements: Claire's impending wedding to Jerry has formed a leitmotif throughout *Aristocrats*; the difficult marriage of Alice and Eamonn, and Judith's problematic liaison with Willie Driver. In the final moments of *The Faith Healer*, Brian Friel takes us into the middle of a far more fundamental 'marriage', beyond class and convenient economy: Frank Hardy's consummation, in violent assassination, with the young male farmers, yesterday's wedding-guests:

> their faces whiter; their carnations chaste against their black suits. . . . We had ceased to be physical and existed only in spirit, only in the need we had for each other. (pp. 375–6)

The whole play has latent and compelling eroticism, the deep shadows of the relationships which are so starkly told: Grace's yearning for Frank; Teddy the pimp, needing

Frank and Grace together, in the van with him; Frank's fatal encounter with the young wedding-guests, pale-faced and threatening in the Donegal dawn.

The Faith Healer complements Friel's earlier play, *The Enemy Within*: Frank Hardy is a twentieth-century St Columba. But Frank goes back to Ireland. His powers of healing and his sense of self-exile in Scotland are deliberately less heroic and much more problematic than Columba's similar commitments were. Columba's intensely communicated physicality is ironically matched by Frank's ineffable 'gift' of healing. Friel's Columba is already defined and contained by the story which the play tells about him. Frank Hardy is actually in our minds, even as the play unfolds, and remains undefined by the dramatic structure which managed to insert him there, beyond the boundaries and limits of the story he recounts of himself. This is a measure of the development of Friel as a dramatist.

The Field Day Theatre Company

The Field Day Theatre Company was set up by Brian Friel and the actor Stephen Rae in 1980. It was inaugurated by a production of *Translations*, generally regarded as Friel's masterpiece, which was premiered in Derry. Field Day is committed to presenting a major production each year, which is premiered in Derry, in Northern Ireland, and then toured north and south of the Border. These productions are jointly financed by the Arts Councils of Northern Ireland and the Republic of Ireland. The list of productions since *Translations*, and including it, indicates that one of Field Day's commitments is to the development of Irish English: Friel's adaptation of Chekhov's *Three*

Sisters in 1981; his own play, *The Communication Cord*, the following year; *Boesman and Lena* by the South African playwright Athol Fugard in 1983; Tom Paulin's *The Riot Act* (which is a version of Sophocles' *Antigone*) in a double bill with Derek Mahon's *High Time* (his own poetic translation of Molière's *Ecole des Maris*); and, at the beginning of 1986, Thomas Kilroy's new play *Double Cross*.

The concern in all these productions of new plays, new versions of plays, and plays from other cultures is the centrality of language to any profound political change. Paulin and Mahon are Irish poets: their translation of European plays into Irish English is an attempt to wrest them away from British English and to break the habit of turning to these existing versions merely because they are there. Friel's translation of Chekhov, as well as his two new plays – especially *Translations* – all reflect his vision of social transformations in the development of language. The South African Fugard has a similar vision of language becoming the motor of social change. Kilroy, Fugard and Friel are, as playwrights, committed to the public practice of language as a means of advancing social change. New words and linguistic structures gain currency through a period of great drama – for instance, Shakespeare and his fellow playwrights in late Renaissance England – and when this richer language is established, through the communality of drama, new ideas can find common expression: society can be transformed.

So important is this enterprise, so entrenched are the social institutions which continue to sustain registers of British English, as the international language of a one-world economy, that Field Day realised that these productions by themselves were inadequate. The Field Day Theatre Company was expanded to include as directors Seamus Deane, David Hammond, Seamus Heaney, Tom Paulin, together with the two founding directors, Friel and Rea. Together they initiated the publication of a series of pamphlets, something in the style of Swift's committed satirical pamphleteering of the eighteenth century. Since 1984, twelve pamphlets have been published.

There is no room here to offer the analysis of these remarkable pamphlets that they deserve; they have a political and artistic importance beyond their modest publication. Some of the concepts raised are especially significant, however, for the development of theatre in Ireland in particular, and for the extension of the frontiers of drama generally.

Pamphlets 1–6 are published in a collection: *Ireland's Field Day* (London, Hutchinson, 1985):

1. Tom Paulin, 'A new look at the language question';
2. Seamus Heaney, 'An open letter';
3. Seamus Deane, 'Civilians and barbarians';
4. Seamus Deane, 'Heroic styles: the tradition of an idea';
5. Richard Kearney, 'Myth and motherland';
6. Declan Kiberd, 'Anglo-Irish attitudes'.

Pamphlets 7, 8 and 9 are published by Field Day under the collective title: FIELD DAY PAMPHLETS: *The Protestant Idea of Liberty*, Derry, 1985:

7. Terence Brown, 'The whole Protestant community: the making of a historical myth';
8. Marianne Elliott, 'Watchmen in Sion: the Protestant idea of liberty';
9. R. L. McCartney, 'Liberty and authority in Ireland'.

Pamphlets 10, 11 and 12 are published by Field Day under the collective title: FIELD DAY PAMPHLETS: *Emergency Legislation*, Derry, 1986:

10. Eanna Mulloy, 'Dynasties of coercion';
11. Michael Farrell, 'The apparatus of repression';
12. Patrick J. McGrory, 'Law and the constitution: present discontents'.

It is unlikely that further pamphlets will be published whilst Field Day carries out its other major publishing commitment to produce a massive two-volume, million-word anthology of Irish English Literature, due for publication.

The first pamphlet, by Tom Paulin, is especially important, 'A new look at the language question', in which he describes succinctly how the English language developed *politically*. Paulin focuses on the confused state of language policies in the Republic and in Northern Ireland, and in literate and oral English registers in use:

> state education in Northern Ireland is based upon a pragmatic view of the English language and a short-sighted assumption of colonial status, while education in the Irish Republic is based on an idealistic view of Irish which aims to conserve the language and assert the cultural difference of the country. . . .

> . . . Spoken Irish English exists in a number of provincial and local forms, but because no scholar has as yet compiled a *Dictionary of Irish English* many words are literally homeless. They live in the careless richness of speech, but they rarely appear in print. When they do, many readers are unable to understand them and have

no dictionary where they can discover their meaning. The language therefore lives freely and spontaneously as speech, but it lacks any institutional existence and so is impoverished as a literary medium. (p. 11)

He then proceeds to show how the absence of Irish English as both oral and literary medium divides the culture of the Irish (in all its social and religious aspects) into political factions. He concludes:

Indeed, a language can live both gracefully and intensely in its literary and political journalism. Unfortunately, the establishment of a tradition of good critical prose, like the publication of *A Dictionary of Irish English* or the rewriting of the Irish Constitution, appear to be impossible in the present climate of confused opinions and violent politics. One of the results of this enormous cultural impoverishment is a living but fragmented speech, untold numbers of homeless words and an uncertain or a derelict prose. (pp. 16–17)

For Tom Paulin, Irish English needs a lexicon and form in order to accommodate the oral language of all of its speakers. For Richard Kearney, the mythology of the culture must be able to encompass the changing experiences of its people. In his pamphlet, No. 5, 'Myth and motherland', he argues for new ideas:

Without mythology, our hopes and memories are homeless; we capitulate to the mindless conformism of fact. But if revered for its own abstract sake, if totally divorced from the challenge of reality, mythology becomes another kind of conformism, another kind of death. We must never cease to keep our mythological images in dialogue with history; because once we do we fossilise. That is why we will go on telling stories, inventing and reinventing myths, until we have brought history home to itself. (p. 80)

Finally, Declan Kiberd links the problem of Irish English literature to the problem of British English literature and criticism in his pamphlet (No. 6), 'Anglo-Irish attitudes'. He shows precisely how the decline of British English is actually concealed as linguistic decline in the nineteenth century by its antipathetic relationship to Irish writers who continue to contribute to the development of English through their literature:

> British literary figures began to find in Ireland all those traits which they feared they were losing in themselves. Inevitably, there was much that was sentimental, and even patronising, in their view. They gave the Irish a reputation for colourful speech which did not always square with the facts, a reputation so powerful that it still clings to those Irish writers who have done most to repudiate it. (p. 97)

Kiberd then lists the twentieth-century Irish writers who have struggled to make English into a stark and forceful language in their literature. He concludes:

> The Irish revival, seen in this light, may be less an explosion of verbal colour, than a dignified assertion of a people's right to be colourless. To give this thesis the extended consideration it deserves would be to risk dismantling one of the most potent myths in the history of Anglo-American criticism of Irish writing. (p. 98)

Translations

Much of the material in the pamphlets outlined above is directly relevant to Friel's two new plays of the early 1980s, *Translations* (1980), and *The Communication Cord* (1983). As before, in Friel's oeuvre, these two plays are very closely linked to each other. Indeed, *The Communication Cord* is a parody: a dramatic, formal and stylistic inversion in the twentieth century, of the nineteenth-century material of *Translations*. Just as *The Faith Healer* was in some senses a toughening up of the relationships depicted in the rather more domestic *Aristocrats*, so *The Communication Cord* warns us against any unreflecting emotional catharsis we might read into *Translations* in the undeniably intense experience of it in performance.

Translations is, first of all, a particularly potent love story: the young Irish woman, Maire, is loved by Manus, a young Irish scholar and teacher with no prospects in his father's hedge-school in Baile Beag (Ballybeg) in the early 1830s. She falls in love with an English soldier, Yolland, who is with the Royal Engineers and is in Ireland to map out the country and change all the names to English ones. Yolland is a close friend of Manus's somewhat anglicised brother, Owen, who is acting as translator for this ordnance survey of the British King's colony, in 1833. Yolland partly falls in love with her, but mainly falls in love with the rural West of Ireland.

The scene in which they finally come together alone and declare their love for each other is the narrative climax of the play. It is a brilliantly constructed scene. Neither of them can understand the other's language – although in the theatre both actors are talking in English. There is therefore deep irony here for the audience, for they are in the position of knowing what each is saying to the other.

The 'uneducated' peasant girl Maire even tries to talk to him in Latin (which she has learned in the hedge-school) but the 'educated' Yolland still thinks she is talking in Irish. He tries to tell her, 'I would tell you how I want to be here – to live here – always – with you – always, always', but she cannot understand his English. Yolland continues, unable to understand her Irish, as though reiteration will help. The audience can hear again that he is not saying that he is going to marry her, but that he is coming to live in Baile Beag (Ballybeg) with her. Maire is for Yolland the fatal attraction of the rural West of Ireland:

> YOLLAND: I've made up my mind. . . .
> MAIRE: Shhh.
> YOLLAND: I'm not going to leave here. . . .
> MAIRE: Shh-listen to me. I want you, too, soldier. . . .
> . . . I want to live with you – anywhere – anywhere at all – always – always. (p. 430)

This is a similar trope to that of Siobhain O Suillibhain's play *Citti*.

At the end of the play Yolland disappears – he has been killed, not by Manus who has lost out in every way, but by some of the young peasant farmers perhaps, presumably in response to the heightened political tension as the true significance of what the British Army is doing becomes apparent. Yolland's commanding officer, Lancey, is prepared to raze the village to the ground in order to find out what has happened to him. Before Lancey's dreadful ultimatum is made public, Manus has decided to leave: the school, his family (father Hugh and brother Owen) whom he regards as both deeply compromised with the

English in their separate ways, and the village community. He takes his leave of his brother Owen:

> MANUS: I had a stone in my hand when I went out looking for him – I was going to fell him. The lame scholar turned violent.
>
> OWEN: Did anybody see you?
>
> MANUS: (*Again close to tears*) But when I saw him standing there at the side of the road – smiling – and her face buried in his shoulder – I couldn't even go close to them. I just shouted something stupid – something like, 'You're a bastard, Yolland.' If I'd even said it in English . . . 'cos he kept saying 'Sorry-sorry?' The wrong gesture in the wrong language.
>
> (p. 432)

The love affair across the tribal divide, with its tragic consequences, is only a part of what the play is about. It is a hook on which to hang a profound analysis of language. Language is also used as a metaphor for the colonial penetration of people's minds. In the first instance, the play depicts the languages taught in the hedge-schools and spoken in rural Donegal among the peasants: Irish, Latin and some Greek – but no English. This gives the peasants a formal classical education, which is epitomised by the peasant figure of Jimmy Jack Cassie, known as the Infant Prodigy: a bachelor in his 60s for whom it is perfectly natural to speak Latin and Greek fluently. He comes to the classes for the company mainly. He is a foil to the Schoolmaster Hugh who is his age-mate. The two of them had a moment of heroic commitment in their lives when they went to fight for Wolf Tone in 1798 – described by Hugh as 'Two young gallants with pikes across their shoulders and the *Aeneid* in their pockets' (p. 445).

There is an exchange in the last moments of the play between Hugh and his anglicised son Owen (who is now conscious of a betrayal of his people). Hugh tells Owen with reference to Jimmy Jack Cassie (whom he always calls James) that 'it is not the literal past, the "facts" of history, that shape us, but the images of the past embodied in language – James has ceased to make that discrimination. . . . We must never cease renewing those images; because once we do we fossilize. . . . Take care, Owen. To remember everything is a form of madness' (p. 445). This clutch of cryptic comments – which comes at a moment in the play when the atmosphere is highly charged and the audience are sensitive to the deeper significance of everything that is said – sums up the burden and responsibilities of a particular sort of knowledge that has come out of the cultural inheritance of Europe. It is also the subject of the pamphlet of Richard Kearney, quoted above.

Maire is at the other end of the spectrum of knowledge among the nineteenth-century Donegal peasants. Maire wants to learn English, and she tells Schoolmaster Hugh what Daniel O'Connell has been saying about the importance of all the Irish becoming masters of the language of their colonial masters:

MAIRE: I'm talking about Daniel O'Connell.
HUGH: Does she mean that little Kerry politician?
MAIRE: I'm talking about the Liberator, Master, as you well know. And what he said was this: 'The old language is a barrier to modern progress.' He said that last month. And he's right. I don't want Greek. I don't want Latin. I want English.   (p. 400)

She wants to learn English – in order to emigrate to

America. It is certainly not the reason why O'Connell wanted the Irish to learn English. She does not want to acquire a new language for the sake of knowledge, but as a means of moving out of her culture completely, to embrace the new materialism. For Manus who intends to marry her this is a double betrayal of her homeland; and even before the arrival of Yolland on the scene, there is already a deep political tension between Maire and Manus. It centres upon an entanglement of language and speaking, knowledge and materialism: faithfulness.

Dominating the play is the 1833 Survey of Ireland. Objectively, and within the fabric of the play, this renaming of every single part of Ireland, every little stream and hillock, is seen as a curiously significant turning point in the history of Ireland's colonisation by Britain: the moment when the English virtually climbed into the minds of the Irish peasantry and broke their independent culture. The potato famines which followed confirmed in the material world what had already taken place in the people's culture. Once the renaming was completed, mass emigration was inevitable in the wake of the famine. The countryside no longer existed as anything that Irish could name.

The two soldiers whom we see on stage as carrying out this task are both reasonable people: Lancey and Yolland. The latter, indeed, is a misfit in the British Army: a representative of British Liberalism, racked with guilt. It is not by accident that Yolland's 'catch-phrase' is 'Sorry-sorry?' in response to anything that is said to him in another language. He is sensitive to all the relationships without language in which he finds himself, and out of this has come an awareness of how partial – and indeed limited – is his materially privileged knowledge. The friendship between him and Owen is quite natural. It is even appealing, and some of the most important ideas of the play come through the pleasant exchanges of this beguiling relationship:

> YOLLAND: The day I arrived in Ballybeg – no, Baile Beag – the moment you brought me in here, I had a curious sensation. It's difficult to describe. It was a momentary sense of discovery; no – not quite a sense of discovery – a sense of recognition, of confirmation of something I half knew instinctively; as if I had stepped. . . .
>
> OWEN: Back into ancient time?
>
> YOLLAND: No, no. It wasn't an awareness of a *direction* being changed but of experience being of a totally different order. I had moved into a consciousness that wasn't striving or agitated but at its ease and with its own conviction and assurance. . . .
>
> . . . I may learn the password but the language of the tribe will always elude me, won't it?. . . .
>
> OWEN: You can learn to decode us. (p. 416)

Hugh joins his son and Yolland and a remarkably effortless intellectual conversation on how place-names can be effectively translated takes place within the framework of the drama. Yolland's awareness of the deeper personal issues is taken up by Hugh, in a politely magisterial way:

> I understand your sense of exclusion, of being cut off from a life here; and I trust that you will find access to us with my son's help. But remember that words are signals, counters. They are not immortal. And it can happen – to use an image you'll understand – it can happen that a civilization can be imprisoned in a linguistic contour which no longer matches the landscape of . . . fact. Gentlemen. (*He leaves*) (p. 419)

Friel's control of the moods in these early scenes enables the issues to surface with crystal clarity. One further character in the play, Sarah, completes the structure of relationships that encompasses the theme of language. Sarah is seemingly dumb. Only Manus believes that she is not, and in the opening moments of the play she is being taught to say her name. She loves Manus for giving her a voice. Ironically, she is the one who discovers Maire's infidelity to Manus; and, with deeper irony, Manus takes it out on Sarah by going cold on her. Lancey's icy threat to the community, made in her presence, has the effect of driving her back into speechlessness. She has learned speech in order to carry one unhappy message to the person who most matters to her: the bleakness of her characterisation beneath its surface appeal reflects the emotional contours of the whole play.

At the end of the play, Hugh quotes Ovid which Jimmy Jack Cassie translates: "'I am a barbarian in this place because I am not understood by anyone'" (p. 443). It is a quotation that could refer to any of the Irish characters; and to Yolland. But not to Lancey. He has changed all the Irish names into English; and now he who has only commands and threats – the voice of the 'civilising' colonial authority – is understood by everyone. In a bleak ending, Hugh tries to renew an image of classical antiquity to explain the ironic destruction of his world – but he cannot even now remember this: what is the purpose of his knowledge? And if he pursues knowledge for its own rewards of an emotional equilibrium – what is the price that he will pay for this? *Translations* offers a complex exploration of language, knowledge and politics.

The Communication Cord
The set of *The Communication Cord* offers the first

interesting comparison with *Translations*: the latter is set in a disused barn in 1833; the former's set is the interior of:

> *a 'traditional' Irish cottage. . . . Every detail . . . is accurate for its time (from 1900 to 1930) . . . It is too pat, too 'authentic'. It is in fact a restored house, a reproduction, an artefact of today making obeisance to a home of yesterday.* (p. 11)

Although physically and spacially the two sets are strikingly similar – for instance with the wooden staircase going up to the loft – the setting of the modern play is not precisely the romantic restoration of the barn of the former hedge-school, but of a cottage of the period of Ireland's political independence from Britain.

The second point of comparison is that the central character of the modern play, Tim Gallagher, is a young linguistics scholar: without tenure in the university in which he lectures; without PhD, which he is still researching; and therefore without prospects. He is a direct 1980s equivalent of Manus. His friend Jack McNeilis is a young, successful barrister, a complete materialist: a twentieth-century personality bred out of the nineteenth-century Owen, Manus' brother. Jack's family are doing up the cottage:

> TIM: I think my grandmother was probably reared in a house like this.
> JACK: Everybody's grandmother was reared in a house like this. Do you like it?
> TIM: It – it – it's very . . .
> JACK: What?
> TIM: Nice.

JACK: 'Nice'! The ancestral seat of the McNeilis dynasty, restored and refurbished with love and dedication, absolutely authentic in every last detail, and all you can say is 'nice'. For one who professes the English language your vocabulary is damned limp. Listen, professor. (*In parody*) This is where we all come from. This is our first cathedral. This shaped our souls This determined our first pieties. . . . (*Laughs heartily*) (p. 15)

A sort of intellectual schizophrenia makes him mock what he restores.

The blighted love of *Translations*, between Manus and Maire, and between Maire and Yolland, compelling in its dramatic intensity, gives way to one-night stands and weekend seductions in the farce of *The Communication Cord*: Tim is 'borrowing' his friend's cottage for the afternoon to impress Susan, the daughter of Senator Donovan. The Senator is having it off with Evette, who is also about to be seduced by Jack. And so on. The farce is accomplished and very funny. The motor of it is the sensible Claire, who initially at least is having an affair with no one, since she was previously stood-up by both Tim and Jack.

In the end the cottage falls down on top of everyone. The significance of this is lightly indicated in the structure of the play. Central to this structure is the subject-matter of Tim's PhD thesis on linguistics. It is on Conversation: 'Language as a ritualized act between two people. . . . The exchange of units of communication through an agreed code' (p. 84). People joke about his thesis; and Tim himself is aware of the social need for self-parody. In fact, the play is a reflexive demonstration of the thesis: it shows the ritualised acts which stand for communication, the impoverishment of language. The bizarre situations and personalities – Nora Dan and the German – highlight the rituals. At the end of the play Tim, sensibly, pairs off with Claire:

> TIM: Maybe the message doesn't matter at all then.
> . . . .
> CLAIRE: It's the occasion that matters.
> TIM: And the reverberations that the occasion generates.
> . . . .
> CLAIRE: And the desire to sustain the occasion.
> TIM: And saying anything, anything at all, that keeps the occasion going. . . .
> CLAIRE: Maybe even saying nothing.
> TIM: Maybe. Maybe silence is the perfect discourse.
> CLAIRE: Kiss me then.   (pp. 85–6)

Mayhem is going on around them. They sustain their kiss to the end of the play, causing the house to fall down. The 'restored' house, which is collapsing, follows in the wake of the collapse of the ritualised and redundant acts of language. The manic nihilism of the play offers a skilful satire on the present Irish *petit bourgeois* state: it is caught between sterile rural romanticism and an arid English language – through which all that people can now express, it seems, are their narrow, materialist aspirations. In these circumstances, silence is indeed the perfect discourse.

5
The Plays of Margaretta D'Arcy and John Arden

Margaretta D'Arcy was born to a Dublin working-class father who fought in the old Irish Republican Army in 1922, and a mother of Russian-Jewish extraction. She was educated in Dublin and worked in the Dublin theatre from the age of 15, and then, when she was 20, in the London theatre where she met John Arden. Arden is English, born in Yorkshire. He was, from the late 1950s, regarded as one of the leading English playwrights whose play, *Sergeant Musgrave's Dance*, is established as a modern classic of the British theatre. Arden is the truly radical British playwright of this century, whose poetic and political vision has negated his white, male, middle-class upbringing. Furthermore, he has transformed this negation into a positive and accomplished art: expressed, especially, through the collaborative drama with Margaretta D'Arcy, and in his novel *Silence Among the Weapons*.

D'Arcy and Arden settled in the West of Ireland, in County Galway and later Galway City, where they have committed themselves and their art, both as writers and performers, to Ireland, to republican and socialist analysis and praxis, and to internationalism and the fight against Third World oppression in a one-world economy. Their commitment to Ireland has put them outside the British theatre Establishment, including the Establishment on the Left. This has been reinforced by the depth and consistency of their social and political analysis, which is expressed not only in their writing but also in the way they see their plays into performance. For substantially the same reasons they are held at arms' length by the Irish theatre Establishment. The excuse of Arden being English is in fact less of a stumbling-block.

For both Arden and D'Arcy, the events and repressions in the North after 1969 represent not so much deep personal trauma as a compelling revelation of European civilisation in crisis in the last quarter of the twentieth century. The unresolved and *unreasonable* violence is seen by them as the means to grasp *rationally* the ironies, paradoxes and contradictions which are normally quite deeply concealed in Western capitalist economies. I imagine that for both of them a retreat to England would be the way to close down radical thought and creativity, while living and working in Ireland is a way of opening up their art and – through that very artistic consciousness – their political actions.

Their lives and their work bring into sharp focus the dilemma of the playwright who is also a political activist. Many avowedly political playwrights in European theatre since the Second World War are political only in so far as the subject-matter of their plays is concerned. The absence of censorship in the developed Free World of plays critical of its social and economic systems succeeds in making such plays appear to contradict their political intention. A few Western playwrights are concerned to relate the ways in which their plays are produced in performance to reflect the political subject-matter. However, the relationship of the committed playwright to political action is, at a crude level, one of governing priorities: artistic development or political action? In the inevitable conflict, which is sacrificed? In fact, in developed economies the division can easily be blurred and the conflict postponed; in underdeveloping economies it cannot. Very few playwrights and performers in the Third World can make a living trying to change their volatile and dangerous societies through their creative art. There is sometimes academic and state patronage for the critical intelligentsia of the country; for the playwright who works with and for the oppressed mass of the population there is none, only imprisonment – usually without trial – or exile.

If the playwright wants to continue working at the base of his or her society then he or she must first learn from the oppressed what their needs are, and then learn to organise at that level: perhaps through farming co-operatives, or trade unions, or women's groups, or through religious organisations. Drama then becomes a task of communicating laterally these needs and extending these organisations. All over the Third World now, in the 1980s, theatre activists – actors, makers of plays, sometimes even writers – are also becoming skilled organisers and communicators: in order to make a more effective drama *with* those people, who really need to change their societies in order to ease their oppression. The drama aesthetic reflects this radical shift in the perceptions of the playwright from the demands of the art form to the needs of the audiences, and to their continuing ability to organise themselves as audiences. This aesthetic demystifies drama – creative inspiration is not a set of secret rules known only to the initiated *writer* – but it does not in any way diminish it as an art. Indeed, Filipino worker and peasant theatre activists insist that it is only good art which makes good politics, and, they add, only active involvement in the politics of change can transform an imaginatively dead and self-reflecting middle-class theatre.

The sort of work which responds to audiences' needs is epitomised by the Filipino activists, and is very similar to the developing drama work of Margaretta D'Arcy in Galway in the mid-1980s. She has moved towards a theatre aesthetic which responds to the needs of some oppressed working women in Galway and Mayo and to their developing ability to organise themselves. This work, though not the drama aesthetic, was briefly referred to in Chapter 2. She has stressed that she no longer uses the same methods of dramatic improvisation which she and Arden used in their plays about Ireland in the 1970s. The women she works with need to gain their confidence; and formal improvisation techniques are often alienating. Since her spells in Armagh jail in 1978 and 1980 as a Republican prisoner of the British state, which included her participation in the no-wash protest in H-Block at the Maze Prison, she has been concerned to work only with women, in small groups and over a much longer period of time, in an attempt to help relieve their oppression. This work is a positive development out of her republican and feminist statement which she published on her release: *Tell Them Everything* (the full title on the cover of the book is *The women in Armagh said to me TELL THEM EVERYTHING and this I have tried to do*, London, Pluto Press, 1981).

This text is an integral part of D'Arcy's and Arden's collaborative and separately-authored Irish oeuvre since 1969. It is important to set out the whole oeuvre on Ireland because the plays are not really separate entities but part of a political and artistic development. In performances by Arden and D'Arcy since 1976, when they constituted themselves as the Galway Theatre Workshop, they have combined and reworked scenes from all of the plays. Thus the written and published texts are really only one aspect of their whole artistic achievement. And, whilst this achievement was being realised, they were actively participating in Ireland's politics, both north and south of the Border. The following are published and unpublished texts in this oeuvre in a roughly chronological order.

The Non-Stop Connolly Show, by D'Arcy and Arden: a massive drama in six parts which runs for 26 hours, about the Irish trade unionist and active revolutionary, James Connolly. This great theatre work of the twentieth century was begun by Arden and D'Arcy in 1969; completed as a written text in 1974; and first performed in a single 26-hour performance at Liberty Hall in Dublin over Easter 1975; published in 1976 as five separate books.

'A Socialist Hero on the Stage', 1976, written in collaboration with D'Arcy, in Arden's collection of essays on the theatre and its public, *To Present the Pretence*: this essay analyses the writing and performance of *The Non-Stop Connolly Show*.

The Little Gray Home in the West, first performed in 1972 in a dramatised reading in London, and published in 1982. It was formerly *The Ballygombeen Bequest* which, as a production, became the subject of a libel action that was only finally settled in 1977.

A Pinprick of History, by D'Arcy, unpublished, performed at The Almost Free Theatre in London, 1977: this is a reflexive play about repression in the Republic of Ireland and the Galway Theatre Workshop which she and Arden set up in 1976 to tour a series of dramatisations by themselves from their plays about repression and imperialism under the collective title *The Menace of Ireland*. It is also about the intimidation from the political parties which they encountered in staging these performances. Subsequent performances of *The Menace of Ireland*, after they had severed themselves from the professional theatre, in 1979, included not only *A Pinprick of History* but also Arden's radio play, *Pearl*, and some work surrounding Robert Owen and the Manchester Enthusiasts which formed the historical background for *Vandaleur's Folly*.

Vandaleur's Folly, by D'Arcy and Arden, first staged by 7:84 Theatre Company in 1978, in a production which toured England and Ireland, published 1981: the play is described as an Anglo-Irish Melodrama, and is about an actual agricultural co-operative which was set up in Ralahine, Ireland, 1831.

Tell Them Everything, by D'Arcy, published in 1981.

What is especially interesting in the interpenetration of these quite separate and different artistic enterprises is the unswerving commitment of the two writers to the social production of their performance and written products. They not only write difficult and radical works: they see them into radical performance, and then see the text-in-performance into print. It is one thing to write a play for the theatre (not a film, or television series) which is 26 hours long with dozens of characters; it is another thing to see it into a performance which hones rather than blunts its political cutting-edge. Indeed, in the early stages of its composition, in 1971, before it had spread to six plays, Arden was approached by the BBC for a radio play as a commissioned work. He offered them the planned play on James Connolly in 1916. Arden records, in 'A Socialist Hero on the Stage', that they rejected it:

'A play on such a subject, they said, might "inflame passions in Northern Ireland".'

(*To Present the Pretence*, p. 110)

Arden does not note, however, the large-scale work on the Easter Uprising in 1916 which was eventually commissioned and broadcast: David Rudkin's *Cries From Casement As His Bones Are Brought to Dublin* (which was discussed in Chapter 1). However, even if D'Arcy's and Arden's Connolly play had been commissioned by the BBC it is unlikely that it would have been broadcast with the same complex Marxist analysis of the continuing conflict between revolution and reform which the stage play developed for its Dublin performance.

Neither Arden nor D'Arcy was content to leave the work after the one 26-hour Easter performance. Arden is at pains, in 'A Socialist Hero on the Stage' to list all the subsequent performances, north and south of the Border, and in London, and the extraordinary difficulties which were put in the way of these, including threats against the lives of the performers and the actual killing of Liam MacMillen who helped to organise the Belfast performances, a few days after the performances there and to whose memory the published version of *The Non-Stop Connolly Show* is dedicated.

The commitment to getting their plays performed, on the one hand, and, on the other, to ensuring that those performances continue to make precise political statements, has led them to preface the published versions of the plays with statements about what each production of each play should aim to achieve. *The Non-Stop Connolly*

215

Show should not be read without a close study of the
Preface, which is reprinted in each of the five books that
contain the work. This Preface is expanded into a much
longer analysis in 'A Socialist Hero on the Stage'. There
is also an Authors' Preface to both the 1981 edition of
Vandaleur's Folly and the 1982 edition of *The Little Gray
Home in the West*. The former Preface is a continuation
of D'Arcy's and Arden's analysis of the relationship of
dramatic fictions to historiography which they began in
their composite record of the creation of *The Non-Stop
Connolly Show*. In addition, the last two substantial
paragraphs of the *Vandaleur's Folly* Preface are repeated,
more or less word for word, with the exception of the title
of the play, as the whole Preface to *The Little Gray Home
in the West*. These paragraphs describe a visit which
D'Arcy and Arden paid to Greece ('In the spring of
1978 . . .' – *Little Gray Home in the West*; '. . . spring of
1979 . . .' – *Vandaleur's Folly*: these conflicting dates are
consistently maintained in each Preface) in which they
confronted the perpetuation of dominant male sexuality
in nearly all the major roles in the classical European
theatre. This idea was further developed at the subsequent
Women-in-Entertainment seminar in London, which
D'Arcy attended. They end each Preface with the
following injunction:

When this play is performed by a professional company,
the male parts are to be played by women.

It should be noted that this is not an instruction to reverse
the roles: the female parts continue to be played by
women. The injunction, in effect, requires each play in
professional performance to be performed by an all-
women company. The careful explanation as to why this

injunction has been made, as well as the particular tone
in which it is made, invites such a company to share in
the political experimentation which the Preface proposes.
It is the authors saying: Look, our dramatic art isn't above
the continuing oppression of women, so let's see what
further insights about male roles in these historical
situations dealt with in these plays can be gained when we
make women play the male parts.

Despite the powerful integration of ideas across the
whole of D'Arcy's and Arden's oeuvre in the 1970s –
including, for example, their jointly authored, Arthurian
play, *The Island of the Mighty* (1972) – I am proposing to
discuss only *The Non-Stop Connolly Show*. Even here, I
cannot offer a comprehensive analysis. The discussion
which follows assumes that the reader has access to the
published text and to the authors' deliberate
demystification of the creation of that text in 'A Socialist
Hero on the Stage', in *To Present the Pretence*, pp. 92–
138. What I want to comment on in the work as a whole
are the same ideas and aesthetic which Arden and D'Arcy
themselves emphasise: the central and unresolved conflict
between revolution and reform; the relationship of
socialism to republicanism in the context of north and
south, and the issue of land in Ireland which continues to
underscore the struggle today; their particular depiction of
women; the emblematic theatre which they have recreated
and its antecedents in carnival and the Corpus Christi
cycle of the medieval theatre. These seem to me to be the
crucial aspects of the work as a written text and aside
from the political action that only a performance of it
might generate.

Paradoxically, despite the emphasis on highly visual
performance elements in the work, reading through the
words-on-the-page-text of the six parts offers a particularly

rich experience – closer to the experience of reading a novel than a normal-length play. The reader is engrossed, not by naturalistic description but by a narrative of epic proportions. All the reader needs to do, as a preparation, is to allow the backcloths to be created in his or her imagination. There are 10 backcloths, which the authors briefly describe. They stress that the backdrops are 'emblematic', in the style of trade union banners, and not at all naturalistic. *Emblematic* is the key word in the play's aesthetic. In relation to the backcloths it means that they have concrete and unequivocal images of all the ideas and concepts which the scene is trying to represent. The conscious effort to visualise these backcloths, as they occur at the beginning of an act, will actually predispose the reader to the sort of heightened poetic language which the characters use. It is a language which is similarly direct and unambiguous; and the verbal images contained in the poetry are sharply outlined by their symbolic reference, in the same way as the pictures on the backcloths.

A good example of an emblematic painting is one given by Arden himself, in the essay 'Ancient Principles', in *To Present the Pretence*: the painting by the medieval Flemish artist Peter Brueghel, 'The Battle Between Carnival and Lent' (*To Present the Pretence*, pp. 12–16). Visual emblems are the radical disruption of the 'conventional' organisation of space, and the superimposition upon the field of view of an alternative, symbolic order. In a similar way, poetry dissolves the conventional ordering of time, creating a powerful present. An example of what I am trying to say could be taken from any part of the play but most appropriately from the beginning of Part One. The backcloth is described as follows:

A view of Edinburgh, slum tenements below the Castle,

which flies the Union Jack from the top turret. (Backcloth I)

The reader needs to envisage a simple, direct drawing of Edinburgh Castle peopled by figures which communicate (1) 'Scotland' and 'Edinburgh'; (2) 'affluence' and 'control'. This is then contradicted by (1) the Union Jack on a turret, with perhaps an appropriate English military figure; (2) slum tenements peopled by other figures. According to Arden's analysis of Breughel's painting, these figures would all be playing roles: looking out of the backcloth, at the audience, advertising themselves as emblems of the social conditions which determine their behaviour. Thus, the view of the backcloth is not at all a naturalistic view of Edinburgh at the turn of the century, but a 'view' of the immanent class war under nineteenth-century imperialism. As audience, we are not looking at a 'snapshot' of what is happening, but at a 'reason' – for what happens next. The reader can fill out the canvas of the backcloth at will. With this in mind we read the next bit of the text:

Enter Mother Connolly (and Grabitall, at the side, lurking).

MOTHER CONNOLLY:

It is the right of every man on earth
(Who for his life must bend his back and work)
To own, control, and finally enjoy
The produce of his labour at its greatest worth.
Did I say every man? Each woman, girl and boy
Is equally entitled to such a right –
If not, why do we live? But yet we have not got it:
Through all of history it has been withheld:
Though frequently, after a fearsome fight,

> Some grudging portion has been slowly granted
> Only because the mighty were compelled
> By greater might of those whom they oppressed.

Grabitall lunges forward and makes his counter speech, which ends:

GRABITALL: . . . . I hold
My domination over all the world –
Three-fourths – two-thirds – at any rate, a lot:
And there is nothing I will not do to stop you getting
what I have got!

A prior imaginative response to a particular backcloth opens the reader's mind to the richness and significance of the language spoken by all characters. The rhythms of their speeches sharpen the significance of their presence on stage as emblems of the formal interaction of the haves and the have-nots.

When the backcloths recur in later sections the reader should also specifically recall the particular backcloth. The backcloth for the Prologue to Part Six, especially (Backcloth 10) has specific echoes of the symbolism of Backcloth 2. Both have as a background an idealised view of the Irish countryside. In the earlier backcloth, however, the foreground has '. . . *a gallows with a hanged man, a round tower, an allegorical female with a wolfhound and a harp*'. The later backcloth foregrounds '*A red-haired woman in a chariot . . . she wears an embroidered robe and brandishes a spear*'. The female in the former is a cliché now, a figure from, and emblem of, the Yeatsian Celtic Twilight; the latter is a figure which constantly recurs in Arden's work and is related to the Earth Goddess, or White Goddess of Robert Graves's book of that title (see Bibliography). The former is a Romantic decoration, accompanying the symbols of the self-reflecting and divided male: a wild landscape, tower and the abyss (the hanging man) – all of which I imagine Arden despises; the latter is part of a magic relating to a previous, female-ordered universe which is deeply undermining of dominant male reasoning. This backcloth – Backcloth 10 – is again a 'reason' for what is about to take place on the stage, namely, Connolly's compromise with his proletarian Marxist reasoning.

Indeed, one kind of exegesis of the whole work could be made through an emblematic analysis of the backcloths. Ranged together they are like a rite of passage for Connolly, as a Promethean protagonist for the oppressed, through the miasma of religion, capitalism and imperialism. A Christian equivalent would be the panels of the Stations of the Cross, although Connolly, unlike Christ, is not situated within the panels as their suffering focus.

Such an exegesis would be likely to miss the actual structure of the work in its six parts, however, for the organisation of the material is less emblematic than literary. The emblematic backcloths and figures in the *mise en scène*, together with the poetic language, secure the continuity and consistency of the material over 26 hours of performance. The dramatic structuring of the parts introduces a counter-balancing diversity. Each part has its own significant *literary* reference. Part One has strong elements of Victorian melodrama: the boy struggles in grinding poverty through his adolescence, enduring hardships, finding his true love in the person of Lillie Reynolds, and nearly losing her in a final climactic chase, which nonetheless leaves the lovers reunited. The whole part has strong, if ironical, Dickensian overtones, especially in the figure of the economically-exploited adolescent.

Part Two has overtones of the Victorian 'improving' work of fiction, centring, in this case, on literacy. Again, the reference is ironical, quoting the model while undermining it. It is very much about the significance and importance of reading and writing in the political struggle: not only allowing oneself to be 'improved' – which novels like *Eric, Or Little by Little* are about – but also learning the necessary communication skills in order to pass on any useful knowledge gained to as many others in conditions of oppression as possible. Connolly does not acquire literacy in order to transit out of his class, but in order to communicate class consciousness to that class. If Part One is fast-moving, Part Two is more reflective and concludes not with an action-packed climax – as Part One does – but with Connolly 'qualifying' as a lecturer and organiser by getting his first 'white-collar' job, as paid organiser to the Dublin Socialist Club.

Parts Three, Four, Five and Six all have three acts (Part Six has, in addition, a Prologue): each has the formal structure of a conventional drama. Part Three takes place in Ireland and shows Connolly as a person initially present at, then participating in the unfolding drama of international politics and wars (in particular, the Boer War in South Africa) which involves the great and the famous: Maud Gonne, W. B. Yeats, Keir Hardie (the first leader of the Labour Party in Britain), G. B. Shaw, the Webbs, Rosa Luxemburg, Kautsky, *etcetera*. Set alongside these scenes are contrasting scenes of the grinding poverty in which the Connollys are forced to live, and in particular with Lillie Connolly's suffering. There is no mawkishness in this: Lillie is allowed an extraordinary awareness of her political role:

LILLIE:

> You need not tell me you believe
> That man has not been born to lead
> Nor woman from his lazy rib-bone built up only to
> serve.
> You need not tell me when we are so poor
> That by my strength behind this tenement door
> Yourself are strengthened all the more
> To stand out in the street and state
> That you at least alone will not accept defeat.
> If I stand out with you our children could not eat.
> All last night I filled my empty arms with hate.
> I now declare it.
> James, what I have said, you need not say again.
>
> (p. 24)

She juxtaposes herself and Maud Gonne:

LILLIE:

> Miss Gonne, I mean Madame Gonne, came round
> here, James,
> while you were in prison this morning.
> She paid for the doctor
> She paid for the rent
> She did almost everything for me it was possible to
> resent
> And now both of us are so grateful
> She was so offhand and cool –
> Had either of us said anything
> We would have felt such a churl and a fool.   (p. 24)

This play, Part Three, is very much the view of great events from a Dublin tenement. Part Four is set in the USA and the careful pace of Parts Two and Three gives way to fast and furious discussion, to highly-charged meetings which turn out to be cliff-hangers, to scheming and corruption. There is a much higher ratio of prose to verse in this part: the characters' dialogue is less deliberate and much more wordy. In addition there is also a great deal of melodramatic action, building up to a climax in which, ironically, the hero, Connolly, loses and the 'baddie' – in this case Sam Gompers, the leader of the American Federation of Labour – wins. This is accompanied by the razmataz of USA electioneering and well-known American tunes with new words. The domesticity is also very public – different from the Dublin tenement where Connolly's family seemed so cut-off from the outside world – and the play generally has an American tone of frankness.

Part Five, which deals with Connolly's return to Ireland, has hardly any domesticity in it, and in this it sharply contrasts with the other play which was set mainly in Dublin, Part Three. In Part Five, Lillie appears briefly in Acts I and III; Nora, Connolly's eldest daughter, only in Act I. The play confronts the awesome complexity of labour relations, international capital and European imperialism in the period 1910 to 1914. The play is a political *tour de force*. It makes use of a number of dramatic devices, not previously used, to lay bare the contradictions as Europe slipped into war and organised Labour movements failed to cope with the pace of events. The reference in this play seems to me to be to plays of the Unity Theatre of the 1930s, and to the political plays such as Brecht's *St Joan of the Stockyards*, and Auden's and Isherwood's *On the Frontier*.

The final play, Part Six, is completely different from the other parts. It is as though, with the increasing pace in the previous play, the dramatic content has burst through a barrier of dramatic form into a completely different sort of theatre. The play makes extensive use of masks and transformations, which, particularly in the War Demons, is reminiscent of the Japanese Kabuki theatre. The whole style creates an intensity, which is both rational and emotional and is akin to the folk theatre of India – Arden and D'Arcy draw attention to this influence in 'A Socialist Hero on the Stage' – like, for example, the Bengali *Jatras*, all-night epic masked dramas, accompanied by music, and which can make a powerful political impact. This play is a fitting and necessary climax to the whole work. If the performance has gone through the night the audience needs this intensity in the dawn to heighten the significance of the whole experience.

Thus, the theatre aesthetic which governs the work as an artistic entity is characterised by an emblematic consistency in the stage images and dialogue. This consistency exists in a diversified dramatic structure. Such thoroughness of artistic purpose is necessitated by the commitment of the playwrights to their subject-matter – James Connolly – and its political content: the central conflict between revolution and reform. They record how they encouraged themselves in their daunting task by making up the following rhyme:

> My name is James Connolly
> I neither smoke nor drink:
> Come to the Theatre for twenty-six hours
> And watch me sit and think.
>
> (*To Present the Pretence*, p. 96)

The conflict in Connolly's life is, on an immediately obvious level, between socialism and capitalism. Of course, Connolly's whole life is single-mindedly devoted to

225

destroying capitalism as an economic system which is unjust and oppresses the majority of the people. But the authors perceive that the deeper conflict is between revolution, which Connolly perceives as the only way to get rid of capitalism, and reform, which actually entrenches a wider, global, injustice and oppression, while seeming to get rid of it in one place. In theatrical terms, they see this conflict as an emblematic battle – like Breughel's battle between Carnival and Lent – in the wider war between capital and labour. It is like a joust:

> Every time the Revolutionist Cause [Connolly's cause] gained ground, the Capitalist lost ground: whenever the Reformists succeeded in muffling a Revolutionary demand, Capitalism was made more secure in its stronghold. (ibid., pp. 98–9)

Thus, Connolly's battles are all fought with proponents of reform *within* the labour movement. The emblematic figure of Grabitall, the figure of the internationalist capitalist who on occasion becomes specific people (J. Pierpoint Morgan in Part Four, Murphy in Parts Five and Six), is seen continually to be using Labour reformists to secure a little for themselves and a lot for him.

This emblematic battle, in a variety of forms and with different antagonists, allows the play of ironies to govern the narrative, which is strongest in the American play, Part Four. In Ireland, the battle becomes disguised as other sorts of conflict. The most intractable of these is the incompatibility, *in Ireland*, between republicanism and socialism:

MILLIGAN: Socialism in the north can never be republican.

CONNOLLY: Republicanism in the south can never be socialist. I've heard both notions *ad nauseam*. I don't believe either. (Part Three, p. 33)

Connolly discovers a link between socialism and republicanism in the pre-Marxist writing of James Fintan Lalor (1807–49). (The scene in which Connolly comes upon Lalor's book, *The Faith of a Felon*, is in Part Three, p. 17. Lalor's writing is contained in Fogarty (ed.) *James Fintan Lalor*, Dublin and London, 1918.) His knowledge of Lalor's writings brings him together with Maud Gonne; and later, in Part Six, with Padraic Pearse, when they join together in the revolutionary thrust which became the 1916 Easter Uprising. Lalor's writing focuses on the need for land to pass into collective ownership: 'The entire soil of a country belongs of right to the people of that country', as Connolly quotes him in the play (Part Three, p. 16). However, this conflict is not resolved, either in the play, or today – as D'Arcy and Arden show in their play, *The Little Gray Home in the West*, which is set in the year in which it was written, 1971. In fact, *The Non-Stop Connolly Show* does not tackle the relationship of the ownership of land and the peasant mode of production to socialism as defined by an urban proletariat. It is the one aspect of the Marxist analysis which underpins the whole play which is fudged – because Connolly himself, like Lenin after him, refused to acknowledge the significance of the peasant culture in the material analysis. This issue has now become the central conflict in Third World economies in the 1980s. What is really significant in *The Non-Stop Connolly Show*, in my view, is the final play, Part Six, in which Connolly breaks all the socialist-materialist prohibitions in joining forces with the culturalist revolutionary Pearce. It is clear, historically, that Connolly's (Marxist) participation in the

1916 Uprising was as a result of a political analysis which allowed for greater significance to be given to the specific cultural-nationalist perspectives of a colonised country like Ireland than Lenin – or Rosa Luxemburg – would ever allow in their economic-materialist analysis.

Arden and D'Arcy prepare for this modification in Connolly's thought in earlier parts, and, in the end, it is in no way a contradiction of his commitment to socialism. Their drama is convincing. But Connolly's political and social perspectives were formed almost entirely out of the urban industrial experience of European imperialism; and oppression was defined for him as the oppression of workers. Because of this, he could not truly perceive the peculiar needs of those bound to the land. As this century has progressed, since Connolly's death, the reformists have actually secured for labour in the developed world – the so-called First World – the material conditions beyond what the revolutionary Connolly fought for. But they did it on the backs of millions of peasants in the Third World, whose suffering today is now greater than it was even under imperialism.

The final point which I wish to make about *The Non-Stop Connolly Show* is the particular way in which women are depicted throughout the six parts. There is a sensitive and purposefully non-patronising portrayal of Lillie Connolly, and also of Nora, Connolly's daughter. Other Irish women revolutionists, like Maud Gonne, Countess Constance Markievicz, Winifred Carney, Alice Milligan, are all accorded their rightful status. Their particular contribution, often overlooked in the historical accounts, is justly recorded. Above all, the playwrights have been concerned to avoid showing women in any way as sex objects – something which a great deal of other left-wing drama about the labour struggle in the early part of this century signally fails to avoid doing under the wholly spurious argument that the political message can only be communicated through a sugar-coating of sex.

The discussion here of this major Irish (and European) play is obviously limited. There need to be much more detailed analyses of the political content and performance of the work than it has received to date. Such discussions could be both within and beyond the parameters set down by the playwrights in their own excellent exegesis.

In addition, there should also be a comprehensive comparison between the intentions of this work, and the intentions of *Pull Down a Horseman* (1966), the play by Eugene McCabe which is entirely about the meeting which took place between Connolly and Pearce and of which there is no written record. This play, and its companion play of 13 years later about Pearce's last days in solitary confinement, *Gale Day* (1979), are based in Freudian psychoanalysis and theatrical naturalism. They are published together, as companion written texts; and together they provide, both in their analysis and theatre aesthetic, a schematic alternative to D'Arcy's and Arden's Marxist theatre discourse.

McCabe's major play, which won a number of awards, *King of the Castle* (1964), provides a further point of comparison with their work, especially *The Little Gray Home in the West*, because both are about land-grabbing in the present-day Republic of Ireland. McCabe's play is a powerful naturalistic drama, set on the land at harvest time, with the economic drives of its central exploitative character rooted in sexual neurosis. Arden's and D'Arcy's original play, *The Ballygombeen Bequest*, intervened politically in an actual land and inheritance dispute in the area in which they were living. It was stopped by a libel action; and the play subsequently became, under its present title, a play about the relationship of the Republic of Ireland today to the republicanism and socialism of Connolly in the 1916 Uprising.

Conclusion

Text: Writing and Performance

One of the issues which this book has touched on, in the course of discussing contemporary Irish drama, is the relationship between Speech (the public performance) and Writing (the published play-text). The basis for this discussion has been

(1) the social production of dramatic art;
(2) the specific reception by audiences of the performance 'text', compared to the specific reception by the reader of the written 'text'; and
(3) an attempt to avoid creating a hierarchy either way between performance 'text' and written 'text' – even though it may seem historically, and within small-scale societies today, that drama in performance has a clear precedence over drama in writing.

Much drama criticism is closet literary criticism. It is also unreflexively concerned with the written 'text'. By

231

'unreflexive' I mean that the way that the critic consolidates the *reader's* interpretation of drama – by printed criticism of plays – is unacknowledged. The critic's control of the meaning of the playwright's text is consistently hidden. This observation may seem paradoxical, given the overtly high status of the drama critic as well as his or her unquestioned role in determining the success or failure of a play on the basis of its initial *performances*.

This needs to be looked at carefully. First of all, the drama critic is making an assessment of the play *in writing*. He or she does not stand up at the end of the performance and offer vocally a judgement to the audience – as is often done by adjudicators in various kinds of performance competitions, though they usually comment on performance skills and not on the semantics and ideology of the performance. Should a drama critic pronounce upon the 'meaning' of a play to an audience immediately after its performance, members of that particular audience would have something to say themselves. I have sometimes wondered what would happen if I stood up at the end of a performance in a Dublin theatre and said 'I am not Irish but I am going to tell you what this play means' or 'I am going to tell you what your opinion of this play should be'. People would certainly have something to say. But I am doing just that in writing this book. So do all drama critics, including critics of First Nights. Academic critics and newspaper critics, in exactly the same way, exploit the status of *print*. Indeed, few critics ever bother to address the audience who were present at the performance with them. Whatever the members of the audience felt is irrelevant. The critic addresses the public at large: those potential audiences who have not yet seen the performance. If they now go to see the performance, they will see it in the context of a written pre-judgement.

Conclusion

Although I acknowledge this reflexivity here, it is obvious that this book nevertheless continues to contribute to the reader's privileged status, and thus to the continuing status of the written 'text', even though its intentions are consistently to deny a privileged status to either readers or audiences – and, indeed, to deny a privileged status to the notion of 'Text'. Being conscious of the reflexive trap does not mean that one can avoid it; but this kind of raised consciousness has significant political implications. I think this is generally the case in a study of the public and communal art of drama, and especially significant in the dramatic art of societies who have experienced European colonisation.

Text and Political Action

Any discussion of Irish drama – or of any indigenous drama which has had to contribute to the destruction of the political hegemony of a colonial authority – is obliged to consider the relationship of the aesthetics of drama to social and political change. In terms of the discussion of 'text' – whether written or in performance – this means rethinking how we assess dramatic representations of social reality. In textual analysis – again, whether this be of written play-texts or of performance texts – we do not need to consider the political and social function of drama. The 'text' has integrity in purely aesthetic terms. This is often referred to as the universal meaning of a particular play. Its meaning is valid within the purely artistic boundaries of the text.

Even within these artistic boundaries it is still possible for a play to pursue a political argument which contradicts its audience's own political perspective and certainties.

The text, in a sense, can attack the ethics of the very people to whom it is being presented in performance, and still communicate with them. The usual tools at the disposal of the playwright to keep social criticism within the boundaries of the 'text' are irony and contradiction. Shaw and Wilde are examples of Irish playwrights – Ironists – who remained 'trapped' within 'Text'.

Since 1969 it has become more difficult for playwrights to complete the text, to join the circle of understanding, to write the whole play. On a superficial level, because there are now no easy solutions to sectarian divisions in the North, and no shared vision of a positive Irish destiny, plays which seek to represent this reality cannot depict solutions, and playwrights cannot write in their own solutions for the sake of artistic niceness. No matter how accurate the characterisation, no matter how authentic the dialogue, and no matter how profound the contradictions depicted within the text, the completion of that text will inevitably undermine all of these, and contradict – or deconstruct – the text itself. A number of Irish playwrights have resorted to disjunctions within the text: a deliberate rupturing of the text's claim to be a representation of reality.

It is not possible, on the other hand, for the playwright to abandon his art and pursue political action: in the campaigns of violence, by the forces of the State and by those opposing it, there is a strong element of unreality and a lack of integrity. The circle of a greater understanding again cannot be made complete.

Some playwrights – Martin Lynch, for example; Arden and D'Arcy; and the playwrights and theatre activists of TEAM, and Project Arts – begin to perceive that the 'play' of an Irish reality can only be 'written' by the community: that is to say, it is made, with the people, in

234

drama workshops. The greater political understanding which occurs in the course of a workshop is shared by those making the drama and those eventually watching it. Their consciousness which comes through drama as a process, and not the texts of plays as products. This raising of consciousness, of a greater political understanding which can form the basis for much more effective action in the future for real social change, becomes the focus and function of drama. This book has made no attempt to discuss these radical strategies which are often only in embryo and seldom fully-fledged. A popular political theatre for social change is much more fully developed amongst the oppressed peasantry and landless wage labourers of the Third World. Such an overtly non-text-based theatre is obviously viewed with deep distrust and derision by those writers and critics committed to the primacy of the dramatic text.

In considering Irish drama since 1969, we can begin to appreciate that an acknowledgment of the absolute integrity of the text *even within the First World* is a corresponding denial of action for social change. I would venture to say that this is a real issue: a crisis in the lives of a number of Irish playwrights. Within the dominant cultures of the First World, the intensity of the debate surrounding the political function of drama reflects a deep resistance to any change which would threaten the highly developed art of drama. Within the Third World, which the First World is consistently underdeveloping, the political function of drama is undisputed (except by only the most compliant indigenous agents of neo-colonialism). The only worthwhile discussion is precisely how drama can become more central to political praxis.

Many playwrights and critics within the First World who resist an erosion of artistic excellence also wish for a more just and equitable distribution of material resources. Unfortunately, the textual quality of drama is inextricably bound up with the increasing affluence of First World societies. This, too, is a real and bitter dilemma for us. Irish drama, within dramatic texts and also beyond them, particularly in the pamphleteering of the Field Day Theatre Company, offers us the perspectives of writers in the ambivalent Irish State, caught between the materialism of its erstwhile colonising neighbour, Britain, and the cultural awareness of other eroded potentialities within the Irish culture. Even as they try to write about these potentialities they feel that the actual process of *writing it out* is suspect: a marginalisation of their understanding of the inadequacy of the existing political agendas; and of the inability of their texts to represent this.

Theatre in Ireland

The problem of a committed but marginalised drama comes most sharply into focus in the theatre in the Gaelic language. In the interface of drama aesthetics and political action, the *Gaeltacht* theatre is the example *par excellence* of the deeper linguistic contradictions within all Irish drama. Gaelic is strongly metaphorical and powerfully vocal. It could be as effective a language for dramatic experiment as English was for the English Shakespeare and his English contemporaries. Yet at the moment when it might find its playwrights, the audiences for a drama in Gaelic are dwindling. For most Irish playwrights, developing a drama in Gaelic is no longer an option. Instead, they have the task of making the language of the colonisers communicate to their Irish audiences the particular understanding which they work towards in the creation of their plays.

Conclusion

Problems in language and utterance lie at the heart of all the drama which we have been discussing. This is so whether it be drama as text or drama as a programme for political action. Before we even begin to make the drama we are constrained by verbal language. Verbal language – whether it be Gaelic, Irish English, or British English – has its own linguistic structures and transformational grammars. Indeed, sentences have actually structured *already* the reality which the performance is attempting to define. Initially we perceive the reality around us in the form of sentences.

Furthermore, not all languages have an equal status in the relationship of their structures to social reality. At an obvious level, a British English reality is in sentences used by the British English. An Irish reality, or a British Irish reality, will need to be in sentences in Irish English, or translated out of the sentences which already express that reality in Gaelic. At its most potent, drama *un*makes the reality of those sentences, in a language beyond verbal language, in order to get at a different reality, a greater consciousness of the illusiveness of semantics and ideology which constitute reality.

Everything in Irish drama now is therefore, consciously, a kind of *translation*: an approximation from one verbal language to another; a movement from one register of English to another; a transference of meaning from words to emblems and acting; the transformation of a structure of linguistics into a structure of drama. All are attempts at a more profound communication among members of Irish society than is normally permitted in normal verbal language usage.

We need to constitute ourselves as audiences. As an audience, at a performance, we collectively focus on the drama being enacted before us: when it is successful, and as it develops into a means of communicating a deeper understanding, it compels us into the very fabric of the fictions: a language of meanings, beyond sentences and words.

All that I have just expressed I have expressed in words and sentences. However, the sense that I hope they communicate ultimately derives not from those words and sentences in a vacuum, but from the important perceptions which the plays of a number of Irish playwrights framed and found an expression for during the past 20 years.

The plays of Brian Friel, especially, offer audiences and readers remarkable insights. Before he wrote them and realised them in performance we did not have the sentences to understand them. His plays, therefore, have provided us with the expression of a deeper understanding. From the individual plays and from his oeuvre we can come to understand more: about Ireland, politically; about the passions in all of us for place, country and identity in this last decade in the twentieth century; and, curiously, about the extraordinary potential of live theatre. What is truly impressive in Friel's accomplishment is the climate of expression which he has created in Ireland in which playwrights and theatre activists – including those in deep disagreement with his work and his persona – can contribute to an extraordinary development in drama.

Bibliography

Plays

(Square brackets [ ] denote year of first stage production. In compiling this bibliography I am aware of its inadequacies. I have used a number of sources but particularly the general bibliography of Brady and Cleeve (1985) and the excellent specialised bibliography in D. E. S. Maxwell (1984). Professor Mikhail's bibliography is of criticism and commentary only.)

JOHN ARDEN AND MARGARETTA D'ARCY
Published works since 1969 (for unpublished work see p. 000).

Plays by Margaretta D'Arcy and John Arden
The Hero Rises Up (London, Methuen, 1969).
The Island of the Mighty (London, Eyre Methuen, 1974).
The Non-Stop Connolly Show:
    Parts 1 and 2: Boyhood: 1868–1889; and Apprenticeship: 1889–1896
    Part 3: Professional: 1896–1903
    Part 4: The New World: 1903–1910
    Part 5: The Great Lockout: 1910–1914

Contemporary Irish Dramatists

Part 6: World War and the Rising: 1914–1916
  (All 5 books first published London, Pluto Press, 1978; reprinted
  as a single volume London, Methuen, 1986).
Vandaleur's Folly (London, Eyre Methuen, 1981).
The Little Gray Home in the West (London, Pluto Press, 1982).

Plays by John Arden
*Two Autobiographical Plays: The True History of Squire Jonathan and
  his Unfortunate Treasure and The Bagman or the Impromptu of
  Muswell Hill* (London, Methuen, 1971).
Pearl (London, Eyre Methuen, 1979).

Commentary by John Arden
To Present the Pretence: Essays on the Theatre and its Public (London,
  Eyre Methuen, 1977).

Commentary by Margaretta D'Arcy
*Tell Them Everything: A Sojourn in the Prison of Her Majesty Queen
  Elizabeth II at Ard Macha (Armagh)* (London, Pluto Press, 1981).

Novel by John Arden
Silence Among the Weapons (London, Methuen, 1982).

BRENDAN BEHAN
The Complete Plays, with an Introduction by Alan Simpson (London,
  Eyre Methuen, 1978).
(Note also: Mikhail, E. H., *Brendan Behan: an annotated bibliography
  of criticism*, Basingstoke, Macmillan, 1984.)

MAEVE BINCHY
Deeply Regretted By (Dublin, Turoe Press with Radio Telefis Eireann,
  1979).
Half-Promised Land [1979].
Ireland of the Welcomes, television play [1980].

JOHN BOYD
Collected Plays 1
  The Flats: The Farm: Guests (Dundonald, Blackstaff Press, 1973;
  revised edition 1981).
Collected Plays 2
  The Street: Facing North (Dundonald, Blackstaff Press, 1982).

ANNE DEVLIN
Ourselves Alone, The Long March and A Woman Calling (London,
  Faber & Faber, 1986) [1985].

Bibliography

Television play
Naming the Names, from her short story of that title in *The Way Paver* (London, Faber & Faber, 1986).

BERNARD FARRELL
I Do Not Like Thee, Doctor Fell (Dublin, Co-op Books, 1979) [1979].
Canaries [1980].
All In Favour Said No! [1981].
Then Moses Met Marconi [1983].
All the Way Back [1985].

Radio plays
Gliding with Mr Gleeson and *Scholarship Trio* [both 1984].

PASCHAL FINNAN
The Swine and the Potwalloper, in *Collection One* (Dublin, Co-op Books, 1979).
Sam [1979].

BRIAN FRIEL
Plays
This Doubtful Paradise (also *The Francophile*) [1959].
The Blind Mice [1963].
The Loves of Cass McGuire (London, Faber & Faber, 1967) [1966].
Lovers (London, Faber & Faber, 1969; new edition, Dublin, The Gallery Press, 1984) [1966].
Crystal and Fox (London, Faber & Faber, 1970) [1970].
The Mundy Scheme, in *Two Plays* (New York, Farrar Strauss, 1970); (*Crystal and Fox* is the other play in this edition).
The Gentle Island (London, Davis Poynter, 1973) [1971].
The Enemy Within (Dublin, The Gallery Press, 1979) [1962].
Volunteers (London, Faber & Faber, 1979) [1974].
Selected Plays of Brian Friel (London, Faber & Faber, 1984) contains:
    Philadelphia, Here I Come! [1964].
    The Freedom of the City [1973].
    Living Quarters [1977].
    Aristocrats [1979].
    Faith Healer [1979].
    Translations (also contains an Introduction by Seamus Deane and Checklist of Works) [1980].
The Communication Cord (London, Faber & Faber, 1983) [1982].

Short stories
The Diviner, contains an Introduction by Seamus Deane (Dublin, The O'Brien Press, 1983).

241

Contemporary Irish Dramatists

Adaptations
Three Sisters, translated from Chekhov (Dublin, The Gallery Press, 1981).
Fathers and Sons after Turgenyev (London, Faber and Faber, 1987) [1987].

ROBIN GLENDINNING
Condemning Violence [1984].
Mumbo Jumbo [1986].

DESMOND HOGAN
A Short Walk to The Sea, in *Collection One* (Dublin, Co-op Books, 1979) [1975].
Sanctified Distances [1976].

Radio play
Jimmy [1977].

ROBERT HOGAN
Seven Irish Plays 1946–1964 (Minneapolis, University of Minnesota Press; Oxford, OUP, 1967 i.e. 1968).

RON HUTCHINSON
Rat in the Skull (London, Methuen & Royal Court Theatre Royal Court Writers Series, 1984; revised post-production, 1985).

JOHN B. KEANE
Plays
Sive (Dublin, Progress House, 1959; revised version, Dublin, Progress House, 1986) [1959].
Sharon's Grave (Dublin, Progress House, 1960) [1960].
The Man From Clare (Cork, The Mercier Press, 1962) [1962].
The Highest House on the Mountain (Dublin, Progress House, 1961) [1960].
Many Young Men of Twenty, in Robert Hogan, *Seven Irish Plays, 1946–1964* (1967 i.e. 1968) [1961].
No More in Dust [1961].
Hut 42 [1962].
The Rain at the End of Summer (Dublin, Progress House, 1968) [1967].
The Year of the Hiker (Cork, The Mercier Press, 1978) [1963].
The Field (Cork, The Mercier Press, 1966) [1965].
Roses of Tralee [1966].
Big Maggie (Cork, The Mercier Press, 1978) [1969].
The Change in Mame Fadden (Cork, The Mercier Press, 1973) [1971].
Moll (Cork, The Mercier Press, 1971) [1972].

Bibliography

Values: three one-act plays (Cork, The Mercier Press, 1973).
The Crazy Wall (Cork, The Mercier Press, 1974) [1974].
The Good Thing (Cork, The Mercier Press, 1975) [1975].
The Buds of Ballybunion (Cork, The Mercier Press, 1978) [1978].
The Chastitute (Cork, The Mercier Press, 1981).

Autobiography
Self-portrait (Cork, The Mercier Press, 1964).
(John B. Keane's prose fiction, the *Letters from . . .* series, and the
Stories from a Kerry Fireside, are published by The Mercier Press).

THOMAS KILROY
Plays
The Death and Resurrection of Mr Roche (London, Faber & Faber,
1969) [1968].
The O'Neill [1969].
Tea and Sex and Shakespeare [1976].
Talbot's Box (Dublin, The Gallery Press, 1979) [1977].
Double Cross (London, Faber & Faber, 1986) [1986].
The Seagull, adapted from the play by Chekhov [1981].

Novel
The Big Chapel (London, Faber & Faber, 1971; new edition, Dublin,
Poolbeg Press, 1982).

HUGH LEONARD
Plays
The Big Birthday [1956].
A Leap in the Dark [1957].
Madigan's Lock [1958].
A Walk on the Water [1960].
Stephen D (London, Evans, 1965) [1962].
The Poker Session (London, Evans, 1964) [1963].
The Saints Go Cycling In, dramatisation of Flann O'Brien's *The Dalkey
Archive* [1965].
Late Arrival of Incoming Aircraft (London, Evans/French, 1968).
The Au Pair Man [1968].
The Patrick Pearce Motel (London, Samuel French, 1971) [1971].
Da (Newark, USA, Proscenium Press, 1975) [1973].
New edition of three plays:
Da/A Life/Time Was (Harmondsworth, Penguin Books, 1981).
(Page references in Chapter 1 refer to the USA edition.)
Irishmen [1975].
Weekend [1982].
Kill [1982].

Some of My Best Friends Are Husbands (after Labiche) [1985].
Pizzazz: 'View from the Obelisk', 'Roman Fever', 'Pizzazz' (London, Faber & Faber, 1986).

Autobiography
Leonard's Last Book (Dublin, Canavan Books, 1985).
Home Before Night (Harmondsworth, Penguin Books, 1979).
Leonard's Year (Dublin, Canavan Books, 1985).

Television scripts (after 1959)
Country Matters; Nicholas Nickleby; Me Mammy; Strumpet City; Good Behaviour

Film scripts
Great Catherine; Herself Surprised; Troubles

MARTIN LYNCH
Dockers [1980].
The Interrogation of Ambrose Fogarty (Dundonald, The Blackstaff Press, 1982) [1982].
Castles in the Air [1982].
Oul Delph and False Teeth [1983].

EUGENE MCCABE
Plays
King of the Castle (Dublin, The Gallery Press, 1978) [1964].
Breakdown [1966].
Swift [1969].
Roma (Dublin, Turoe Press in association with Radio Telefis Eireann, 1979); includes the short story 'Roma' by McCabe, published earlier.
Pull Down a Horseman/Gale Day (Dublin, The Gallery Press, 1979); [*Pull Down a Horseman* was first produced in 1966; *Gale Day* was first produced in 1979]

Prose fiction
Victims, a novel (Cork, The Mercier Press, 1979).
Heritage and Other Stories (Dublin, Irish Books Media, 1985).

Television scripts
A Matter of Conscience; The Funeral; Cancer/Heritage/Seige, trilogy on contemporary Ulster.

FRANK MCGUINNESS
Plays
The Factory Girls [1982].

244

Bibliography

Borderlands [1983].
Gatherers [1983].
Baglady/Ladybag [1985].
Observe the Sons of Ulster, Marching Towards the Somme (London, Faber & Faber, 1986) [1985].
Innocence [1986].

Television script
Scout.

Tom MacIntyre
Plays
Eye Winker Tom Tinker [1972].
Jack Be Nimble [1976].
Find the Lady [1977].
Doobally Black Way [1979].
The Great Hunger, adapted from the poem by Patrick Kavanagh [1983].
The Bearded Lady [1984].
Rise Up Lovely Sweeney [1985].
Dance for your Daddy [1987].

Prose fiction
Dance the Dance, a novel (London, Faber & Faber, 1970).
The Harper's Turn, short stories (Dublin, Gallery Books, 1982).

M. J. Molloy
The Old Road [1943].
The Visiting House, in R. Hogan (ed.), *Seven Irish Plays* (Minneapolis, University of Minnesota Press, 1967) [1946].
The King of Friday's Men (Dublin, James Duffy, 1954): also in J. C. Trewin (ed.), *Plays of the Year* (London, P. Elek, 1949; Newark, USA, The Proscenium Press, 1975) [1948].
The Wood of the Whispering (Dublin, Progress House, 1961; also Newark, USA, The Proscenium Press, 1975) [1953].
The Will and the Way [1955].
The Paddy Pedlar (Dublin, James Duffy, 1954; also Newark, USA, The Proscenium Press, 1975) [1952].
Daughter from Over the Water [1958].
A Right Rose Tree [1958].
The Wooing of Duvesa [1964].
The Bride of Fontebranda [1975].
Petticoat Loose (Newark, USA, The Proscenium Press, 1982) [1979].
(All references in Chapter 2 quote from the USA edition of the plays.)

Contemporary Irish Dramatists

THOMAS MURPHY

(With Noel O'Donoghue) *On The Outside* (Dublin, The Gallery Press, 1976; new edition, 1984) [1974].

A Whistle in the Dark (Dublin, The Gallery Press, 1984) [1961].

A Crucial Week in the Life of a Grocer's Assistant, revision of an earlier play, *The Fooleen* (Dublin, The Gallery Press, 1978) [1969].

The Orphans, A Drama Supplement in *The Journal of Irish Literature*, III (3), Sept. 1974 [1968].

Famine (Dublin, The Gallery Press, 1977; new edition, 1984) [1968].

The Morning After Optimism (Cork, The Mercier Press, 1973) [1971].

On The Inside [1974].

The Sanctuary Lamp (Dublin, Poolbeg Press, 1976) [1975].

The J. Arthur Maginnis Story.

The Blue Macushla [1980].

The Gigli Concert (Dublin, The Gallery Press, 1984) [1983].

Conversations on a Homecoming, revision of an earlier play, *The White House* [1985].

Bailegangaire (Dublin, The Gallery Press, 1987) [1985].

Adaptations
The Vicar of Wakefield, from Oliver Goldsmith's novel.
She Stoops to Conquer, from Oliver Goldsmith's play.
The Informer, from Liam O'Flaherty's novella.

ULICK O'CONNOR
The Dream Box [1969].
The Dark Lovers [1974].
Three Noh Plays: The Grand Inquisitor/Submarine/Deidre (County Dublin, Wolfhound Press, 1980) [1978].
Execution [1985].

STEWART PARKER
Plays
Spokesong (London, Samuel French, 1979) [1975].
Nightshade (Dublin, Co-op Books, 1980).
Catchpenny Twist (Dublin, The Gallery Press, 1980).
Northern Star [1984].

Scripts for television/radio
Iris in the Traffic, Ruby in the Rain (for television).
The Traveller (for radio).
I'm a Dreamer, Montreal (for radio).

GRAHAM REID
Plays
The Death of Humpty Dumpty [1979].

Bibliography

The Closed Door [1980].
Remembrance (London, Faber & Faber, 1985) [1984].
Callers [1985].

Television scripts
The Hidden Curriculum.
*The Billy Plays: Too Late to Talk to Billy/A Matter of Choice/A Coming
    to Terms for Billy/Lorna* (London, Faber & Faber, 1987); formerly
    published, *Billy: Three Plays for Television* (1984).
Ties of Blood, 6 plays for television (London, Faber & Faber, 1986).

DAVID RUDKIN
(D. R. has written a number of television, radio, stage and screen plays,
as well as translations and adaptations from other languages and cultures.
Given below are bibliographical references for the two Northern Irish
plays discussed in Chapter 1.)
Cries from Casement as his Bones are Brought to Dublin (London, British
    Broadcasting Corporation, 1974).
Ashes (London, Pluto Press, 1978; offset from the Samuel French
    edition, 1974) [1974].

JIM SHERIDAN
Mobile Homes (Dublin, Co-op Books, 1978) [1976].
(With Neil Jordan) *Journal of a Hole.*
Karak.
Spike.

PETER SHERIDAN
Liberty Suit (Dublin, Co-op Books, 1978).
Emigrants (Dublin, Co-op Books, 1979).
No Entry.
Down All the Days.

SAM THOMPSON
Over the Bridge, edited and introduced by Stewart Parker (Dublin, Gill
    and Macmillan, 1970) [1960].

General Bibliography

(The following bibliography contains selected works
referred to in the book, including African and other Third
World references; and to various other methodological

source works not mentioned, but used in the study of drama.)

JOHN BANVILLE, *Birchwood* (London, Panther, 1984; first published 1973).

——, *Doctor Copernicus* (London, Panther, 1980; 1976).

——, *Kepler* (London, Panther, 1983; 1981).

ANNE M. BRADY and BRIAN CLEEVE, *A Biographical Dictionary of Irish Writers* (Mullingar, The Lilliput Press, 1985).

DANIEL CORKERY, *The Fortunes of the Irish Language* (Cork, The Mercier Press, 1968; 1954).

SEAMUS DEANE, *Celtic Revivals: Essays in Modern Irish Literature* (London, Faber & Faber, 1985).

——, *A Short History of Irish Literature* (London, Hutchinson, 1986).

LIAM DE PAOR, *The Peoples of Ireland: From prehistory to modern times* (London, Hutchinson, 1986).

MICHEL DE GHELDERODE, *The Death of Doctor Faust* in *Seven Plays*, Vol. II (London, MacGibbon and Kee, 1966).

P. J. DOWLING, *The Hedge Schools of Ireland* (Cork, The Mercier Press, 1968; 1935).

THE DRUID THEATRE COMPANY, *Druid: The First Ten Years* (Galway, Druid Performing Arts, 1985).

KIER ELAM, *The Semiotics of Theatre and Drama* (London, Methuen, 1980).

MICHAEL ETHERTON, *The Development of African Drama* (London, Hutchinson, 1982).

——, 'Peasants and Intellectuals: An Essay Review', *Convergence*, XIV (4), (1981); reprinted from *Africa*, 51 (4) (1981).

THE FIELD DAY THEATRE COMPANY, *Ireland's Field Day* (London, Hutchinson, 1985), contains the Field Day Pamphlets Nos 1–6:

    No. 1: Tom Paulin, 'A new look at the language question'

    No. 2: Seamus Heaney, 'An open letter'

    No. 3: Seamus Deane, 'Civilians and barbarians'

    No. 4: Seamus Deane, 'Heroic styles: the tradition of an idea'

    No. 5: Richard Kearney, 'Myth and motherland'

    No. 6: Declan Kiberd, 'Anglo-Irish attitudes'

Field Day Pamphlets: The Protestant Idea of Liberty (Derry, Field Day, 1985) contains the Field Day Pamphlets Nos 7–9:

    No. 7: Terence Brown, 'The whole Protestant community: the making of a historical myth'

    No. 8: Marianne Elliott, 'Watchmen in Sion: the Protestant idea of liberty'

    No. 9: R. L. McCartney, 'Liberty and authority in Ireland'

Field Day Pamphlets: Emergency Legislation (Derry, Field Day, 1986) contains the Field Day Pamphlets Nos 10–12:

Bibliography

No. 10: Eanna Mulloy, 'Dynasties of coercion'

No. 11: Michael Farrell, 'The apparatus of repression'

No. 12: Patrick J. McGrory, 'Law and the constitution: present discontents'

ATHOL FUGARD, *Boesman and Lena* (London, Oxford University Press, 1973).

——, *Statements: Three Plays – Sizwe Bansi is Dead/The Island/Statements After an Arrest under the Immorality Act* (London, Oxford University Press, 1978; 1974).

JAMES GIBBS, *Wole Soyinka* (Basingstoke, Macmillan, 1986); (Wole Soyinka's plays are published in *Collected Works* by Methuen, London).

ROBERT GRAVES, *The White Goddess* (London, Faber & Faber, 1981; 1946).

ROBERT HOGAN, *After the Irish Renaissance* (London, Macmillan, 1968).

HILARY LAWSON, *Reflexivity, the post-modern predicament* (London, Hutchinson, 1985).

COLIN MACCABE, *Theoretical Essays: film, linguistics, literature* (Manchester, Manchester University Press, 1985).

THOMAS MANN, *Doctor Faustus*, trans. H. T. Lowe-Porter (Harmondsworth, Penguin, 1968; 1947).

D. E. S. MAXWELL, *A Critical History of Modern Irish Drama, 1891–1980* (Cambridge, Cambridge University Press, 1984).

PHILOMENA MUINZER, 'Evacuating the Museum: the Crisis of Playwriting in Ulster', *New Theatre Quarterly*, 9, III (9) (Feb., 1987).

NGUGI WA THIONG'O, *Decolonising the Mind: The Politics of Language in African Literature* (Nairobi, Heinemann Kenya, and London, James Currey, 1986).

FLANN O'BRIEN, *Stories and Plays* (London, Grafton Books (Collins), 1986), contains *Faustus Kelly*, by Myles na gCopaleen (1950).

——, *The Dalkey Archive* (London, Grafton Books (Collins), 1986; 1964).

MICHEL PECHEUX, *Language, Semantics and Ideology*, trans. Harbans Nagpal (Basingstoke, Macmillan, 1982; 1975).

JUNE SCHLUETER, *The Plays and Novels of Peter Handke* (Pittsburgh, USA, University of Pittsburgh Press, 1981). (Peter Handke's plays are published in English translation by Methuen, London.)

KATE SOPER, *Humanism and Anti-Humanism* (London, Hutchinson, 1986).

WOLE SOYINKA, *Myth, Literature and the African World* (Cambridge, CUP, 1976).

CAROLYN SWIFT, *Stage by Stage* (Dublin, Poolbeg Press, 1985).

JANET WOLFF, *The Social Production of Art* (Basingstoke, Macmillan, 1981).

PETER WORSLEY, *The Three Worlds: Culture and World Development* (London, Weidenfeld & Nicolson, 1984).

Index

Index

Index

252

Index